THE ART OF THE
Limerick

1

MISTRESS TOWL.

There was an Old Woman named Towl,

Who went out to Sea with her Owl,

But the Owl was Sea-sick,

And scream'd for Physic ;

Which sadly annoy'd Mistress Towl.

Published by Harris & Son, corner of St. Pauls, New London

THE FIRST LIMERICK IN THE FIRST LIMERICK BOOK
from the British Museum (British Library) copy of
The History of Sixteen Wonderful Old Women . . .
1820/21, Harris & Son, Corner St. Paul's
Church-Yard (author and artist unknown).

THE ART OF THE
Limerick

CYRIL BIBBY

M.A., M.Sc., Ph.D., Dip.Ed., F.L.S., F.R.S.A.

THE RESEARCH PUBLISHING CO.
52 Lincoln's Inn Fields · London

True ease in writing comes from art, not chance,
As those move easiest who have learn'd to dance.
'Tis not enough no harshness gives offence;
The sound must seem an echo to the sense.
                    Alexander Pope, 'Essay on Criticism'

© CYRIL BIBBY, 1978
ISBN 0 7050 0053 2
Printed in England for The Research Publishing Co.
(Fudge & Co. Ltd.), London

Acknowledgements

First, I must thank my daughter Gillian (whose gift of a limerick book first set me upon the serious study of this type of verse) and my other children (Helen, John and Peter) whose early enjoyment of the silly stories and rhymes which I used frequently to make up for their amusement helped my own sense of fun to resist erosion by the passing years. As for Frances my wife, her ears have long been the sole auditors of my more private verses, and to her I am indebted for that sort of utterly honest criticism which is possible only between the closest of friends.

This book is primarily one of literary criticism, and (whilst, I hope, appealing equally to the general reader) it should be of particular value to serious students of literature. I have, therefore, included in the critical apparatus many references to publications in which limericks have previously been printed (in some cases, simply to provide a more recent source for readers without access to major libraries containing earlier material). This, however, does not in the great majority of cases imply anything about original authorship. Indeed, in the case of limericks, the attribution of authorship poses a problem of peculiar difficulty. More than any other verse-form, they circulate mainly orally, with many a modification in passage, and are eventually printed (if at all) as a sort of composite effort to which a number of unknown hands have contributed. One might, in fact, well say:

> Those rhymesters, Anon. and Trad.,
> Wrote much that is morally bad
>   In poems on panties,
>   And salty sea-shanties –
> In limericks, too, I would add.

In some cases, however, one can feel fairly certain about original authorship, and I acknowledge with gratitude the granting of permission to quote some such verses (as also in the case of illustrations). If, by any chance, I have anywhere failed in this respect, I would say:

5

> If there be any author of verse
> (Whether excellent, weakish or worse)
>> Who resents an omission
>> To obtain due permission,
> From apology I'm not averse.

My gratitude must also be expressed to the invariably helpful staffs of many libraries, especially those of the British Museum, Cambridge University, Kingston upon Hull College of Education, the Bodleian, the Liverpool Picton, and the Universities of London and Hull. Then there are those who have so freely given of their advice or scholarship or skills, and in particular Mr. Jim Abraham, Mr. David Brown, Mrs. Eileen Brown, Professor P.M. Brown, Mr. Brian Catchpole, Mr. J.M. Cohen, Dame Daphne du Maurier, Professor A.T. Hanson, Mr. Christopher Isherwood, Mr. Paul Jennings, Mr. John Lehmann, the Earl of Limerick, Mr. Roy MacGregor-Hastie, Mr. Tom Martin, Professor B. Moloney, Professor A.F. Norman, Sir Frederick Osborne, Professor Arthur Pollard, Father Anthony Skillen, Professor Ninian Smart and Mrs. Muriel Walton. To summarise my indebtedness:

> All these to my help gladly came;
> They sought neither favour nor fame:
>> If, despite all this aid,
>> Mistakes have been made,
> The author alone is to blame.

C.B.

Contents

The limerick is precious, an exquisite
thing; like a good Burgundy, it should not
be taken indifferently, too often, or in
unduly large quantities. Only a fool, I
repeat a fool, would gulp down a glass of
Chambertin, or read this book in one sitting.

'Count Palmo Vicarion'
(Christopher Logue)

Beware of the limerick bore;
From a seemingly infinite store
    He trots out more verse
    Where the scansion gets worse
But the subject's the same as before.

Paul Jennings

I

Limericks in General

Once really immersed in the study of limericks, one finds that questions keep cropping up to which the answers are so generally taken for granted that few people even realise that they exist. Who invented the limerick – or did it simply evolve? If the latter, how far back may its history be traced? How standard is the limerick's form, even in such basic features as scansion? Then there is the mystery of the origin of the word 'limerick': does it really derive from the town of that name, or is this merely a traditional belief? And what factors make some verses very good limericks and others very poor ones?

One thing is certain: a limerick is nothing if it is not either clever or funny. But humour is a many-sided thing, and no one has ever succeeded in producing a really satisfying analysis of its nature. Some idea of the complexity of the matter may be gained by glancing at the index of Roget's *Thesaurus*. From 'humour', it leads to amusement, diversion, fun, frolic, merriment, jollity, joviality, buffoonery, pleasantry and wit. Follow 'wit', and one comes to farce, jocosity, waggery, whimsicality, smartness, repartee, ridicule, scintillation and word-play. A third route leads to salacity, impurity, impudicity, obscenity, ribaldry, smut, bawdry and pornography. There is not one of these many inter-grading terms which cannot be illustrated by a limerick.

It has been said that "The alternative qualities of the limerick . . . are wit and fantasy. And the wit is almost invariably less a matter of story than of situation"[1], but this is an over-simplification. To begin with, story and situation cannot always be separated, and certainly not in one of the most famous of all limericks, which dates from at least 1873 and is sometimes attributed to Lewis Carroll:

> There was a young lady of Riga,
> Who went for a ride on a tiger;
>   They returned from the ride
>   With the lady inside,
> And a smile on the face of the tiger.[2]

9

Then there are other very different cases, in which the wit lies in clever presentation of metaphysical mystery, as in Monsignor Ronald Knox's verse on philosophical idealism and in its even more ingenious reply:

> There was a young man who said, "God
> Must find it exceedingly odd
>   To see that this tree
>   Continues to be
> When no one's about in the quad."[3]

> Dear Sir, your astonishment's odd,
> *I'm* always about in the quad.
>   And that's why the tree
>   Continues to be,
> Since observed by, yours faithfully, God.[4]

Many varieties of humour were long ago charted by Carolyn Wells, that indomitable American woman born in 1862, whose great *Book of Humorous Verse* included headings of 'Banter', 'Satire', 'Cynicism', 'Burlesque', 'Bathos', 'Parody', 'Whimsey' and 'Nonsense'. And, she emphasised, "Absence of sense is not necessarily nonsense . . . By far the most meritorious and interesting kind of nonsense is that which embodies an absurd or ridiculous idea, and treats it with elaborate seriousness"[5]. Moreover, as De Quincey once remarked, "None but a man of extraordinary talent can write first-rate nonsense"[6]. Wyndham Lewis claims that "It is generally difficult to convince the average Englishman that nonsense can mean something"[7] – but let us not forget that old author-unknown saying, "A little nonsense now and then is relished by the wisest men".

One variety of humour is tied up with tongue-twisting effects, as in:

> There was an old Russian named Mowski –
> Voulezvousvillivitcheochowski;
>   His horse he called Schwewski,
>   His cow, Paderewski,
> And his little dog, Bowwowwowwowski.[8]

and (with the American pronunciation of 'tutor' as *too-ter*):

> A tutor who taught on the flute
> Tried to teach two young tooters to toot.
>   Said the two to the tutor,
>   "Is it harder to toot, or
> To tutor two tooters to toot?"[9]

Indeed, many U.S. verses depend for full effect upon the 'correct' transatlantic pronunciation (in this next case, 'fertile' as *fer-till*):

> A remarkable figure has Myrtle,
> A retractable tail like a turtle;
> > But though she has never
> > Been called cute or clever,
> She annually proves to be fertile.[10]

Similar considerations apply to regional differences of speech inside England. Edward Lear presumably pronounced 'gone' as *gorn*:

There was an Old Man at a Junction,
Whose feelings were wrought with compunction,
When they said "The Train's gone!" He exclaimed "How forlorn!"
But remained on the rails of the Junction.[11]

A northerner would fully appreciate a limerick in which 'grass' rhymed with 'ass', but not one in which it rhymed with 'farce', while in parts of Yorkshire 'woman' would rhyme with 'human'. Interestingly enough, this sort of variation in pronunciation was explicitly exploited in *Punch* as early as 1863:

> There was an old girl of Newcastle,
> Who wore a great tassel, or tarsel;
> > It made her so proud
> > That folks said, quite loud,
> "Her pride wouldn't make a *small* parcel".[12]

What applies geographically also applies historically and socially. In the nineteenth century, even so inveterate a traveller as Lear was insular enough to use good old British pronunciations of place names, irrespective of how mere foreigners might imagine that their own great cities should be pronounced:

There was an Old Person of Prague,
Who was suddenly seized with the plague;
But they gave him some butter, which caused him to stutter,
And cured that Old Person of Prague.[13]

– which recalls W.J. Prouse's serious poem of the same period, extolling "the beautiful city of Prague [whose] longitude's possibly vague"[14]. In more recent times. the highly educated intimates of the Rev. Charles Inge would doubtless have found the rhyming of this verse of his to be immaculate:

> There once was a Madame called Tussaud,
> Who loved the grand folk in 'Who's Who' so,

> That she made them in wax,
> Both their fronts and their backs,
> And asked no permission to do so.[15]

but it would seem strange to the less cultured millions who speak of Madam *Tuss-ord* rather than of Madame *Too-soe*.

In some sense related to the tongue-twisters are those limericks which use a triple-rhyming effect in the last line, thus:

> The bottle of perfume that Willie sent
> Was highly displeasing to Millicent;
>   Her thanks were so cold,
>   They quarrelled, I'm told,
> Through that silly scent Willie sent Millicent.[16]

and, with the additional complication of typographical abbreviation, this verse:

> She frowned and called him Mr.
> Because in sport he Kr.
>   And so in spite
>   That very night
> This Mr. Kr. Sr.[17]

This abbreviation device, incidentally, had been early exploited by Mark Twain:

> A man, hired by John Smith and Co.,
> Loudly declared that he'd tho.
>   Men that he saw
>   Dumping dirt near his store,
> The drivers, therefore, didn't do. .[18]

Another verbal device sometimes used to enliven the limerick is the pun, of which Lewis Carroll made good use in a verse composed to amuse Vera Bellinger, one of his many little girl friends:

> There was a young lady of station,
> "I love man!" was her sole exclamation;
>   But when men cried, "You flatter!"
>   She replied, "Oh, no matter!"
> Isle of Man is the true explanation.[19]

And Oliver Wendell Holmes, that almost compulsive punster, made especially clever play on the name of America's most famous preacher of the period:

The Reverend Henry Ward Beecher
Called a hen a most elegant creature.
   The hen, pleased with that,
   Laid an egg in his hat –
And thus did the hen reward Beecher.[20]

Punning has become somewhat *de trop* among England's intelligent-sia, but it still survives healthily in the U.S.A.:

There was an old maid of Genoa;
I blush when I think what Iowa.
   She's gone to her rest,
   And it's all for the best;
Otherwise I would borrow Samoa.[21]

One clever punning limerick is based upon the brand-names of American beers:

A lovely young girl named Anne Heuser
Declared that no man could surprise her;
   But a fellow named Gibbons
   Untied her Blue Ribbons,
And now she is sadder Budweiser.[22]

A variant on this 'Anne Heuser' (*Anheuser*) verse explores the pos-sibilities of 'Schlitz' in her pants. So far, however, nobody seems to have exploited the potential of other brands such as 'High Life', 'Smooth 'N' Spicy', 'Koch's', 'Poker' and 'Horny Bull'.

   Other limericks amuse by means of a variety of linguistic tricks. This, from New Orleans, has what is virtually a verbally disjunctive riddle in each line:

A certain young pate who was addle
Rode a horse he alleged to be saddle.
   But his gust which was dis
   For his haps which were mis
Sent him back to his lac which was Cadil.[23]

while this verse makes clever play on the names of Gertrude Stein, Jacob Epstein and Albert Einstein:

There's a wonderful family called Stein,
There's Gert and there's Ep and there's Ein;
   Gert's poems are bunk,
   Ep's statues are junk,
And no one can understand Ein.[24]

Bergson exaggerated when he wrote, "one accentuates humour by descending deeper and deeper into the evil that exists"[25], but he had an important point. Cicero recognised it long ago with his reference to the rôle of 'derision' in humour, as did Freud with his 'release of inhibition'. However much one may deplore such moral imperfections of mankind, there is no denying their existence. Sometimes, indeed, as Hazlitt reminded us, "We laugh at a thing merely because we ought not. If we think we must not laugh, this perverse impediment makes our temptation to laugh the greater; for by endeavouring to keep the obnoxious image out of sight, it comes upon us more irresistibly"[26]. Perhaps, however, we may take a little comfort from one of Samuel Butler's Erewhonian 'Sunchild Sayings': "When the righteous man turneth away from the righteousness that he hath committed, and doeth that which is a little naughty and wrong, he will generally be found to have gained in amiability what he has lost in righteousness"[27]. At any rate, the fact is that almost everybody relishes ruthless limericks like these:

> A youthful beef-packer named Young,
> One day, when his nerves were unstrung,
> Pushed his wife's ma – unseen –
> In the chopping machine,
> Then canned her and labelled her 'Tongue'.

> There was a young lady of Malta,
> Who strangled her aunt with a halter.
> She said, "I won't bury her,
> She'll do for my terrier;
> She'll keep for a month if I salt her".[28]

Almost everybody, also, enjoys limericks which their particular microsocial group finds indiscreet enough to provide some slight thrill of taboo-defiance but not so shocking as to be utterly unacceptable. I remember, as a lad of eight or nine, a small tremor of pleasure at so minuscule a misdemeanour as speaking out loud the words 'belly' and 'hell' in rhymed disguise:

> A wonderful bird is the pelican,
> His beak holds more than his belican;
> He takes in his beak
> Enough food for a week,
> But nobody knows how the helican.[29]

(The original version of this, incidentally, has been attributed to Dixon Merritt, an old-type veteran Florida newspaper man.)

Few children today would find this at all 'daring', but there are still
many to whom audible indications of indigestion are mirth-making:

> I sat next to the Duchess at tea,
> Distressed as a person could be.
>> Her rumblings abdominal
>> Were simply phenomenal –
> And everyone thought it was me![30]

And any reference to female underwear is quite widely found either
amusing or embarrassing or mildly stimulating:

> There was a young lady of Tottenham,
> Her manners – she'd wholly forgotten 'em.
>> While at tea at the Vicar's,
>> She took off her knickers,
> Explaining she felt much too hot in 'em.[31]

So one may mark a continuous progression of the shocking, from
the slightest impropriety down eventually to sheer pornography. It
would be tedious and distasteful to exemplify each stage on the
downward slope, but one general point is worth noting. Provided it
is skilfully composed, and especially if it also embraces an ingenious
or unexpected idea, a limerick tends to be particularly appealing
when it manages to offend more than one sort of propriety – that is,
so long as it does not offend so grossly as to produce revulsion. And,
for the more highly cultured, an additional bonus may be provided
by improprieties of a quite different kind. Gershon Legman has
remarked that "non-college people simply do not find it easy to
understand . . . all the trick geographical rhyming and other purely
formal and intellectual ornamentation of the limerick"[32]; but that is
only half the story. There is also, for those who have been nurtured
in the finer nuances of metre and rhyme, the thrill of 'getting away'
with outrageous literary liberties quite impermissible in almost
every other variety of verse. Thus, "bawdy limericks . . . represent
for the educated group a sort of private revolt against the rules of
prosody and propriety, at one and the same time"[33].

Unfortunately, it cannot be said that higher education has so far
done much to promote scholarly study of the limerick. Indeed, to
me as a scientist, accustomed to check and double-check assertions
before presuming to put them into print, it came as rather a shock to
find how frequently literary writers seem to quote and requote
received statements without any properly rigorous investigation. I
was, for example, excited to find, in Ernest Rhys's *New Book of Sense
and Nonsense*, a near-limerick from Boccaccio's *Decameron*:

> My Brunetta, fair and feat, no, no.
> Why should you say so? Oh, oh!
>   The meat of my master
>   Takes you for no taster.
> Go from the kitchen, go.[34]

However, since Boccaccio wrote in Italian, it seemed an obvious precaution to check in a couple of other translations (the Bibliophilist and the Folio Society editions), and in neither could I find anything approaching a limerick. So, to the native Mursia Milano edition – only to discover that this apparent Italian proto-limerick, which has been quoted by a succession of commentators, is little more than the metrical invention of an English translator. Even more exciting was a passage in F.A. Wright's *Greek Social Life*: "The invention of limericks also was a favourite diversion at ancient Athenian symposia, and Aristophanes at the end of *The Wasps* gives half a dozen specimens"[35], with this verse given as an example:

> An amateur, driving too fast,
> From his car to the roadway was cast;
> And a friend kindly said, as he bandaged his head –
> "Mr. Cobbler, stick to your last".[36]

Wright was a Professor of Classics: surely he could be relied on? But another translation, by Benjamin Rogers, proved to be not even remotely limerickal:

> There was a man of Sybaris, do you know,
> Thrown from his carriage, and he cracked his skull,
> Quite badly too. Fact was, he could not drive.
> There was a friend of his stood by, and said,
> "Let each man exercise the art he knows".[37]

Where, then, did the truth lie? Back again to the original text, and even my little Greek (checked by a graecist friend), was enough to satisfy me that the second version was very much nearer to Aristophanes. So much for yet another myth!

Baring-Gould has asked, "Why . . . should anyone *want* to write about such an indecorous form of verse as the limerick?"[38], which seems to me as much a confusion of sensibility with structure as if one were to speak of a five-lined form of morality. Nor do I accept the widely held view that the best examples are necessarily the most indecent. The limerick has covered a vast range of subject matter, is capable of considerable flexibility in metre, and is notable for the marvellous ingenuity of rhyming which its practitioners have displayed. Hilaire Belloc was justified in objecting to the common confusion of levity with frivolity, and I agree with the anonymous writer who averred that "a successful limericker must be regarded as a better poet than many writers of modern free verse"[39]. Moreover, I reject the not uncommon contemporary literary heresy, that writing which simply oozes amorphously out of its author is somehow superior to that which is severely disciplined. There is much good poetry without either rhyme or regular metre, but I strongly suspect that Kingsley Amis was right when he said that "usually it's a case of shying away from hard work"[40]. Or, as Robert Conquest once put it, to write poetry without any metrical restraints is rather like playing tennis without a net. A.P. Herbert overstated things when he wrote, "The limerick . . . is the most difficult of all forms of metrical composition – that is, to do perfectly"[41], but at least it is a form in which success is unmistakeable and inadequacy cannot be covered by a smokescreen of opaque verbiage about 'creativity'.

Perhaps David MacCord has best encapsulated in a single verse the widely captivating appeal of this *genre*:

> Well, it's partly the shape of the thing
> That gives the old limerick wing;
>   Those accordion pleats,
>   Full of airy conceits,
> Take it up like a kite on a string.[42]

II

How Pleasant to Know Mr. Lear!

Nearly everybody seems to know that the limerick was invented by Edward Lear – and nearly everybody is wrong.

Not that the man-in-the-street may be overmuch blamed for this misapprehension: after all, it has been shared by many scholars. Indeed, as early as 1898, the limerick form had been virtually defined by one 'M.H.', in *Notes and Queries*, as "the nonsense verse as written by Lear"[1]. And even that great *aficionado* of the form, Langford Reed, wrote this in 1924:

> Although at the Lim'ricks of Lear
> We may feel a temptation to sneer,
> We should never forget
> That we owe him a debt
> For his work as the first pioneer.[2]

The myth has been perpetuated by a long line of writers who should have known better, including a quite recent contributor to the 'New Revised Edition' of *Chambers's Encyclopaedia*[3].

The truth is that Lear did not invent the limerick: he popularised it. Nor is there the slightest excuse for the neglect of this simple truth by so many so-called literary critics. After all, Lear himself had stated the position quite plainly in his introduction to *More Nonsense Pictures, Rhymes, Botany &c.* "Long years ago," he wrote, "in the days when much of my time was spent in a country house, where children and mirth abounded, the lines beginning, 'There was an Old Man of Tobago', were suggested to me by a valued friend, as a form of verse lending itself to limitless variety for Rhymes and Pictures, and thenceforth the greater part of the original drawings and verses for the first *Book of Nonsense* were struck off "[4]. As a matter of fact, the authentic original man of Tobago was not an old man at all: he was a sick man. The verse, probably by R.S. Sharpe and illustrated by a cartoon usually attributed to Robert Cruikshank, was first printed in 1822 in *Anecdotes and Adventures of Fifteen Gentlemen*, issued by John Marshall, a small London publisher of that period:

> There was a sick man of Tobago
> Liv'd long on rice-gruel and sago;
> > But at last, to his bliss,
> > The physician said this –
> "To a roast leg of mutton you may go."[5]

Nevertheless – and typically of the loose scholarship which seems to have suffused this field of study – references to the 'original' 'old' man are still being made today by pseudo-scholarly writers on the subject.

Lear was a loveable and most fascinating character. Born in Highgate in 1812, he was next to youngest of twenty-one offspring of a reputedly (but not in fact) Danish-descended stockbroker, whose financial speculations led him first to penury and later to prison. Edward was a delicate child (asthmatic, bronchitic, and mildly epileptic), but he had great natural talents and an enormous capacity for hard work. By the age of fifteen he was keeping himself as a commercial artist and, two years later, was commissioned to paint parrots for the Zoological Society of London. Like some other great men of his generation, he not only survived his comparative lack of schooling, but seems actually to have benefited by it. "I am always thanking God", he once wrote, "that I was never educated, for it seems to me that 999 of those who are so, expensively and laboriously, have lost all before they arrive at my age 47 – and remain like Swift's Strulbruggs – cut and dry for life."[6]. He became fairly competent in five languages and was erudite in an eclectic (if rather disorganised) fashion.

He seems to have been a compulsive worker at his profession of illustrating natural history and travel books. In 1865, for example, he produced 200 sketches in Crete, 145 in the Corniche, and 125 in the Nice-Cannes neighbourhood. At the age of 62, still practising as a 'wandering artist', he sent back home from India (in the space of six months) nearly 600 drawings, 9 sketch-books and 4 journals. No wonder that he described himself as "a very energetic and frisky old cove"![7]. In this necessarily peripatetic existence, his perennial itch to be ever on the move must have been a benison. His book-illustrating did not pay particularly well, but on his travels he often held exhibitions of his work (especially of his landscape paintings) and sold sufficient to earn a fairly comfortable living. And his personal charm was such that his friends found him patrons and his patrons became his friends. He even gave private painting lessons to Queen Victoria.

Lear's most important early supporters were the Stanley family, four of whom he served as successive Earls of Derby. The 13th Earl

commissioned him at the age of twenty to illustrate a handbook for
the estate menagerie at Knowsley, near Liverpool, and thenceforward he was a frequent guest at their grand family residence. He
immediately became a firm favourite with the younger generation,
for whom (at first with no thought of publication) he devised many
of his best absurdities. When eventually he dropped the *nom-de-plume* 'Derry Down Derry', by which he had unsuccessfully sought
to protect the serious artist from public association with nonsense,
he added this dedication:

TO THE

GREAT-GRANDCHILDREN, GRAND-NEPHEWS, AND GRAND-NIECES

OF EDWARD, 13th EARL OF DERBY,

THIS BOOK OF DRAWINGS AND VERSES

(the greater part of which were originally made and composed for their parents)

IS DEDICATED BY

THE AUTHOR

EDWARD LEAR

LONDON
1864   8

Lear received a mere £125 (but this, it should be remembered, was
in 1861 money) for the third edition of 2000 copies of his first *Book of
Nonsense*, and vast numbers of his more serious drawings and paintings were never sold at all, but occasionally he allowed himself wild
dreams of what he would do if ever he were to become really
wealthy. If, for example, he were to get £18,000(!) for his 200
Tennyson illustrations (which, in fact, he never managed to sell at
all), he would buy himself a "chocolate coloured carriage speckled
with gold, driven by a coachman in green vestments and silver
spectacles wherein sitting on a lofty cushion composed of muffins
and volumes of the Apocrypha" he would "disport himself all about
the London parks to the general satisfaction of all pious people"[9].
Here, of course, is the real key to Lear's unique success as a
nonsense-writer: he was himself a nonsensical person. As he put it in
his own self-mocking eight-verse self-portrait:

How pleasant to know Mr. Lear!
    Who has written such volumes of stuff !
Some think him ill-tempered and queer,
    But a few think him pleasant enough.

His mind is concrete and fastidious,
    His nose is remarkably big;

There was an old man of Peru,—who watched his wife makeng a stew,
Till once by mistake, in a stove she did bake, that unfortunat man of Peru

22

There was an Old Man of Peru,
Who watched his wife making a stew;
But once by mistake, in a stove she did bake,
That unfortunate Man of Peru.

A MANUSCRIPT ORIGINAL OF A LEAR LIMERICK.
Above – Lear's sketch with accompanying verse,
from H.W. Liebert, 1975, *Lear in the Original . . .* New York, H.P. Kraus.
Below – The illustration as it appeared in the 1846 *Book of Nonsense.*
Between – The verse laid out in four-line form.

His visage is more or less hideous,
　　His beard it resembles a wig.

He has many friends, laymen and clerical;
　　Old Foss is the name of his cat;
His body is perfectly spherical,
　　He weareth a runcible hat.

He reads but he cannot speak Spanish,
　　He cannot abide ginger-beer;
Ere the days of his pilgrimage vanish,
　　How pleasant to know Mr. Lear![10]

One can almost see and hear the Stanley children hooting with laughter at limericks in similar vein. The preposterous proboscis appeared again in 'There was an Old Person of Tring, who embellished his nose with a ring' and in 'There was an Old Man, on whose nose, Most birds of the air could repose'. It appeared afloat in 'There was an old man in a barge, Whose nose was exceedingly large', with still higher flights of fantasy in the 'old man of West Dumpet, Who possessed a large nose like a trumpet' and in the 'old person of Cassel, Whose nose finished off in a Tassel'. As for the luxuriant beard, one of Lear's limericks had 'Two Owls and a Hen, four Larks and a Wren' building their nests in it. His rotundity may be reflected in the 'old man, who when little, Fell casually into a kettle; But, growing too stout, He could never get out, So he passed all his life in that kettle'. Lear's restlessness shewed in 'There was an Old Man on a hill, Who seldom, if ever, stood still'; his irascibility in the 'Old Man of Peru', who 'tore off his hair, And behaved like a bear'; his valetudinarianism in the 'Old Man of Vienna, Who lived upon Tincture of Senna' and in the 'old man of the Dargle, Who purchased six barrels of Gargle'. His melancholy came out in the 'Old Man of Cape Horn, Who wished he had never been born"; his nervousness in the 'Old Person of Rhodes, Who strongly objected to toads'; his general feeling of inadequacy in the 'Old Man of Corfu, Who never knew what he should do'. And, of course, his immense amiability in the 'Old Man of the Isles, Whose face was pervaded with smiles'.

Then there were all those queer fictitious characters from Smyrna, Portugal, Madras, Crete, Buda, Calcutta – their creator could have been any one of them. Perhaps he was all of them: nobody ever knew Edward Lear better than he knew himself. "Nonsense was the safety-valve of his consciousness responding to most of his approaches to himself and his environment. It became ultimately a world in itself specially created by him as a refuge from the trials and tribulations of life . . . It was as though he lived a double life, one in

the realm of sense and the other in that of nonsense; and he had the
power of transmuting himself from one to the other at will"[11]. And,
as a result:

> There once was an artist named Lear
> Who wrote verses to make children cheer.
>> Though they never made sense,
>> Their success was immense,
> And the Queen thought that Lear was a dear.[12]

Children cheered to such effect that his nursery books were read and
re-read to the point of physical destruction, and extant copies of
early editions are extremely rare.

In Liverpool's Picton Library, however, I found an intriguing
volume, possibly one of a private printing (without either pagina-
tion or name of any publisher) produced for presentation to some of
Lear's friends, which from internal evidence may well have been
made at the time of the 1854 edition of his first *Book of Nonsense*. The
Picton book is inscribed in manuscript to "Professor Nicholls this
congenial tribute of respect – Similius simili gaudet"[13], and each of
its 73 pages consists of a single limerick, in some cases with manuscript corrections. The first verse reads:

> There was an Old Derry Down Derry,
> Who loved to see little folks merry;
>> So he made them a Book,
>> And with laughter they shook,
> At the fun of that Derry Down Derry.

followed by:

> There was an Old Man of Nepaul
> From his horse had a terrible fall;
>> But, though split quite in two,
>> By some very strong glue
> They mended that Man of Nepaul.

and then by:

> There was a young lady of Hull,
> Who was charged by virulent bull;
>> But she seized on a spade,
>> And called out, "Who's afraid?"
> Which distracted that virulent bull.[14]

– both of these latter two, by the way, being in different page
positions from their places in most publicly available editions. There
are two different versions of the 'Old Man of the West':

There was an Old Man with a nose,
Who said, 'If you choose to suppose
    That my nose is too long,
    You are certainly wrong!'
That remarkable Man with a nose.

There was a Young Lady whose nose
Was so long that it reached to her toes;
    So she hired an Old Lady
    Whose conduct was steady,
To carry that wonderful nose.

FOUR PREPOSTEROUS PROBOSCIDES.

Illustrating Lear's preoccupation with physiognomic peculiarities.

There was an Old Man, on whose nose
Most birds of the air could repose;
But they all flew away
At the closing of day,
Which relieved that Old Man and his nose.

There is a young lady, whose nose
Continually prospers and grows;
When it grew out of sight,
She exlaimed in a fright,
'Oh! Farewell to the end of my nose!'

Facing page and upper this page – from 1846 Book of Nonsense.
Lower this page – from 1872 More Nonsense . . .

> There was an Old Man of the West,
> Who wore a pale plum-coloured vest;
>   When they said, "Does it fit?"
>   He replied "Not a bit!"
> That uneasy Old Man of the West.
>
> There was an Old Man of the West,
> Who never could get any rest;
>   So they set him to spin
>   On his nose and his chin,
> Which cured that Old Man of the West.[15]

but, strangely enough, their respective illustrations are inappropriately transposed.

The first (1846) edition, probably published by Thomas McLean (although no publisher is given in the British Museum – now the British Library – catalogue), appeared in two parts, of 47 and 37 lithographed plates respectively. The second (1854) edition, still under the *nom de plume* 'Derry Down Derry', was of 73 plates. The third (1861) edition, in which Lear acknowledged his authorship and which had the imprint of Routledge, Warne and Routledge, consisted of 111 folios. By 1863, the tenth edition had appeared. Some editions open 'sideways' to give a page much wider than its length, thus accommodating with great ease the horizontally elongated beards, noses, donkeys, frying pans etc. which characterise so many of Lear's nonsense drawings. Advantage was also sometimes taken of this wide page to print the stanzas in a 'centred' three-line setting, rather than in the now almost invariably used five-line form, thus:

> There was a Young Lady whose chin resembled the point of a pin,
> So she had it made sharp, and purchased a harp,
> And played several tunes with her chin.

> There was an Old Person of Cadiz, who was always polite to all ladies,
> But in handing his daughter, he fell into the water,
> Which drowned that Old Person of Cadiz.[16]

There is, incidentally, a good deal to be said for this three-line lay-out. It gives a certain unity to the presentation of the person in the first long internally rhyming 'double' line, then similarly to the main action in the rather shorter internally rhyming second 'double' line, with crisp emphasis on the 'pay-off' consequence in the short third line. Elsewhere, there are examples of Lear's limericks set out as quatrains, with an internal rhyme halfway through the third 'double' line, thus:

There was an Old Derry Down Derry,
Who loved to see little folks merry;
So he made them a book,
And with laughter they shook,
At the fun of that Derry Down Derry.

LEAR'S ORIGINALLY PSEUDONYMOUS *BOOK OF NONSENSE* title-page from the (? printed 1854) 'presentation' volume, Liverpool Picton Library. Accompanying verse is:

There was an old Man of Bohemia,
Whose daughter was christened Euphemia,
Till one day, to his grief, she married a thief,
Which grieved that old Man of Bohemia.[17]

For Lear, 'nonsense' expressed itself in a total unity of word and picture – with the latter often more important than the former. With him, it was not a case of just writing something and then getting somebody else to illustrate it. And that, no doubt, is one reason why his products are still vastly more appealing to children than most later imitations.

Nor, of course, did Lear confine himself to limericks. His second book, *Nonsense Songs, Stories, Botany and Alphabets*, published in 1871, included those three classics, 'The Owl and the Pussy-Cat', 'The Jumblies', and 'Calico Pie', but contained not a single limerick. His 1872 *More Nonsense, Pictures, Rhymes, Botany, &c.* did include 100 illustrated verses of this sort, but their general heading, 'One Hundred Nonsense Pictures and Rhymes', perhaps indicates Lear's own order of priority between the two inter-related components of each unit. Then, in 1877, *Laughable Lyrics: a Fourth Book of Nonsense Poems, Songs, Botany, Music, &c.* was again limerickless, but included those wonderful inventions, 'The Dong with a Luminous Nose' and 'The Pobble who has No Toes'. Finally, there was the posthumous 1895 publication, *Nonsense Songs and Stories*, consisting largely of selections from the earlier four volumes, but memorable especially for 'The Heraldic Blazon of Foss the Cat', with its sketches of 'Foss Couchant', 'Foss, a untin', 'Foss rampant', Foss dansant', 'Foss, regardant', 'Foss Pprpr.' and 'Foss, Passant'.

His unity of verse and illustration, I suspect, may be one main reason why Lear usually repeated the person of the first line of his limericks in the fifth. Since the verse was to illustrate the drawing at least as much as the drawing was to illustrate the verse, it must have seemed natural enough to concentrate attention once more in the final line upon the subject of the unity. Thus, although it is true that "Part of the charm of the limerick is the surprise, the sudden swoop and unexpected twist of the last line"[18], it is also true that there was some positive gain in Lear's general final-line repetition. Yet, despite many unwarranted assertions to the contrary, several of his limericks do not in fact end the last line with the same word as the first. Sometimes he repeats the gist of the second line:

There was an Old Man of the Nile,
Who sharpened his nails with a file;

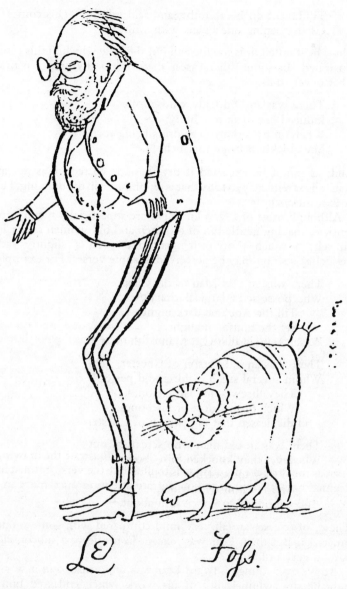

EDWARD LEAR AND HIS CAT 'FOSS'.

sketch from a letter by Lear to Hallam Tennyson, 16 June 1884, by kind permission of Lord Tennyson and Lincolnshire Library Service (Tennyson Research Centre).

> Till he cut off his thumbs, and said calmly, "This comes
> Of sharpening one's nails with a file!"[19]

– but, be it noted, it is the file and not the Nile which in this case is
illustrated. In some other cases, there is no rhyming repetition
whatsoever, thus:

> There was an Old Lady whose folly
> Induced her to sit in a holly;
> Whereon by a thorn, her dress being torn,
> She quickly became melancholy.[20]

And, as might be expected if my thesis is correct, it is not any
generalised tendency to folly that is emphasised in the drawing, but a
face of melancholy.

Although most of Lear's limericks are superficially merely nonsensical, making gentle fun of old men and old women rather like
himself, a much more astringent and even a slightly sado-
masochistic strain may be perceived in some verses. For example:

> There was an Old Man of the Cape,
> Who possessed a large Barbary Ape;
>   Till the Ape one dark night
>   Set the house on alight,
> Which burned that Old Man of the Cape.

> There was an old Person of Chester,
> Whom several small children did pester;
>   They threw some large stones,
>   Which broke most of his bones,
> And displeased that old person of Chester.

> There was an old man who screamed out
> Whenever they knocked him about;
>   So they took off his boots
>   And fed him with fruits,
> And continued to knock him about.[21]

These, of course, are all very mild compared with some modern
limericks. But then, Lear was (except in his deepest subconscious
core) a very mild man.

Above everything, Edward Lear was whimsical, and it was the
light-hearted whimsicality of his work which endeared him to
nearly every nursery in the land. Despite his arduous life-long
labours as an artist of nature, at which he continued until shortly
before his death in San Remo in 1888, it is not by his paintings that

we now remember him. The irony of his accidentally-achieved immortality was well expressed by Langford Reed in this verse:

> A goddess, capricious, is Fame;
> You may strive to make noted your name,
> But she either neglects you
> Or coolly selects you
> For laurels distinct from your aim.[22]

III

Why 'Limerick'?

No one, consulting the obvious standard works of reference, would find much reason to doubt that the limerick type of verse was so called after the Irish town of that name, for there apears to be a most impressive near-unanimity among authoritative dictionaries and encyclopaedias on this matter.

According to the *Oxford English Dictionary*, the word is "Said to be from a custom at convivial parties, according to which each member sang an extemporized 'nonsense verse', which was followed by a chorus containing the words 'Will you come up to Limerick?' "[1]. The *Oxford Companion to English Literature* says much the same. From the other side of the Atlantic, *Webster's Third New International Dictionary* tells us that the derivation is "probably from the occurrence of the words 'Will you come up to Limerick?' in a chorus sung by the whole group at a party after verses extemporized by individuals"[2]. In the *American Heritage Dictionary of the English Language* we likewise read, "From the line 'Will you come up to Limerick?' "[3]; while *Funk & Wagnalls New Standard Dictionary* says, "Limericks were usually extemporized compositions produced at convivial parties in Ireland by each individual in turn, while the entire party joined in singing a chorus in which were the words, 'Will you come up to Limerick?' "[4]. The *Universal English Dictionary* provides a minor variation in the actual words of the chorus, which it gives as 'Won't you come up, come up, come up to Limerick'[5] – a wording also given in Scott's *Current Literary Terms*. Another minor variation, 'We'll all come up, come up, come up to Limerick'[6], appeared in Cassell's 1909 *Encyclopaedic Dictionary*; and the 1959 edition of *Brewer's Dictionary of Phrase and Fable* says virtually the same. Yet further confirmation is apparently provided by the 1952 *Concise Etymological Dictionary* and by *The Chambers Twentieth Century Dictionary*. As for the 1967 edition of *Everyman's Encyclopaedia*, it writes quite unambiguously of "the town after which it [the verse-form] is named"[7]. And if, for the sake of final certainty, one refers to the 1970 *Encyclopaedia Britannica*, there also one finds quoted the view that "the name derives from a song . . . the chorus of which was 'Will you come up to Limerick?' "[8]. Even Gershon Legman, probably the most erudite of all limerick anthologists, surprisingly wrote, in his great (albeit unfortunately offensive) collection *The Limerick*, that the name was "appropriated from that of the town in Ireland"[9].

It is true that several of these statements do not unambiguously assert in so many words that the verse-form is named after the town, but the cumulative impression to that effect is unavoidable and overwhelming. Methought that the 'authorities' did agree too much; and, the more I searched in vain for any substantial evidence, the more I became convinced that this was a conspicuous case of authority feeding upon authority. It seems to have started as far back as 1898, when J.M. Murray wrote, in *Notes and Queries*, "Certain it is that a song has existed in Ireland for a very considerable time, the construction of the verse of which is identical with that of Lear's"[10]. It probably continued as a popular belief precisely because it appears so 'obvious'. Then, in 1924, Langford Reed gave great impetus to this theory by the definiteness of his claim for it – since when very few commentators seem ever to have questioned it.

Reed dedicated his *Complete Limerick Book* to "the picturesque and ancient city of Limerick . . . the 'birthplace' of one of our most popular national recreations"[11]. "The Limerick", he went on to say, "apparently derives its name from a song, popular at convivial gatherings in Ireland about a century ago, in which each of an interminable set of verses dealt with the adventures of an inhabitant of a different Irish town, something in the manner of the modern Limerick, and had to be invented on the spur of the moment, each line by a different singer, after which the whole company roared out a chorus commencing with the invitation, 'Will you come up to Limerick?' "[12]. Later, in his 1937 *My Limerick Book*, he delivered himself of further detail: "Here is a spot of information which all possessors of this book ought to have. It concerns a discovery I made thirteen years ago . . . The name 'Limerick' is indirectly connected with the Treaty of Limerick (1691) which brought peace between England and Ireland and released many thousands of trained Irish soldiers for service as mercenaries in 'The Irish Brigade' in France . . . Throughout the ninety years' service of the Brigade, something like a million Irishmen served in it . . . To cut a long story short, the form of the rhyme which had been so popular in France, became equally popular among her Irish Allies . . . and . . . when . . . this form of verse became so popular in England as to require a general title, the one already used in Ireland was adopted. And that's how the Limerick got its name"[13].

Now it is a fact that, following the Treaty of Limerick, an Irish Brigade, mainly organised in that city and largely recruited from that county, did serve in France. Its cavalry, moreover, was commanded by the Earl of Limerick and its infantry by Sir John Fitzgerald, the local member of parliament. It is also quite likely that its members may have become familiar with a few old French verses of limerick form, including a version of 'Hickory Dickory Dock':

> Digerie, Digerie, doge,
> La souris ascend l'horloge,
>   L'horloge frappe,
>   La souris s'échappe,
> Digerie, digerie, doge.[14]

Moreover, Reed made a good point when he drew attention to a footnote in Boswell's *Life of Johnson*, referring to a French verse about a young lady named Caliste, who appeared at a masquerade during the fierce contentions between the followers of the Spanish priest Miguel de Molinos and those of the Dutch theologian Cornelius Jansen:

> "On s'étonne ici que Caliste
> Ait pris l'habite de Moliniste.
>   Puisque cette jeune beauté
>   Ote à chacun sa liberté,
> N'est-ce pas une Janseniste?"[15]

But Reed seems never to have published any hard evidence which he may have found for his 'Irish Brigade' theory of the origin of the term 'limerick'; nor even, so far as is known, did he disclose it to any other person. We are simply left to take everything on trust.

There has been a handful of doubters about Reed's Franco-Irish theory. Ronald Knox once pointed out that the reputed wording of the chorus:

> Won't you come up, come up,
> Won't you come up, I say,
> Won't you come up, come all the way up,
> Come all the way up to Limerick?

is in nothing remotely approaching limerick form. This particular ground of objection, however, is a weak one, for quite commonly a chorus takes different form from the individual verses. More generally, an unsigned article in the 1960 *Children's Encyclopaedia* says, "Nothing is known about the first limerick nor where the name came from" and (very guardedly) "Some people believe that it came

from an old song about a town in Ireland, 'Will you come up to
Limerick?' "[16]. Karl Beckson, editing the 1961 *Readers' Guide to
Literary Terms*, remarks of the term 'limerick' that "its origin . . . is
not definitely known"[17]. The 1968 *Encyclopedia Americana* says
fairly cautiously, "the name may be connected with the Irish city of
Limerick"[18]. The 1970 Centenary Edition of *Brewer's Dictionary of
Phrase and Fable* quotes the theory, but adds "there is no real evidence
for this"[19]. And J.M. Cohen, who contributed the relevant article in
the 1970 edition of the *Encyclopaedia Britannica*, has written to me
privately, "The Langford Reed theory is plausible, but unsupported
by evidence"[20].

Some few anthologists and critics have been properly reserved –
H.I. Brock, for example, wrote in 1947 that "nobody has been able
to find more than a tenuous link between the limerick as a verse form
and the Irish city and county of that name"[21]. In 1965, Guy Boas was
much more sceptical, indeed scathing: "We are asked to believe that
a limerick is so called because a convivial chorus, we are not told of
whom, on an unspecified occasion joined in an unknown refrain
'We'll all come up to Limerick' after each singer had improvised a
limerick . . . This in its woolliness is research gone mad"[22]. But
perhaps the most astringent of the sceptics was Carolyn Wells, the
pioneer American scholar in this field. Within a year of Reed's
announcing his great 'discovery', she wrote, "To link up the matter
with a song, 'Won't you come up to Limerick' – is a mere fancy,
founded on no truth whatever"[23]. It may be worth adding that, as
recently as 1974–75, neither the Limerick City Library nor *The Irish
Times* was able to turn up anything at all (in response to a request by
me) in the way of evidence for the common belief.

The only properly critical conclusion is that, until somebody has
devoted to this mystery something approaching the indefatigable
literary scholarship which Iona and Peter Opie have given to the
historical origin of nursery rhymes, it will be idle to draw any firm
conclusion about the origins of the term 'limerick'. And, in the
meanwhile, I would suggest that the absence of any specifically
French word for this variety of verse argues strongly against an
ultimately French origin. My guess, for what it is worth, is that we
shall eventually discover multiple origins over a long period of time
and a wide range of tongues, and that the real problem is that of
identifying the factors which led to the limerick's remarkable proliferation in England.

Langford Reed felt that he must "pay tribute to the place where the
first Limerick was perpetrated", and he went on to perpetrate (here,
surely, *le mot juste*) this verse:

> All hail to the town of Limerick
> Which provides a cognomen, generic,
>> For a species of verse
>> Which for better, or worse,
> Is supported by laymen and cleric.[24]

Since it seems to have become regarded as almost mandatory to essay the far from easy task of putting 'Limerick' into a limerick, perhaps I may express the present state of my own feelings about the reputed connexion between these two as follows:

> It is said that the name comes from Limerick
> (A place that's Hibernian, not Cymric):
>> I'm not too impressed
>> And beg to suggest
> That the legend is probably chimeric.

There is, incidentally, another somewhat similar case of an *ex cathedra* assertion of this sort becoming, by virtue of frequent repetition, almost unquestioned literary dogma. It relates to the origin of the term 'Mother Goose', used – as it still is widely in the U.S.A. – in relation to nursery rhymes and stories. The original Mother Goose is commonly believed to have been a Bostonian housewife, Elizabeth Goose, born in 1665, who step-mothered ten children in addition to six of her own. One of her daughters married Thomas Fleet, a printer, who was said to have taken down the rhymes from his mother-in-law's own lips and later to have published them in her name. This account appears in any number of reference books, and does not seem to have been seriously questioned until the Opies' edition of the *Oxford Dictionary of Nursery Rhymes* appeared in 1951. This admirable husband-and-wife team, who were not content to continue merely quoting 'authorities' but actually conducted research, found that most American 'Mother Goose' books are evidently based upon John Newberry's eighteenth century English edition of *Songs for the Nursery, or Mother Goose's Melodies for Children*. Moreover, some old German tales of this type were formerly referred to as being by 'Frau Gosen', while as early as 1650 the term 'contes de la Mer-Oie' (the earlier French form of 'Mère-Oie', 'Mother Goose') was current in France. And, despite the most assiduous search, the Opies quite failed to find a single surviving copy of the original reputed Thomas Fleet publication – which they characterised as "the most elusive 'ghost' volume in the history of American letters"[25]. They finally concluded that this almost universally accepted story owes its warranty entirely to one man, John

Fleet Eliot (a great-grandson of Thomas Fleet), who first put it into print in *The Boston Transcript* in 1860.

Thackeray's *Irish Sketch Book* also seems to count against Reed's theory. This most observant nineteenth century note-taker spent some time in Limerick in 1842. Yet, although he was always on the look-out for literary oddities, he "doubts very much whether he has anything to say about Limerick that is worth the trouble of saying or reading"[26] – apart, that is, from a paean in praise of Mr. Cruise's hotel. Moreover, although Thackeray had about ninety verses in the 'Caxton' edition of his *Lyra Hibernica*, not a single one is of recognisably limerick form. And yet – and yet! It never pays to jump to hasty conclusions on the basis of purely negative evidence. Burrowing away amongst earlier printings, I came across this verse, the first of a sequence in similar form, in the 1899 'Pocket Book' edition:

> You've all heard of Larry O'Toole,
> Of the beautiful town of Drumgoole;
>   He had but one eye,
>   To ogle ye by –
> Oh, murther, but that was a jew'l!
>   A fool
> He made of the girls, did O'Toole.[27]

So at least it is established that Thackeray either collected or composed 'Irish' stanzas in perfect limerick form, with the normal five lines followed by a single-footed and then a three-footed line. And, perhaps significantly, the character 'Larry O'Toole' had previously appeared in the novel *Phil Fogarty*, which dealt with the adventures of an Irish force fighting in France.

To cast doubt upon the Irish origin of the term 'limerick' is not, of course, to deny the pre-Lear existence of limericks in Ireland. The two questions, though often confused, are quite distinct. In County Limerick itself, for example, there was in the little village of Croom (on the river Maigue) an eighteenth century group of priests, pedagogues and publicans who seem to have been strongly addicted to such verses. Two of them in particular, Séan ó Tuama (John O'Toumy, or O'Tuomy) and Aindreas MacCraith (Andrew McCrath), were prolific in the *genre*. That is, if one may rely upon the English-language translations produced by Clarence Mangan a century later. To the eye untutored in Erse, the original versions are less convincingly limerickal, as may be seen from this specimen:

> *Is duine mé dhiólas leann lá,*
> *'S chuireas mo bhuión chum remcâis,*

Mura mbeadh duine im chuideachta dhiólfas
Mise bheas thíos leis in anthráth.[28]

The Maigue poets often met in O'Toumy's inn, where the landlord poetically boasted:

I sell the best brandy and sherry,
To make my good customers merry;
      But at times their finances
      Run short, as it chances,
And then I feel very sad, very!

Here's brandy! Come fill up your tumbler;
Or ale, if your liking be humbler;
      And while you've a shilling,
      Keep filling and swilling –
A fig for the growls of the grumbler!

I like, when I'm quite at my leisure,
Mirth, music and all sorts of pleasure;
      When Marjery's bringing
      The glass, I like singing
With bards – if they drink within measure.[29]

To which his very candid friend McCrath replied:

O'Toumy! you boast yourself handy
At selling good ale and bright brandy,
      But the fact is your liquor
      Makes everyone sicker;
I tell you that, I, your friend Andy.

But your poems and pints, by your favour,
Are alike wholly wanting in flavour,
      Because it's your pleasure,
      You give us short measure,
And your ale has a ditch-water savour!

You bow to the floor's very level
When customers enter to revel,
      But if one in shy raiment
      Takes a drink without payment
You score it against the poor devil.[30]

Doubtless one important reason why the Limerick-limerick theory has so long held such almost undisputed sway is that nobody has ever yet produced any credible alternative – just as the Genesis theory of creation had to wait for centuries before being confronted by Darwin's theory. Naturally enough, when first I began probing at this problem, the initial field for investigation of possible alternative origins was that of personal names. If that fascinating bird the petrel could be called after St. Peter, and tontine clubs after the early Italian banker Lorenzo Tonto, and syphilis after the shepherd-hero Syphilus, might not the limerick similarly be named for some historical or fictional figure? Since the fourth Earl of Sandwich, who found that the most convenient form of sustenance during his long sessions at the gaming table was cold beef between slices of toasted bread, inspired that handy word 'sandwich'; since 'wellington boots' were so named after the great Duke of Wellington; since the 'mackintosh' raincoat, so admirably suited to the unpredictable rains of his native hills, was named after Charles Mackintosh; since the 'raglan' style of overcoat-shouldering recalls Lord Fitzroy Somerset, first Baron Raglan; and since women's 'bloomers' immortalised the American suffragist Mrs. Amelia Bloomer; why should not limericks be called after somebody of that name? Perhaps one of the Earls of Limerick, or one of its Bishops, or even some long-forgotten so-named denizen of London's literary underworld? But, sadly, the most diligent search has quite failed to discover a single plausible contender for the palm. Of course, there might have been somebody with 'Limerick' as a forename (it sounds no more unlikely than 'Clerihew', which became the name of a type of verse invented by Edmund Clerihew Bentley). But, if so, the individual concerned has so far eluded me. No, that apparently promising path of exploration eventually petered out in an empty desert.

There is however, another way in which new words are sometimes invented – simply on the spur of the moment, by somebody of lively linguistic ingenuity, arising out of a particular conversational context and compounded of two or more already existent words. Could 'limerick' possibly have been created in this way? Once one starts speculating and investigating along these lines, a few hitherto unrelated factors begin to fall into an interesting pattern. For the mystery is not merely that of the origin of the word. There are also the facts that it did not come into general use until half a century after the verse-form was popularised by Lear; that once in use it spread with astonishing rapidity; and that its etymology seems to have sunk into almost total oblivion almost immediately. Gershon Legman believes that the first appearance was "at some time between 1882 and 1898, possibly in the columns of the sporting newspaper, *The Pink 'Un*"[31], while the first thoroughly established use was on 6th October 1898, when the 'Contents' list of the magazine *Cantab* included "Illustrated Limericks"[32]. And it is round about this year that several interesting considerations concatenate.

In 1899, Rudyard Kipling published his schoolboy story, *Stalky and Co.*, and already the word 'limerick' was evidently sufficiently widely known to be used in the tale quite casually, without a word of explanation. Stalky and his bosom pals M'Turk and Beetle, deeply immersed in an ingenious plot connected with the school's volunteer cadet corps, decide that their arch-enemy Mr. King, a housemaster, must be 'rotted' ('ragged'). Says Stalky to Beetle, "Then you've got to rot King, my giddy poet. Make up a catchy Limerick, and let the fags sing it"[33]. Yet already the origin of the word was shrouded in mystery, for in November 1898 a correspondent to *Notes and Queries* had asked, "When and why did the nonsense verse as written by Lear acquire the name of 'Limerick'?[34]." Nobody seemed to know the answer, but in the following month there was a reply: "A nonsense verse such as was written by Lear is wrongfully so called . . . Who applied this name to the indecent nonsense verse first it is hard to say"[35]. So, if in general people at that time applied the word 'limerick' only to indecent verses in this form, was there perchance another word for decent ones? Yes, there was such a word; and, although it must have been of very limited circulation and very short-lived, it has left just a trace. "A 'learic' . . .", wrote Matthew Russell in February 1898, "is a name we have invented for a single-stanza poem modelled on the form of the *Book of Nonsense*"[36]. Over half a century later, Ernest Weekley suggested that "the choice of the word 'limerick' may have been partly due to the somewhat earlier 'learic', coined, on 'lyric', by Father Matthew Russell"[37].

But this still leaves the problem of why 'learic' should have been modified to 'limerick', and of why (at least initially) the latter should have related especially to the less reputable specimens of the form. Now, it also happens that the year 1898 was that in which the great Walter Skeat, founder of the English Dialect Society, was honoured by a massive *festschrift*. In *The English Dialect Dictionary*, dedicated to Skeat, the word 'limmer' appeared, with the meanings of "A scoundrel, rascal, rogue" and "A prostitute, strumpet, a loose, immoral woman or girl"[38]. What term could be more suited to the unsavoury sorts of character which crop up in so many limericks? No doubt, in 1898, the small and close-knit group who constituted London's literary world of that time would have browsed in the great new dialect dictionary and exchanged chit-chat about their more interesting gleanings. Some, indeed, must have been reminded that the word 'limmer' had earlier been used both by Sir Walter Scott and by George Borrow. In *Waverley*, "Kate and Matty, the limmers, gaed off wi' twa o' Hawley's dragoons"[39], while in *Lavengro* there is the exclamation, "Leave my husband in the hands of you and that limmer!"[40]. The word 'limmer', incidentally, was also used as an adjective, and it seems quite possible that the form 'limmeric' might have been used adjectivally.

How easy now it becomes to imagine a perfectly credible scene of creation! Round about 1898 (in an English period *par excellence* of all kinds of glossic ingenuity), somewhere in Belgravia or Clapham or St. John's Wood, or perhaps in the billiard room of a West End Club, somebody asks, "Have you heard this learic?", and recites one which is a bit off-colour. Somebody else rejoins, "I should call that a 'limmeric', dear chap". Those who understand, chortle; those who are mystified receive an explanation. Within a month the witticism has circulated all over clubland; within another month everyone has forgotten the precise circumstances of its origin. The word appears in print with one 'm' and a 'k' as 'limerick'; it drives 'learic' out of circulation; and soon everybody is assuming some connexion with the town in Ireland. Such a suggestion may seem too highly suppositious if not quite preposterous; nevertheless this is precisely the sort of haphazard manner in which things often do happen in real life.

I am not, as a matter of fact, at all sure that I even have very much faith in my own suggestion. It is probably just as likely that the common belief, though unproven, may be correct. But, at least, this 'limmer'–'learic' hypothesis does incorporate a fair number of hard facts and is therefore worthy of being propounded – if only in order to provide some sort of plausible alternative to Reed's 'Irish' theory. Perhaps, faced now with two conflicting hypotheses, for neither of which there is any firm evidence, some scholar some day will really set to and solve the problem.

IV

Pioneers and Precursors

"The pre-history of the Limerick", Gershon Legman has assured us, "is remarkably easy to trace"[1]. Well, maybe. Perhaps it is – provided that one is not too particular about precisely what constitutes a limerick, and provided also that one does not examine too critically some of the claims which have been made about so-called early examples.

But at least one thing seems quite certain: the earliest known publications consisting exclusively of limericks, in quite recognisably modern form, appeared in London between 1820 and 1823. They were very small 'chap books' (a term derived from the Old English word 'céapmann', a merchant or pedlar), hawked about the streets by vendors, some of whom specialised in the libellous, the obscene, or the politically subversive. But *The History of Sixteen Wonderful Old Women, illustrated by as many engravings: exhibiting their Principal Eccentricities and Amusements*, issued in 1820/21 by Harris and Son, at the Corner of St. Paul's Church-Yard (the original publisher of *The Comic Adventures of Old Mother Hubbard*) was a delightful little children's book. Nursery rhymes had for some time been featuring 'old women' of one sort or another, so the general choice of subject for these new verses was natural enough. Harris's publication is today extremely rare, but there are copies in the British Museum and in the Osborne Collection at Toronto.

Some of the subjects were entirely admirable:

> There was an Old Woman of Leeds,
> Who spent all her time in Good Deeds,
>   She worked for the poor
>   Till her fingers were sore,
> That pious Old Woman of Leeds.[2]

Others had a virtue (in this case, thrift), but took it to such excess as almost turned it into a vice:

> There was an Old Woman of Norwich,
> Who liv'd upon nothing but porridge,

> Parading the town,
> She turned cloak into gown,
> That thrifty Old Woman of Norwich.[3]

One was an undoubted flirt, despite her unfortunate physiognomy:

> There liv'd an Old Woman at Lynn,
> Whose Nose very near touch'd her chin,
>   You may easy suppose
>   She had plenty of Beaux;
> This charming Old Woman of Lynn.[4]

Another was evidently addicted to lotteries:

> There was an Old Woman of Ealing,
> She jump'd till her head touch'd the Ceiling
>   When 2 1 6 4
>   Was announc'd at her Door;
> As a prize to th'Old Woman of Ealing.[5]

Yet another seems to me of especial interest, as being almost certainly the original source of Lear's famous nonsense-song, 'The Owl and the Pussy-Cat', who also went to sea:

> There was an Old Woman named Towl,
> Who went out to Sea with her Owl,
>   But the Owl was Sea-sick,
>   And screamed for Physic;
> Which sadly annoy'd Mistress Towl.[6]

His drawing for 'The Owl and the Pussy-cat' is basically the same as that for the earlier 'Old Woman named Towl' limerick, but with the owl in place of the old woman amidships and the pussy-cat replacing the owl astern. (Incidentally, his manuscript sketch for a limerick 'There was an Old Person of Harrow' – which was not in fact published in either of his two 'Nonsense' books – is quite evidently based upon the illustration to the 1820/21 'Old Woman of Harrow', but with the man pushing the woman in a barrow from right to left instead of from left to right.)

Within not much more than twelve months, John Marshall (Harris's great competitor in the production of children's chap books) published *Adventures and Anecdotes of Fifteen Gentlemen*, all the verses of which have recently been reprinted in Jean Harrowven's 1976 *The Limerick Makers*. The author is believed to have been Richard Scrafton Sharpe, a Bishopsgate grocer, and the illustrations were probably by Robert Cruikshank. Some of the verses display quite

THE OWL AND THE PUSSY-CAT

The Owl and the Pussy-cat went to sea
    In a beautiful pea-green boat,
They took some honey, and plenty of money,
    Wrapped up in a five-pound note.
The Owl looked up to the stars above,
    And sang to a small guitar,
'O lovely Pussy! O Pussy, my love,
    What a beautiful Pussy you are,
        You are,
        You are!
What a beautiful Pussy you are!'

THE PROBABLE DERIVATION OF 'THE OWL AND THE PUSSY-CAT'.

Above – illustration and first verse, from Lear's 1871 *Nonsense Songs* . . .
Compare with frontispiece plate, from the anonymous 1820/21 *The History of Sixteen Wonderful Old Women* . . . , British Museum (British Library) copy.

There was an Old Woman of Harrow,
Who visited in a Wheel barrow,
    And her servant before,
    Knock'd loud at each door;
To announce the Old Woman of Harrow.

There was an Old Person of Harrow
Who bought a mahogany barrow,
    For he said to his wife
    'You're the joy of my life!
And I'll wheel you all day in this barrow!'

ANOTHER LEAR DEBT TO THE FIRST LIMERICK BOOK.

Above – the fifth limerick in the 1820/21 *The History of Sixteen Wonderful Old Women* . . .
Below – sketch and verse by Edward Lear (not published in his lifetime), from A. Davidson & P. Hofer, 1953, *Teapots and Quails* . . , London, John Murray.

considerable humour, satire or wit. Apart from the celebrated Man
of Tobago, there were several other characters from lands overseas –
a feature very much followed later by Lear:

> There was a poor man of Jamaica,
> He open'd a shop as a baker;
>> The nice biscuits he made
>> Procured him much trade
> With the little black boys of Jamaica. [7]

> As a little fat man of Bombay
> Was smoking one very hot day,
>> A bird called a Snipe
>> Flew away with his pipe,
> Which vex'd the fat man of Bombay. [8]

> A Tailor, who sailed from Quebec,
> In a storm ventur'd once upon deck;
>> But the waves of the sea
>> Were as strong as could be,
> And he tumbled in up to his neck. [9]

And this next verse, remarkably enough, was still circulating orally
in Liverpool, virtually unchanged, a good century later:

> There was an old soldier of Bicester,
> Was walking one day with his sister,
>> A bull, with one poke,
>> Toss'd her into an oak
> Before the old gentleman miss'd her. [10]

In 1823, 'A Lady' produced *Little Rhymes for Little Folks: or A
Present for Fanny's Library*, in which for the first time an animal
appeared as the main character in a limerick:

> There was once a nice little dog, Trim,
> Who ne'er had ill temper or whim;
>> He could sit up and dance,
>> Could run, skip, and prance –
> Who would not like little dog Trim? [11]

Taken as a whole, the impressive thing about the limericks in these
three pioneer publications is their high degree of prosodic and
subject-matter sophistication. With few exceptions, their scansion
and rhyming are almost flawless. In several, there is absolutely no
repetition of line-ending words. There is even, in one of the verses

quoted, a place-name of peculiar pronunciation (or, starting from pronunciation, of peculiar spelling) – a feature later much exploited by some modern limerickers. The main characters are, almost invariably, clearly delineated individuals with specified idiosyncrasies or occupations. And sometimes there is even a remarkably modern-seeming final-line 'punch'.

These chap books of children's verse appeared when Lear was about eight to ten years old, and I feel sure that he must have seen them. But, if so, the *finesses* of their verses, to judge by his own later compositions, failed to make much impression on him. In the December of 1845, *Punch* informed its readers that "our old friends the Man of Tobago, the Sailor [*sic*] of Bister [*sic*], &c., &c., have been excluded from the Most Gracious Schoolroom, to make room for an entirely new class of picture-books, containing short-rhymed lessons in history, taste, and morality, calculated to instruct as well as amuse the Royal Infants" [12]. The Queen, in fact, was never quite the strait-laced old lady which modern mythology would have her, and in her earlier days she was in some ways quite a gay young thing. But, even if in 1845 limericks were excluded from the royal nursery, it could not have been for long. A year later, Lear's first nonsense book was off the press, and light-hearted limericks were soon being read to and repeated by infants of every social degree.

It is my belief that an important part of the hidden history of limericks lies in oral circulation by juveniles, and at this point a brief diversion on the general theme of children's verse in limerick form is necessary. Without pausing here to define too closely what precisely constitutes a limerick, it is easily demonstrable that the characteristic rhyme and rhythm patterns are much more widespread than has hitherto been generally recognised. Perhaps they have been largely overlooked because our educational system (and especially our higher education system) is eye-dominated, and few scholars seem capable of recognising a limerick unless it is printed in five lines with the third and fourth indented a few ems. In order to compensate for this quite common inadequacy, I have re-arranged some of the verses quoted below, into the orthodox limerick lay-out.

Let us examine one of the comparatively few traditional nursery rhymes which has been previously recognised as a limerick:

Hickory, dickory, dock,
The mouse ran up the clock;
    The clock struck one,
    The mouse ran down,
Hickory, dickory, dock. [13]

This verse was originally used as a counting-out rhyme for children's games – and appears probably to contain, in its first and fifth lines, corruptions of the ancient Westmorland shepherds' telling-numbers, 'hevers' (eight), 'devers' (nine) and 'dick' (ten). There is, incidentally, a very interesting variant:

> Dickery, dickery, dare!
> The pig flew up in the air;
>> The man in brown
>> Soon brought him down –
> Dickery, dickery, dare![14]

It has been very credibly suggested that the 'pig' was the Lord Protector of England, Richard (son of Oliver) Cromwell. And that the 'man in brown' was a 'Brownfriar', a 'monk' – in fact none other than that General Monk who 'brought him [Cromwell] down' in 1660. This rather elaborate disguise (though it would have been transparent enough at the time) may well have been thought in those dangerous days to be not only witty but also wise.

It can not be safely assumed that the juvenile retailers of such politically pointed verses must be innocently unaware of their real significance. Nor that children would be disinclined to circulate political verse among themselves. In 1935, when the helpless Abyssinian tribesmen were being bombed by the Italian air force, this verse was chanted by children in our streets:

> Roll along, Mussolini, roll along,
> You won't be in Abyssinia long;
>> You'll be sitting on the plain
>> With a bullet in your brain,
> Roll along, Mussolini, roll along.[15]

And young children do not merely repeat verses of topical political or social reference: they actually invent them. Thus, during and soon after the second world war, the German *Führer* was made into a figure of fun:

> Hitler, you are barmy,
> You want to join the army;
>> Get knocked out
>> By a big Boy Scout,
> Hitler, you are barmy.[16]

Eventually a multi-verse epic emerged, from which I quote just two exemplars:

In 1941
Old Hitler ate a bun;
    He got an ache,
    Which made him quake,
In 1941.

In 1942
Old Hitler felt quite blue;
    He left his pants
    In the middle of France,
In 1942.[17]

There is a particularly interesting trio of children's street-limericks, evidently modified successively from the days of Jack the Ripper (active 1888-89), through those of South Africa's President Kruger (died 1904), to those of the film cartoon character Mickey Mouse (from 1928):

Jack the Ripper's dead,
And lying on his bed;
    He cut his throat
    With Sunlight soap,
Jack the Ripper's dead.

Pool old Kruger's dead,
He died last night in bed;
    He cut his throat
    With a bit of soap,
Poor old Kruger's dead.

Mickey Mouse is dead
He died last night in bed;
    He cut his throat
    With a ten bob note,
Mickey Mouse is dead.[18]

Naturally enough, children have also produced limericks or near-limericks with just a sufficient degree of 'daringness' to provide the delicious mild thrill of taboo-word utterance:

Mickey Mouse was in his house,
Taking off his trousers;
    Then his mum
    Smacked his bum
And chased him round the houses.[19]

This element of the slightly shocking crops up also in the exploratory activities of an unnamed mouse:

Shocking, shocking, shocking,
A mouse ran up my stocking;
    When it got to my knee,
    Wow! what did it see?
Shocking, shocking, shocking.[20]

Similarly that popular fictional detective 'Dick Barton' was enlisted
in the service of the mildly scandalous:

Temptation, temptation, temptation,
Dick Barton went down to the station;
    Blondie was there,
    All naked and bare,
Temptation, temptation, temptation.[21]

But by no means all such usage of fictional characters is either
politically pointed or sociologically referential or even mildly
improper. Most often it is simply amusing, as in this example:

Popeye, the sailor man,
He lived in a caravan,
    He bought a pianner
    For six and a tanner,
Popeye, the sailor man.[22]

Then there is that song which children used to chorus around
campfires in the 1930s, blithely unaware (as apparently have been
most adult commentators since then) that they were singing
limericks:

I went to the animal fair,
And who do you think was there?
    The grey baboon
    By the light of the moon
Was combing his golden hair.

The monkey fell out of his bunk,
He fell on the elephant's trunk;
    The elephant sneezed
    And fell on his knees,
And what became of the monk
    -ey, monkey, monkey, monk?[23]

So one may continue, discovering limericks among children's
verses of various degrees of antiquity or recency. This example was
first recorded in about 1815:

Feedum, fiddledum, dee,
The cat's got into the tree.
   Pussy, come down
   Or I'll crack your crown,
And toss you into the sea.[24]

The following variant, recorded comparatively recently, specifies the type of tree concerned:

Diddlety, diddlety, dumpty,
The cat ran up the plum tree;
   Half a crown
   To fetch her down,
Diddlety, diddlety, dumpty.[25]

And the specification is interesting, since for some mysterious reason cats in folk verses seem to have had a continuing special affinity with plum trees, going back to at least one case recorded as early as 1609. That such a connexion should have survived for over three centuries, evidently being repeated and varied from mouth to mouth throughout this long period, should serve as a salutary warning against relying too much on the exclusive authority of print.

Forty years before Harris published his *Sixteen Wonderful Old Women*, an Italian 'Punch and Judy' man, one Piccini, was travelling round England with a show which included this lullaby in approximately limerick form:

Dance a baby, diddy,
What can mammy do wid'ee,
   But sit in her lap
   And give 'un some pap,
And dance a baby, diddy?[26]

And in about 1820 this still universally popular pair of verses (derived from or utilised by Robert Southey) appeared:

What are little boys made of?
What are little boys made of?
   Frogs and snails
   And puppy-dog tails,
That's what little boys are made of.

What are little girls made of?
What are little girls made of?
   Sugar and spice
   And all that's nice,
That's what little girls are made of.[27]

There is thus ample evidence that limericks and the like had existed in child-verse long before Lear was born. They can be identified in nursery rhymes, lullabies, counting-out chants, and disguised political comment. Children formerly enjoyed them, as they still do, as a medium for the *sub rosa* defiance of authority, for mildly exciting titillation, for relieving feelings of aggression, and above all as sheer innocent nonsense. That is to say, in precisely those main manners which apply with adults. Many nursery rhymes were probably not initially produced for children, but derived from verses originally composed as adult ballad, bawdy, joviality, religious ritual, or political satire. And it is probably no accident that the earliest collections of detergised limericks, written specially for children, were published in just about the period when juveniles were first beginning to be sharply delineated from adults, almost as if they were different animals instead of just younger ones.

It is also now clear (and much has been collated by Legman) that limericks and near-limericks existed in adult literature long before 1820. But he erred in asserting that, by about 1740, "the limerick form, now fully achieved in all its particulars, had so often been turned to the uses and abuses of satire . . . drinking, wenching, and other 'low professions', that no one . . . could have saved it as a lyric form, and . . . the limerick metre was abandoned altogether to the uses of nonsense and nursery rhymes"[28]. Look, for example, at this verse by Henry Austin Dobson (1840-1921):

> In after days when grasses high
> O'er-top the stone where I shall lie,
> > Though ill or well the world adjust
> > My slender claim to honour'd dust,
> I shall not question nor reply.[29]

By the common definition, its third and fourth lines are too long for a limerick, but it has the *aabba* rhyme-pattern and, if spoken out with the stresses that its tenderly yearning spirit demands, its rhythm-pattern also is nearly limerickal. And there is really no doubt at all in the case of 'Song to Ceres' by Leigh Hunt (1784-1859), of which one verse runs:

> Laugh out in the loose green jerkin
> That's fit for a goddess to work in,
> > With shoulders brown
> > And the wheaten crown
> About thy temples perking.[30]

Very much to the point also is Thomas Moore (1779-1852), that remarkable son of a Dublin grocer and spirit-dealer, who was contributing to *Anthologia Hibernica* by the age of fourteen, published his *Odes of Anacreon* in 1800 and his *Juvenile Poems* (under the pseudonym 'Edward Little') in the following year, and eventually became the darling of London's literary 'society'. He is popularly best remembered for 'The minstrel boy to the war has gone' and 'The harp that once through Tara's halls', but his prolific output included an enormous range of subjects, sentiments and scansion. Some of his poems were both lyrical and basically limerickal (in this case, two 'limericks' forming each stanza):

> The time I've lost in wooing,
> In watching and pursuing
>   The light that lies
>   In women's eyes,
> Has been my heart's undoing.
> Though Wisdom oft has sought me,
> I scorn'd the lore she brought me,
>   My only books
>   Were women's looks,
> And folly's all they've taught me.[31]

In the same collection is a poem, lyrical in mood and religious in essence, each twelve-line verse consisting of two quintains in limerick form followed by a rhyming couplet refrain:

> Oh, where's the slave so lowly
> Condemned to chains unholy,
>   Who, could he burst
>   His bonds at first,
> Would pine beneath them slowly?
> What soul, whose wrongs degrade it,
> Would wait till time decay'd it,
>   When thus its wing
>   At once may spring
> To the throne of Him who made it?
>   Farewell, Erin, – farewell, all,
>   Who live to weep and fall.[32]

And, as a final indication of Moore's varied and masterly use of this metre, here is part of a long politically-inspired poem built up entirely from 'limerick' quintains:

> Oh, the sight entrancing,
> When morning's beam is glancing

O'er files arrayed
With helm and blade,
And plumes in the gay wind dancing!
When hearts are all high beating,
And the trumpet's voice repeating
    That song whose breath
    May lead to death,
But never to retreating!

Leave pomps to those who need 'em –
Adorn but Man with Freedom,
    And proud he braves
    The gaudiest slaves
That crawl where monarchs lead 'em.[33]

A close contemporary of Moore was Thomas Love Peacock (1785-1866) and he, too, sometimes composed poetry of similar prosody. His two-act musical farce, *The Three Doctors*, of which the British Museum has a holograph manuscript of about 1811, includes a three-verse 'Farrier's Song', completely in limerick form and starting thus:

Oh! if I can carry her!
Oh! if I can marry her!
    I'll leave alone
    Black, bay, and roan,
And be no more a farrier.[34]

Some ten years later, following a comment by William Wilberforce (M.P. for Kingston upon Hull) that "The Rich have means of concealing their transgressions which the Poor have not"[35], Peacock produced (under the *nom-de-plume* 'Dives') his political satire, 'Rich and Poor; or Saint and Sinner'. Its six verses are not perfect limericks, by reason of the non-rhyming final word of each first line, but they are pretty nearly so. Here are three of its stanzas:

The poor man's sins are glaring;
In the face of ghostly warning
    He is caught in the fact
    Of an overt act –
Buying greens on Sunday morning.

The rich man's sins are hidden
In the pomp of wealth and station;
    And escape the sight
    Of the children of light,
Who are wise in their generation.

> The rich man is invisible
> In the crowd of his gay society;
>> But the poor man's delight
>> Is a sore in the sight
> And a stench in the nose of piety.[36]

On the other side of the Irish Sea, Charles O'Flaherty (1794-1824), son of a Dublin pawnbroker, similarly sometimes wrote in approximately limerick style. He did so in his 'Humours of Donnybrook Fair' (not to be confused with the poetically superior eighteenth century street-ballad of similar name), which consisted of thirteen verses, each effectively a limerick plus a two-line 'supplement', thus:

> Oh! 't was Dermot O'Nowlan McFigg,
> That could properly handle a twig.
>> He went up to the Fair
>> And kicked up a dust there,
> In dancing the Donnybrook Jig,
>> With his twig.
> Oh! my blessing to Dermot McFigg![37]

Baring-Gould has also quoted Morris Bishop as claiming that the *Poems* of Edward Lysaght (b. 1763), a Munster barrister, "include a serious celebration of Ireland in Limerick form and also a series of limericks in Irish"[38]. Unfortunately, I was unable to find in that collection more than one verse of even approximately limerick form, and none that could be unambiguously so called.

Whatever may have been the case in Ireland, there is no doubt at all about the existence of limericks in Scotland during the eighteenth century and earlier. Allan Ramsay's *Tea-Table Miscellany*, first published in 1724, includes 'Katy's Answer' to the young laird who had suggested that they should "gae to some burn-side and play":

> My mither's ay glowran o'er me,
> Tho' she did the same before me:
>> I canna get leave
>> To look to my loove,
> Or else she'll be like to devour me.

> Tutor my parents with caution
> Be wylie in ilka motion;
>> Brag well o' ye'r land,
>> And there's my leal hand,
> Win them, I'll be at your devotion.[39]

In the same miscellany, there is a tender love song, 'The Beautiful
Singer', of which two verses follow:

> Singing charms the bless'd above,
> Angels sing, and saints approve;
>   All we below
>   Of heaven can show,
> Is that they both sing and love.
>
> Anna, with an angel's air,
> Sweet her notes, her face as fair;
>   Vassals and Kings
>   Feel, when she sings
> Charms of warbling beauty near.[40]

Even earlier, before 1640, *The Roxburgh Ballads* had been appearing in broadsheet form, among them 'Mondayes Work', a series of
verses to be sung to the tune of 'I owe my hostesse money'. And
here, it is worth noting, there is not only the rhyme and rhythm of
the limerick, but each stanza relates to a separate individual, whose
name terminates the first line and sets the scheme of rhyming:

> Good morrow, neighbour Gamble,
> Come let you and I go ramble:
>   Last night I was shot
>   Through the brains with a pot
> And now my stomach doth wamble.
>
> Gramarcy, neighbour Jinkin,
> I see thow lovest no shrinking,
>   And I, for my part,
>   From thee will not start:
> Come fill us a little more drink in.[41]

Also among these ballads was 'The Innocent Country-Maid's
Delight, or, A Description of the Lives of the Lasses of London'.
Each of its eight verses starts with what is in effect a limerick (some
printed in five lines, some in four):

> Each lass she will paint her face,
> To seem with a comely grace,
>   And powder their hair,
>   To make them look fair,
> That Gallants may them embrace:
>
> The more to appear in pride,
> They often in coaches ride,

Drest up in their knots,
Their jewels and spots,
And twenty knick-knacks beside:

There's nothing they prize above
The delicate Charms of love,
They Kiss and they Court, they're right for the Sport,
No way like the Turtle-dove:[42]

In this ballad, however, each 'limerick' verse continues with an
additional three lines (not printed above).

One can even find the limerick rhyme-scheme, with approxima-
tions to its rhythm-scheme also, as far back as the fifteenth–sixteenth
century Franciscan friar, William Dunbar. Here is the first verse of
one of his delicate love-poems:

Sweet rois of vertew and of gentilnes,
Delytsum lyllie of everie lustynes,
    Richest in bontie and in bewtie cleir,
    And everie vertew that is held maist deir,
Except onlie that ye ar mercyles.[43]

and here the first of a sequence of ten stanzas about a vision of St.
Francis:

In freiris weid full fairly haif I fleichit,
In it haif I in pulpet gon and preichit
    In Derntoun Kirk and eik in Canterberry;
    In it I past at Dover our the ferry
Throw Piccardy, and thair the peple teichit.[44]

It does appear, then, that something closely approaching the
limerick was slowly evolving in Scotland over a period of several
centuries.

It is, however, south of the border in England that perhaps the
most striking examples of early limericks, quasi-limericks and
proto-limericks are to be found. The question is, how 'proto' can a
verse be before it loses all claim to comparative consideration?

Several commentators have noted (but some have much exaggerated) a faintly limerick-like quality in the stanzas of the oldest popular song in the language. One version goes:

Sumer is icumen in,
Llude sing cuccu!
Groweth sed, and bloweth med,
And springeth the wude nu.

> Ewe bleateth after lamb,
> Lhouth after calve cu,
>   Bulluc sterteth, bucke verteth,
> Music sing cuccu![45]

The element of resemblance resides partly in the internal rhyming of
the third line, and comes out more strongly if one rewrites each verse
in five lines instead of four. But, of course, the first line does not
rhyme with the second and last. This applies also to a fourteenth
century verse (of which versions vary) preserved in the Harleian
Manuscripts:

> The lion is wonderly strong,
> And ful of wiles of wo;
>   And whether he playe
>   Or take his preye,
> He can not do bot slo. [*slay*][46]

By the time we reach the sixteenth century, there is a stanza which
has been claimed to be a near-limerick written by Queen Elizabeth:

> The daughter of debate
> Who discord aye doth sow,
>   Hath reaped no gain
>   Where former reign
> Hath taught still peace to grow.[47]

But in its original form this perhaps consisted of only two lines, the
first terminating with the word 'sow'. If so, it would be an example
of 'Poulter's measure', with alternating twelve-syllable and
fourteen-syllable lines (said to be so-called because fourteen was at
one time termed a 'poulterer's dozen'). Moreover, there seems some
doubt whether perhaps the word 'reign' should not read 'rule', in
which case the limerick-approximation becomes somewhat insub-
stantial. There is, however, the characteristic limerick metre in a
four-verse moralisation (based on the newly introduced tobacco)
written by the Protestant divine Robert Wisdome, of which one
stanza reads:

> The Indian weed, withered quite,
> Green at morn, cut down at night,
>   Shows thy decay.
>   All flesh is hay:
> Thus think, then drink Tobacco.[48]

And, by 1606, there was a madrigal, also about the 'weed', which
similarly had the limerick rhyming:

> O metaphysical Tobacco,
> Fetched as far as from Morocco,
>> Thy searching fume
>> Exhales the rheum,
> O metaphysical Tobacco.[49]

Meanwhile, Shakespeare himself had been using something approaching the limerick form of verse. In *King Lear*, Edgar emerges from a hovel disguised as 'poor Tom' of Bedlam, and calls to the King, "Away! The foul fiend follows me!". Then, as Gloucester approaches with his torch flickering in the distance, Edgar cries, "This is the foul Flippertigibbett", and chants his spell:

> S'Withold footed thrice the 'old:
> He met the Night-mare and her nine fold;
>> Bid her alight
>> And her troth plight –
> And aroint thee, witch, aroint thee.[50]

The Flippertigibbett was a dancing devil; S'Withold was probably the Anglosaxon Saint Withold (a protector from sorcery) or perhaps Saint Vitalis (a protector from calamities); the 'old is the wold; and the Night-mare is either a witch's familiar in the form of a female horse who sat on the sleeper's chest and caused bad dreams, or possibly an Old English incubus who had nothing whatever to do with a mare. Incidentally, Isaac D'Israeli (father of Benjamin, the famous prime minister) printed in his fascinating *Curiosities of Literature* one of those 'Tom-a-Bedlam' songs, which go back to the half-naked wandering beggars who tramped the land after Henry VIII dissolved the monasteries (and with them many of their associated almshouses). Here is part of one of them, with modernised spelling:

> From the hag and hungry goblin
> That into rags would rend ye,
>> All the spirits that stand
>> By the naked man,
> In the book of moons defend ye!

> The moon's my constant mistress,
> And the lovely owl my marrow;
>> The flaming drake,
>> And the night-crow, make
> Me music, to my sorrow.[51]

Not quite limericks, but not too far from them.

In *Hamlet*, Shakespeare similarly has Ophelia, distraught and hair in disarray, singing these mad-verses to the music of her lute:

> And will a' not come again?
> And will a' not come again?
>   No, no, he is dead,
>   Go to thy death-bed,
> He never will come again.

> His beard was as white as snow,
> All flaxen was his poll,
>   He is gone, he is gone,
>   And we cast away moan,
> God ha' mercy on his soul![52]

And in *Othello*, Iago calls for wine and bursts into this song:

> And let me the canakin clink, clink;
> And let me the canakin clink;
>   A soldier's a man;
>   Oh, man's life's but a span;
> Why, then, let a soldier drink.[53]

Then there is Stephano's song in *The Tempest*, about a ship's crew who "Loved Moll, Meg and Marian, But none of us cared for Kate":

> For she had a tongue with a tang,
>   Would cry to a sailor, "Go hang":
> She loved not the savour of tar nor of pitch,
> Yet a tailor might scratch her where'er she did itch –
>   Then to sea, boys, and let her go hang.[54]

This might almost be described as a sort of 'anti-limerick', with the third and fourth lines longer instead of shorter than the other three.

By Ben Jonson's time, the quite complete limerick form was being used in Court masques, a species of entertainment probably imported by Henry VIII from Italy, where it had evolved from the older carnival. In 1621, Jonson presented to James I his *Masque of the Metamorphosed Gypsies*, which so pleased the King that shortly afterwards he made Jonson his Master of the Revels. One of the songs sung by Patrico, a wandering hedge-priest, includes these stanzas:

> The faery beam upon you,
> The stars to glister on you;
>   A man of light,
>   In the noon of night
> Till the fire-drake hath o'ergone you!

The wheel of fortune guide you,
The boy with the bow beside you;
 Run aye in the way,
 Till the bird of day
And the luckier lot betide you.

To the old, long life and treasure!
To the young, all health and pleasure!
 To the fair, their face
 With eternal grace,
And the soul to be loved at leisure!
To the witty, all clear mirrors;
To the foolish, their dark errors;
 To the loving sprite,
 A secure delight;
To the jealous, his own false terrors![55]

Now let us look at a couple of stanzas from Robert Herrick's 1648 love-poem, 'The Night-piece: to Julia':

Her Eyes the Glow-worms lend thee,
The Shooting Starres attend thee;
 And the Elves also,
 Whose little eyes glow,
Like the sparks of fire, befriend thee.

Then Julia let me wooe thee,
Thus, thus to come unto me:
 And when I shall meet
 Thy silv'ry feet,
My soule Ile poure into thee.[56]

No doubt here about the limerickality of these verses! No doubt, either, about these less well known lines from Herrick's misogynist poem 'Upon Jone and Jane':

Jone is a wench that's painted;
Jone is a Girle that's tainted;
 Yet Jone she goes
 Like one of those
Whom purity had Sainted.

Jane is a Girle that's prittie;
Jane is a wench that's wittie;
 Yet, who wo'd think,
 Her breath do's stinke,
As so it doth? that's pittie.[57]

Now jump just eighty years, to John Gay's *Beggar's Opera*, with
MacHeath singing in a tavern near Newgate after he has been be-
trayed by Peachum with the connivance of the whores Betty Doxy
and Suky Tawdry:

> At the tree I will suffer with pleasure,
> At the tree I will suffer with pleasure;
>> Let me go where I will,
>> In all kinds of ill,
> I shall find no such furies as these are.[58]

And, before another century had passed, complete illustrated and
hand-coloured chap books of children's limericks were being
hawked about the streets of London.

With this history of English verses containing from early times
each of the individual elements which together constitute the
limerick form, and with examples of those elements being brought
together at different periods in various combinations, and at intervals the cropping up of stanzas with almost perfect limerick prosody, what need is there to search overseas for origin? Can one really
doubt – without necessarily claiming it for this country exclusively –
that the limerick is as native an English growth as the oak tree?

V

What Precisely is a Limerick?

Part of the difficulty in deciding how far back the limerick may be traced in English literature lies in the lack of any precise definition of the form. Yet this is perhaps no bad thing; for, while too great laxness makes all argument meaningless, excessive strictness produces only pedantry.

What, for example, is one to say of Thomas Moore's delicate love-poem, 'The Young May Moon', of which the first verse runs:

> The young May moon is beaming, love,
> The glow-worm's lamp is gleaming, love;
>   How sweet to rove
>   Through Morne's grove,
> When the drowsy world is dreaming, love!
> Then awake! – the heavens look bright, my dear,
> 'Tis never too late for delight, my dear;
>   And the best of all ways
>   To lengthen our days
> Is to steal a few hours from the night, my dear![1]

This has immensely more sophisticated sentiment and expression than one normally associates with limericks, and yet as to rhyming and scansion it consists of perfect limerick quintains modified only by the addition of 'love' or 'my dear' at the ends of the longer lines.

Or what are we to make of some verses by the Rev. Patrick Brontë (father of that extraordinary trio of novelist sisters, Anne and Charlotte and Emily), who was born but two years before Moore and whose poetry is today virtually unknown? His 1811 'The Cottage Maid' is a sequence of twentyfour stanzas, all written in so nearly limerick form that one almost (although, doubtless, wrongly) feels that he must have deliberately decided to avoid it by perpetrating perversely non-rhyming final lines. Here are two typical verses:

> Aloft on the brow of a mountain
> And hard by a clear running fountain,

> In neat little cot,
> Content with her lot,
> Retired, there lives a sweet maiden.
>
> To novels and plays not inclined,
> Nor aught that can sully her mind;
> Temptations may shower –
> Unmoved as a tower,
> She quenches the fiery arrows.[2]

Only fourteen years earlier, the Quaker publisher William Darton had written a highly moral and charmingly illustrated chap book, *A Present for Little Girls*, and in it there was a series of verses calculated to arouse compassion for the afflicted. This is a typical stanza:

> Good people all, both great and small,
> I'm blind and cannot see,
> To my surprise, I lost my eyes,
> Beneath a great oak tree.[3]

This is quite definitely not a limerick, but there is something faintly limerick-like about it. On the other hand, I would maintain that the following traditional nursery rhyme is as near to a limerick as little matter:

> Goosey, goosey, gander,
> Whither shall I wander?
> Upstairs,
> Downstairs,
> In my lady's chamber.[4]

The same applies to this riddle-me-ree (solution: 'a thorn in the foot'), whose origins go back a long way into history:

> I went to the wood and I got it;
> I sat me down and I sought it;
> I kept it still
> Against my will,
> And so by force home brought it.[5]

And nobody seems to have noticed that one of our most popular Christmas carols is written in limerick form throughout, as these two verses, despite being set in four lines rather than five, exemplify:

> We three Kings of Orient are;
> Bearing gifts we traverse afar,
> Field and fountain, moor and mountain,
> Following yonder star.

> Frankincense to offer have I,
> Incense owns a Deity nigh,
> Prayer and praising, all men raising,
> Worship Him, God most high.[6]

Are we to deny verses the name of limerick solely because their subject matter is sacred?

It is a long time since Philip Sidney remarked, "Now swarme many versifiers that neede never aunswere to the name of Poets"[7]: I would only add that today there are too many who call themselves poets but do not even deserve the lesser name of versifier. By contrast, consider one who, while scarcely a poet, was a versifier of genius. The first of the Savoy operas was staged in 1875, at a time when limericks were becoming really popular, and it was not long before W.S. Gilbert was making use of the form. It is to be doubted whether he consciously and deliberately 'wrote in limericks' – but is a thing to be denied its proper name merely because its fabricator may not have had that name in mind? Take, for example, that immensely amusing song in *The Sorcerer* (1877):

> Oh, my name is John Wellington Wells,
> I'm a dealer in magic and spells,
> > In blessings and curses
> > And ever-filled purses,
> In prophecies, witches and knells.[8]

Or look at this duet by the 'Fleshly Poet' Bunthorne and the 'Idyllic Poet' Grosvenor in *Patience: or, Bunthorne's Bride*, which begins with a stanza undeniably consisting of two limericks (that is, if suitably stressed):

> When I go out of door,
> Of demozels a score
> > (All sighing and burning,
> > And clinging and yearning)
> Will follow me as before.
> I shall, with cultured taste,
> Distinguish gems from paste,
> > And 'High diddle diddle'
> > Will rank as an idyll,
> If I pronounce it chaste!

and which includes several limerickal four-liners such as these two:

> A most intense young man,
> A soulful-eyed young man,

An ultra-poetical, super-aesthetical,
Out of the way young man.

A pallid and thin young man,
A haggard and lank young man,
A greenery-yallery, Grosvenor Gallery,
Foot-in-the-grave young man.[9]

Then, in *The Yeoman of the Guard: or The Merryman and his Maid*,
there is a long song by Sergeant Meryll's daughter Phoebe, Colonel
Fairfax and the strolling singer Elsie, which is an almost perfect
sequence of limericks from beginning to end. Space allows here only
three stanzas, consisting in all of five limericks:

A man who would woo a fair maid
Should 'prentice himself to the trade,
        And study all day,
        In methodical way,
How to flatter, cajole and persuade;
He should 'prentice himself at fourteen,
And practise from morning to e'en;
        And when he's of age,
        If he will, I'll engage,
He may capture the heart of a queen!

It is purely a matter of skill,
Which all may attain if they will:
        But every Jack,
        He must study the knack
If he wants to make sure of his Jill!

If he's made the best use of his time,
His twig he'll so carefully lime
        That every bird
        Will come down at his word,
Whatever its plumage or clime.
He must learn that the thrill of a touch
May mean little, or nothing, or much;
        It's an instrument rare,
        To be handled with care,
And ought to be treated as such.[10]

And, in his thirteen-verse 'Sir Guy the Crusader', Gilbert had earlier
used a form of rhyming (*abbab* instead of *aabba*) which is a kind of
'counter-limerick':

> Sir Guy was a doughty crusader,
>> A muscular Knight,
>> Ever ready to fight,
> A very determined invader
> And Dickey the Lion's delight. [11]

Untermeyer has remarked that "Now and then some foolhardy experimenter attempts to extend the limerick . . . all such changes destroy the character and compactness of the pure form. To the *aficionado*, there cannot be a six-line limerick any more than there can be a fifteen-line sonnet" [12]. Two such experiments, both evidently of American origin, follow:

> There was a strange student from Yale
> Who put himself outside the pale.
>> Said the judge: "Please refrain,
>> When passing through Maine,
> From exposing yourself again in the train –
> Or you'll just have to do it in jail". [13]

> The conductor, with voice like a hatchet
> Observed to a cellist from Datchett,
>> "You have twixt your thighs,
>> My dear, a great prize –
> An instrument noted for beauty and size –
> And yet you just sit there and scratch it!" [14]

Neither of these efforts does very much to invalidate Untermeyer's judgement. Some other unidentified author once even went to seven lines:

> There wanst was two cats of Kilkenny,
> Each thought there was one cat too many,
>> So they quarrelled and fit,
>> They scratched and they bit,
>> Till, barring their nails
>> And the tips of their tails,
> Instead of two cats, there warnt any. [15]

No; with each increase in the number of lines there seems to be a loss of impact.

Then there have been a few lengthenings of the fifth line, such as these two:

> There was a young man of Japan
> Whose limericks never would scan:

When they said it was so,
He replied, "Yes, I know,
But I always try to get as many
          words into the last line as ever I possibly can!"[16]

There was a young poet of Trinity
Who, although he could trill like a linnet, he
          Could never complete
          Any poem with feet,
Saying, "Idiots,
          Can't you see
          That what I'm writing
          happens
          to be
          Free
Verse?"[17]

Both of which are amusing enough ploys for their first few times of
playing, but would become tedious with repetition. Compactness,
indeed, is of the very essence of the limerick (although we should
never forget G.K. Chesterton's pithy remark, "Somebody once said
that brevity is the soul of wit, when he obviously meant to say that
wit is the soul of brevity . . . the brevity is only the body, and the wit
the spirit"[18]).

This remark perhaps justifies Norman Douglas's addition of two
very short lines to one of his indecent verses, whose indecency is
redeemed by its ingenuity:

There was a young fellow named Skinner
Who took a young lady to dinner;
          At half past nine
          They sat down to dine,
And by quarter to ten it was in her.
          What, dinner?
          No, Skinner! [19]

There have also been efforts at verying not the number or length of
lines, but other elements of the standard form. W.S. Gilbert, for
example, is said to have produced this pseudo-limerick in non-
rhyme:

There was a young man of St. Bees
Who was stung in the arm by a wasp;
          When they said, "Does it hurt?",
          He replied, "No, it doesn't;
It's a good job it wasn't a hornet!"[20]

presumably as a play upon Edward Lear's original:

> There was an Old Man in a tree,
> Who was horribly bored by a Bee;
> When they said, "Does it buzz?"
> He replied, "Yes, it does,
> It's a regular brute of a Bee!"[21]

And somebody else once engaged in some clever crypto-rhyming, which becomes clear if 'fork' is mentally replaced by 'spoon', 'flesh' by 'meat', and 'quick' by 'soon':

> There was an old man of Dunoon,
> Who always ate soup with a fork,
> For he said, "As I eat
> Neither fish, fowl nor flesh,
> I should finish my dinner too quick".[22]

To the prosodical purists, of course, it is not a question of considering whether any divergence from the standard rhyme-scheme, still less from the standard number or length of lines, might be permissible. They are prepared to specify minutely every detail of required rhyme and scansion. "The limerick", according to Beckson and Ganz's *Reader's Guide to Literary Terms*, "consists of five anapaestic lines rhyming *aabba*. The first, second and fifth lines are trimetre and the third and fourth dimetre"[23]. Ridout and Witting's *Facts of English* also states quite dogmatically that "The LIMERICK is written in anapaestic metre"[24]. Similarly, *Webster's New Collegiate Dictionary* gives "a light verse form of 5 anapaestic lines of which lines 1, 2 and 5 are of 3 feet and rhyme, and lines 3 and 4 are of 2 feet and rhyme"[25]. The *Encyclopaedia Britannica* says that "Most limericks are . . . roughly anapaestic"[26] and the *Encyclopedia Americana* agrees that limericks are "generally in five anapaestic lines"[27]. Baring-Gould follows these authorities, saying, "there are usually nine 'beats' in lines one, two and five; six 'beats' in lines three and four; the third, sixth and ninth 'beats' in lines one, two and five are accented: ditty-*dum*, ditty-*dum*, ditty-*dum*. Scholars call this *anapestic rhythm* or *foot*"[28].

At the risk of appearing foolhardy, I simply refuse to submit to this weight of near-unanimous 'scholarly' authority. E.V. Knox, it is true, did not accept the anapaest dogma, but asserted equally firmly the almost exact opposite, that a good Limerick should have "the consecutive fluency of conversational prose, the metre remaining faultlessly dactylic throughout"[29]. (A dactyl has a 'long' followed by two 'shorts' (*dum*-di-di) rather than the anapaest's two shorts followed by a long (di-di-*dum*).) Yet neither of these claims can stand up against the sheer facts of the case. For example, many of the old classic limericks are neither in anapaests nor in dactyls, but in amphibrachs, which are three-syllabled feet in the order short, long, short (di-*dum*-di), as in:

$$| \; \cup \quad - \cup | \cup \quad - \cup | \cup \quad - \cup |$$
There was an old woman of Harrow

But the trouble about this sort of argument is that, faced with a challenge to his own favoured metrical analysis, an advocate can always find so many ways of evading it. If a foot is one syllable short of what his claim requires, he will reply that this is simply an example of 'elision' or 'suppression'. If there is one syllable too many at the start of a verse, then it is 'anacrusis' (the prefixing of a syllable to provide a sort of 'take-off '). If the end of a line is one syllable short, then that is 'catalexis' or 'stopping short'. Or another failure to fit the asserted pattern of stressing may be explained – or explained away – by being described as due to a 'silence' or to an 'acephality'. And in this way, by a suitable selection of technical prosodic terms, almost anything can be forced into the favoured pattern – 'poetic licence' indeed!

The truth is that many different types of metrical feet have been successfully used in limerick-making. As T.S. Omond somewhat mordantly once remarked, "Prosodical pontiffs should least of all claim infallibility"[30]. In any event, most of the disputation between anapaestians and dactylians seems to me mere pedantry, reminiscent of the conflict between Big-Endians and Little-Endians in Lilliput, whose fanaticism for breaking an egg at one end or the other led to six rebellions followed by three years of open warfare. To see why this is so, the terminology of the debate must be examined, and for this it is necessary to go back briefly to classical times.

In the Greek and Latin languages, syllables may be fairly precisely differentiated as either 'long' or 'short', with these terms having their simple and obvious meanings: that is to say, as taking more or less time to pronounce. Verse can be analysed by the length or 'quantity' of its syllables, with the 'macron' sign $(-)$ used for longs and the 'breve' sign $(\cup)$ for shorts. Sometimes syllable length is produced by the vowel sound itself (as in the English word 'pipe' as opposed to the short 'pip'), but it may also be the result of a short vowel followed by two or more consecutive consonants (as in 'pitch'). The various possible combinations of two or three (occasionally four) longs and/or shorts constitute the classical 'feet', whose different sorts have been given recognised standard names. 'Metre' is thus precisely what the word implies: it is a measure of time taken in pronunciation. And different metrical patterns produce different rhythmical effects – just as different sound-rhythms are produced by walking, running and hop-skip-jump.

But each language has its own metrical quality, and that of English lies in stress and rhythm rather than in syllabic length. It is so rich in consonants that we have learned to make light work of them, sometimes even slurring them almost to the point of extinction. In some words a single syllable (such as 'fire' or 'hour' or 'spasm') may read virtually as two, while in other cases a trisyllable (such as 'violet') may be mouthed more quickly than many a disyllable. And, in an especially casual or deliberately comical context, as with the 'particularly deep young man' in Gilbert and Sullivan's *Patience*, even a pentasyllable may trip off the tongue so lightly as to count as less than half its normal length. Verse is, after all, mainly to be heard rather than perused, and that is why the terms and techniques of metrical analysis are bound to vary from one tongue to another. As Thomas Campion (c. 1575-1620) commented more than three centuries since, "The ear is a rational sense, and a chief judge of proportion"[31]. Or, as Swinburne somewhat sarcastically remarked much later, "A dunce like myself measures verse . . . by ear and not by finger"[32]. For many centuries, indeed, it seems scarcely to have occurred to our best English poets that they should even try to scan by the rules of classical prosody. Then, with the revival of Latin and Greek learning in the sixteenth and early seventeenth centuries, some of them began to do so.

Edward Bysshe, in his 1702 pioneer manual of prosody, *The Art of English Poetry*, had already emphasised that "the structure of our verses . . . [does not lie] . . . in feet composed of long or short syllables, as the verses of the Greeks and Romans"[33]. And yet throughout the eighteenth century there was a continuing stream of contributions to the perhaps rather futile task of forcing English verse into the framework of Graeco–Latin metrical feet. In the nineteenth, a few of our poets actually succeeded in doing so: it was a triumph of sheer technical skill over basic linguistic incompatibility. But other poets of the period followed a contrary path, some of them seeking what they saw as an entirely novel approach. Coleridge, for example, in his preface to 'Christabel', wrote: "the metre . . . is not, properly speaking, irregular, although it may seem so from its being founded on a new principle: namely, that of counting in each line the accents, not the syllables. Though the latter may vary from seven to twelve, yet in each line the accents will be found to be only four"[34]. Here is the first stanza:

'Tis the middle of night by the castle clock,
And the owls have awakened the crowing cock;
Tu-whit! – Tu-whoo
And hark, again! the crowing cock,
How drowsily it crew.[35]

Coventry Patmore, in an essay appended to his poems, proclaimed
that accents must be separated by what he called 'isochronous intervals'. Ruskin, in his *Elements of English Prosody*, scanned by a music-
like notation. In this, he was later strongly supported by Omond,
who wrote, "to scan by syllables alone is like trying to read a page of
music, taking account exclusively of notes, and paying no attention
to pauses or 'rests' "[36]. And G.M. Hopkins actually developed a
complex system of symbols for 'stress', 'half-stress', 'slack', 'equal
stress', 'rests', 'outriders', 'vowel-chimes', 'chromatic vowel-runs'
etc. These were all elements in his extraordinarily flexible 'sprung
rhythm', in which the scanning was "by accents or stresses alone,
without any account of the number of syllables"[37]. Moreover, as
Hopkins wrote in the posthumously published manuscript preface
to his poems, "it is natural in Sprung Rhythm for the lines to be *rove
over* . . . the scanning runs on without break"[38]. Thus, from his
'Pied Beauty':

Glory be to God for dappled things –
For skies of couple-colour as a brinded cow;
For rose-moles all in stipple upon trout that swim.[39]

The intriguing question now arises: could a sort of limerick possibly be written in so irregular a form as sprung rhythm? And the
answer is that, at just about the time when Hopkins was experiment-
ing with his new-found poetic freedom, W.S. Gilbert did precisely
that. When his *Bab Ballads* appeared in 1869, he could never even
have heard the word 'limerick', but the five-lined stanzas of 'The
Story of Prince Agib' may perhaps be counted as limericks of a sort
(provided, of course, that they are appropriately stressed):

Of Agib, who amid Tartaric scenes,
Wrote a lot of ballet-music in his teens:
His gentle spirit rolls
In the melody of souls –
Which is pretty, but I don't know what it means.

Oh! that day of sorrow, misery and rage,
I shall carry to the Catacombs of Age,
Photographically lined
On the tablet of my mind,
When a yesterday has faded from its page![40]

Nevertheless, it is sometimes tactically wise to contest a case upon one's adversary's own ground, and perhaps I may most effectively make my point by fabricating a few limericks in a fair variety of 'feet'. For these following efforts, composed more or less off-the-cuff, I make no greater claim than that they serve my present purpose, which is to challenge the dogmatic anapaestists and dactylists alike. First, in two-syllabled feet (using the traditional symbols, but to indicate 'accent' or 'stress' rather than 'length' of syllables):

Iambus (⌣ —)

There was	a man	called Sam,
Who liked	to eat	cold ham;
	He thought	it nice
	To cut	a slice
And spread	it with	plum jam.

Trochee (— ⌣)

Once a	man called	Harry
Found it	wise to	marry
	Mary's	father
	Said, "I'd	rather
Now you	didn't	tarry."

A verse in spondees (— —) throughout would be too heavy for the light-hearted limerick spirit, while one in pyrrhics (⌣ ⌣) would be too flabby; but it would be perfectly possibly to produce limericks in either.

Next, in the three most common of the eight possible types of three-syllabled feet:

Anapaest (⌣⌣—)

There was once	a young man	of Cologne,
With a heart	that was hard	as a stone;
	He took oats	from a horse
	With no trace	of remorse,
And deprived	a poor dog	of its bone.

Dactyl (—⌣⌣)

Once a young	woman of	Cottingham,
Laying out	bulbs before	potting, 'em,
	Pouring on	merrily
	Weedkiller,	verily
Only suc	ceeded in	rotting 'em.

Amphibrach (◡–◡)

There once was	a maiden	of Arden
Who thought, as	she lay in	the garden,
	"If caught in	this nudeness,
	I think there's	no rudeness
So long as	I mutter,	'Beg pardon!' "

A molossus (–––) stanza would be even heavier than one in spondee, and in tribrach (◡◡◡) even flabbier than in pyrrhic. But the other three possible three-syllabled measures, provided that their disadvantageous tendency to weight is turned to advantage by suitable selection of theme, are not impossible to use, and could even be quite amusing in stanzas deliberately recited and accented in a measured and mock-dolorous (if somewhat distorted) manner:

Bacchine (◡––)

Among all	the foul vice	of Hong Kong
Are good folk	who still count	it quite wrong
	To flaunt out	that crude sight
	Of deep shame,	a red light,
So each night	they play long	at mahjong.

Antibacchine (––◡)

Weep tears as	you hear this	foul story.
Bold knights in	proud search of	great glory,
	All ambushed	next morning,
	Denied a	fair warning,
Thus came at	long last to	graves gory.

Amphimacer (–◡–)

Once our friend	denizened	Waterloo;
Then he moved,	trying out	Timbuktoo:
	Sad to say,	never more
	Shall he see	homeland shore.
Weep a tear,	friends most dear,	boo–hoo–hoo!

And, if all this be not considered sufficient to demolish the prosodical dogmatists, here finally is just one more verse by way of make-weight, written in 'third paeon' (one of the many possible sorts of four-syllabled feet):

Third Paeon (˘˘–˘)

There was once a	tricky fellow,	Ebenezer,
Who decided	to put Aunty	in the freezer;
	When they said, "You're	not a nice man,"
	He replied, "But	I'm an ice man
And I only	did it just so	as to tease 'er".

But there is more to any form of verse than its mere rhyming and metre. Just as the sonnet has always seemed especially suited to the expression of tender passion, so there is something about the limerick peculiarly appropriate to nonsense, bawdy and wit. A writer in *The Times Literary Supplement* once described the type as being "essentially liturgical, corresponding to the underlying ritual of Greek tragedy, with the *parodos* [initial entry] of the first line, the *peripeteia* [change of situation] of the second, the *stichomythia* [development from earlier statements] of the two short lines . . . and the *epiphaneia* [final showing] in the last"[41]. This is perhaps making rather heavy weather of things, but many of the best examples do seem to have something of such a ritual pattern of progression. They also have some other qualities listed by Clifton Fadiman: "development, variety, speed, climax and high mnemonic value"[42]. They have, as Paul Jennings has remarked, "a kind of inevitability, a quality of something just found lying there, occurring naturally, like the first diamonds"[43]. And for the most perfect result, Morris Bishop has affirmed, "The structure should be a rise from the commonplace reality of line one to logical madness in line five"[44]. In some sense, one might say that the limerick is to poetry in general what the caricature is to graphic art.

As nearly always happens when one seeks a strict definition of anything sufficiently alive to have any character, in the final analysis one fails. But, even though one may not succeed in defining a rhinoceros, the animal is very easily recognisable when seen. Similarly, my unsuccessful search for a perfect definition of the limerick has not been waste of time, because during the search all sorts of interesting facts have been turned up and many things have become much clearer. One ends up still unable to define precisely what constitutes a limerick, but able to exercise better judgement about what makes a good one. Such as this play upon prosodical measure:

> There was a young Scot named McAmiter,
> Who bragged of excessive diameter;
>   Yet it wasn't the size
>   That opened their eyes,
> But the rhythm – trochaic hexameter.[45]

VI

Popularity Post-Lear

It was immediately following the 1863 reprint of Edward Lear's first nonsense book that limericks first became really popular, both in England and across the Atlantic. In that year, at the height of the American Civil War, John Wilkes's radical periodical, *The Spirit of the Times*, printed twentythree 'Nursery Rhymes for the Army', by 'L.L.D.'. These letters probably stood for the surname of Charles Godfrey Leland, who also in that year produced anonymously a slim limerick volume, entitled *Ye Book of Copperheads*, directed against the so-called 'copperhead' defeatist opponents of Abraham Lincoln. Then, in March 1864, the north's Sanitary Commission sponsored *The New Book of Nonsense*, with profits for the benefit of war-sufferers. This was so successful that it was quickly followed by *Ye Book of Bubbles*, and that in turn by *Inklings for Thinklings*. These volumes imitated Lear's nonsense book not only in the general nature of their contents, but also in format and in the unity of each limerick with its accompanying illustration.

Some of the verses had no sort of specifically American slant, but were clearly of English connotation, as in this case:

> There was a young lady of Bath,
> Whose figure was thin as a lath;
> > If you stuck up a pin
> > You'd swear it was twin
> To this vertical lady of Bath.[1]

Others were recognisable developments from identifiable Lear limericks:

> There was an old man and his wife,
> Who lived in the bitterest strife;
> > He opened the stove,
> > Pushed her in with a shove,
> And cried, "There, you pest of my life".[2]

But there were some referring unambiguously, if sometimes cryptically, to Civil War personalities or places. Here is Abraham

Lincoln, who was not quite the devoted negro-liberator of popular mythology:

> To a very black man from Ethiopia,
> Old Abe said – "Pray go to Utopia –
>   The bears will be nice
>   And there'll be plenty of ice,
> You troublesome man of Ethiopia".[3]

And here is a very clever verse, which refers not only to the charismatic General Robert E. Lee, commander-in-chief of the southern Confederate Army, but also to the now scarce-remembered General George G. Meade (commander of the northern army of the Potomac), to Fort Mead in Florida, and to the strangely named little town of Tea in South Dakota:

> There was an old person named Lee,
> Who came to the north to take Tea;
>   But they offered him Mead(e),
>   And as that disagreed,
> He concluded to try Tennessee.[4]

Yet other limericks portrayed U.S. stereotypes which are still recognisable, such as the somewhat precious Bostonian intellectual:

> There was a young person of Boston,
> And the vaguest of doubts she was tossed on.
>   Of effect and of cause
>   She discoursed without pause:
> Remarkable person of Boston![5]

It was also in 1863 that, back in England, *Punch* first went in for limericks in a big way. On 10th January of that year, the humorous weekly announced its intention of printing a series until every town in the Kingdom had been immortalised. And during the succeeding seven weeks some excellent efforts appeared:

> There was a young lady of Crewe,
> Whose eyes were excessively blue;
>   So she got an old fellow
>   To rub them with yellow,
> And so they turned green, which is true.

> There was a young lady of Oakham,
> Who would steal your cigars and then soak 'em
>   In treacle and rum
>   And then smear them with gum,
> So it wasn't a pleasure to smoke 'em.

There was a discreet Brigadier,
Very fond of Four Thousand a-year;
Who, when he heard the guns rattle,
Fiercely cried—"Ha! the battle!"—
Then complacently slid to the rear.

TWO ILLUSTRATED LIMERICKS FROM THE AMERICAN CIVIL WAR.

This page and facing page – from the 1864 The New Book of Nonsense . . . , *Philadelphia.*

To a very black man from Ethiopia,
Old Abe said—"Pray go to Utopia—
  The bears will be nice
  And there'll be plenty of ice,
You troublesome man of Ethiopia."

The author(s) and illustrator of these two verses (which were reprinted in Carolyn Wells, 1925, *Book of American Limericks*, New York, Knickerbocker Press) are unknown.

> There was a young lady of Denbigh,
> Who wrote to her confidante, "N.B.
>   I don't mean to try
>   To be married, not I,
> But where can the eyes of the men be?"[6]

Interestingly enough, this last verse, changed only by the substitution of 'Tenby' for 'Denbigh', reappeared some sixty or so years later as a prizewinner in a competition for original limericks conducted by a London daily paper! Fortunately, the fraud was exposed and the prize withdrawn.

But *Punch's* project terminated abruptly on 28th February, reputedly because of the submission of a disconcerting number of bawdy and sacrilegious limericks. Nor indeed, would it be surprising if this were true, for the period was one of considerable *sub rosa* obscenity. Although I have been unable to trace an extant copy, it seems established that in 1868 *A New Book of Nonsense*, probably the earliest printed collection of erotic limericks, was published in London. Two years later there came, under the amusingly inappropriate fake imprint of 'Oxford, at the University Press, on behalf of the Society for Promoting Useful Knowledge', over fifty indecent limericks in a remarkably titled volume, *Cythera's Hymnal, or Flakes from the Foreskin: a Collection of Songs, Poems, Nursery Rhymes, Quiddities, etc.* Then, similarly claiming Oxford parentage but actually printed by the small London firm of Cameron, there appeared in succession two erotic periodicals which between them printed over sixty limericks. *The Pearl: a Monthly Journal of Facetiae and Voluptuous Reading* survived for eighteen issues in 1879 and 1880. Its successor, called *The Cremorne: A Magazine of Wit, Facetiae, Parody, Graphic Tales of Love, etc.*, cashed in on the notoriety of the Cremorne 'pleasure gardens' off the King's Road in Chelsea. (Some of these indecent periodical issues were privately reprinted in the U.S.A. during the 1930s.)

Although many of London's 'respectable' citizens circulated pornographia of this sort, many more enjoyed hearing, reading and writing perfectly decent limericks, some of which had a witty acerbity lacking from most light verse of today. It is only fairly recently that a privileged cultural meritocracy has begun to develop that peculiar academic *hauteur* which seems to combine contempt for the tastes of the common man with incessant demands for large handouts from the public purse. During the nineteenth century, it was quite usual for men of distinction to contribute cheerfully to the admirable cause of ordinary conviviality. They produced charades, limericks, satires and 'squibs' of all sorts, without any hypersensitive agonising about their possible effect upon scholarly reputations. In 1872, the brief-lived Cambridge humorous magazine, *The Light Green*, published a set of limericks written by Arthur Hilton under the *nom de plume* 'Edward Leary'. Unfortunately, some of the accepted attributions of authorship during that period can not now be proved and must be taken more or less on trust. But Coulson Kernahan has recalled an after-dinner occasion when, the conversation turning upon a special number of *The Graphic* devoted to 'Poets of the Day', "Swinburne ran through the pictured poets . . . composing, on the spur of the moment, nonsense verses and Limericks that hit off with delicate humour or mordant irony the personal or poetical peculiarities of the different 'bards', as he called them"[7].

Rossetti liked to castigate his more or less eminent contemporaries, which invests his surviving limericks with special interest. This is what he had to say of his friend, the bald and bewigged poet-painter, William Bell Scott:

> There once was a painter named Scott
> Who seemed to have hair, but had not.
> He seemed to have sense:
> 'Twas an equal pretence
> On the part of the painter named Scott.[8]

Of that easily offended but pugnacious painter Whistler (who once produced a book called *The Gentle Art of Making Enemies*), he wrote:

> There's a combative Artist named Whistler
> Who is, like his own hog-hairs, a bristler:
> A tube of white lead
> And a punch on the head
> Offer varied attractions to Whistler.[9]

Perhaps his most venomous verse was directed at the poet-critic, Robert Buchanan, who had hidden an unfavourable review under a pseudonym:

> As a critic, the Poet Buchanan
> Thinks Pseudo. much safer than Anon.;
> Into Maitland he shrunk,
> But the smell of the skunk
> Guides the shuddering nose to Buchanan.[10]

But, to do Rossetti's sometimes cruel sense of humour justice, he also applied it to himself. In his later years he was distinctly corpulent, and his publisher was the London firm of Ellis:

There's a publishing party, named Ellis
Who's addicted to poets with bellies:
      He has at least two –.
      One in fact, one in view –
And God knows what will happen to Ellis.[11]

The limericks of 'Lewis Carroll', on the other hand, were generally, as would be expected, just rather gently humorous, as these two:

There was once a young man of Oporto,
Who daily got shorter and shorter;
      The reason, he said,
      Was the hod on his head,
Which was filled with the heaviest mortar.

His sister, named Lucy O'Finner,
Grew constantly thinner and thinner;
      The reason was plain:
      She slept out in the rain,
And was never allowed any dinner.[12]

Lewis Carroll has also been fairly securely credited with this, seen in
a newspaper clipping probably from *The Whitby Gazette:*

There was a young lady of Whitby
Who had the bad luck to be bit by
      Two brown little things
      Without any wings
And now she's uncomfy to sit by.[13]

John Galsworthy is reputed to have written this verse:

An angry young husband called Bicket
Said: "Turn yourself round and I'll kick it;
      You have painted my wife
      In the nude to the life.
Do you think, Mr. Greene, it was cricket?"[14]

and Arnold Bennett this:

There was a young man of Montrose
Who has pockets in none of his clothes.
      When asked by his lass
      Where he carried his brass.
He said, "Darling, I pay through the nose".[15]

Rudyard Kipling was evidently no great genius at the game, to judge
by his inferior variant of 'A Tailor, who sailed from Quebec':

There was a small boy of Quebec,
Who was buried in snow to his neck.
    When they said, "Are you friz?"
    He replied, "Yes, I is –
But we don't call this cold in Quebec".[16]

Nor, apparently, was Robert Louis Stevenson:

There was an old man of the Cape
Who made himself garments of crêpe.
    When asked, "Do they tear?"
    He replied, "Here and there;
But they're perfectly splendid for shape".[17]

As we move into the next overlapping generation and out from
the field of letters into that of philosophy, Bertrand Russell comes
into the picture:

There was a young girl of Shanghai
Who was so exceedingly shy
    That, undressing at night,
    She turned out the light
For fear of the All-seeing Eye.[18]

Then to the legitimate stage, with Seymour Hicks:

There was a young lady of Zenda,
Whose language was loving and tender,
    She said to her beau,
    "Down to Richmond we'll go,
And we'll dine at the Star and – Suspender".[19]

And to music hall with Charles Coburn, best remembered by 'Two
Lovely Black Eyes' and 'The Man who Broke the Bank at Monte
Carlo':

A charming young lady named Nelly
Once danced herself almost to jelly;
    The doctors declared
    That her life might be spared
If she stayed for a week at Pwllheli.[20]

During these decades around the turn of the century, there was
also a great output of limericks in the U.S.A., especially at first in
some little magazines such as *Chap Book* and *The Lark*. This latter,
described by Carolyn Wells in 1902 as "the only periodical of any
merit that has ever made intelligent nonsense its special feature"[21],

was edited by Gelett Burgess, famed for his 'Purple Cow' verses.
Soon a few little books began to appear, among them Anthony
Euwer's 1917 *Limeratomy*, which celebrated various parts of the
body in stanzas such as this:

> The hands, they were made to assist
> In supplying the features with grist,
>> There are only a few –
>> As a rule about two –
> And are hitched to the front of the wrist.[22]

In 1925, 'Shaemus Witherspoon' (said to have been H.B. Swope,
editor of *The New York World*) produced *The Glimerick Book*, a
collection of 'mystifying limericks'. More to my liking is a delightful
English volume of 1908, *Lyrics, Pathetic and Humorous, from A to Z*,
by Edmund Dulac, whose Lear-like absurdities (which applied also
to their accompanying colour-illustrations) may be savoured in this
specimen, selected almost at random:

> *K* was a kind-hearted King
> Who once taught a bird how to sing,
>> By knocking a pan
>> With the knob of a fan,
> And a kettle tied on to a string.[23]

As the twentieth century got into its stride, wider and wider
sectors of the population acquired the taste, and by 1907/8 England
was in what can only be described as a 'limerick boom'. Any number
of competitions, normally with a sixpenny postal order entrance fee,
were conducted by such weekly magazines as *London Opinion, Tit-
Bits* and *The Referee*, soon to be followed by very nearly every
newspaper in the land. These were several specialist journals, and
even some fee-charging 'professors' prospering from the advice
which they sold. (One of these 'professors' misapprehendingly tried
to place an advertisement with the London office of the Irish *Limerick
Times*!) Some of the awards offered in these competitions were very
substantial indeed. On one occasion *London Opinion* gave ten first
prizes of £50 apiece (worth about £500 in today's money) for the best
final lines to this limerick, which I print as completed by one of the
winners:

> There was a young lady of Ryde,
> Whose locks were consid'rably dyed,
>> The hue of her hair
>> Made everyone stare,
> "She's piebald, she'll die bald!" they cried.[24]

The manufacturers of 'Traylee' cork-tipped cigarettes offered a prize of £3 per week for life, and this munificent reward was won pretty easily:

> That the Traylee's the best cigarette,
> Is a 'tip' that we cannot forget.
>> And in buying, I'll mention
>> There's a three pound a week pension;
> Two good 'lines' – one you give, one you get.[25]

The same firm then promoted a second competition, this time for a country villa completely furnished by Waring & Gillow, plus a horse and trap, plus £2 per week for life. Then yet a third competition, with a first prize of £1000.

Eventually, the National Anti-Gambling League argued that the huge numbers of entries made "The whole business . . . manifestly a gigantic gamble, not a competition in literary skill", and that "Corruption is spreading all over the country, and the rising generation is being led into gambling habits which all the efforts of teachers, moralists, and preachers will not be able to eradicate"[26]. The League lobbied vigorously (but unsuccessfully) for legislation to make the competitions illegal, and a question in the House of Commons elicited, on 17th July 1908, the astonishing information that "The public in the last six months of the year, would have bought, in the ordinary way, between 700,000 and 800,000 sixpenny postal orders. They had actually bought no less than 11,400,000"[27]. *Punch* published a cartoon of the Postmaster-General remarking, as he looked at a goose which had just laid a golden egg, "It's a silly bird and wants its neck wrung, but it lays an egg that just suits me"[28].

In 1904, a perceptive contributor to *Punch* had commented, "The value of the Limerick as a handmaiden to history has not been sufficiently considered . . . Many . . . phases of modern life can find adequate record in its irresponsible jocundity. Other chroniclers jumble, hesitate, doubt and stammer; the Limerick goes straight to the point, touching the events of the moment"[29]. And this can be well illustrated from the pages of *Punch* itself. In 1892, for example, there were enormous sales for *The Stickit Minister*, a novel by the Rev. Samuel Rutherford Crockett of the Penicuik manse, and its financial success was celebrated thus:

> An ingenious person named Crockett
> Ascended to fame like a rocket;
>> His Minister (Stickit)
>> Was such a good trick, it
> Expanded his publisher's pocket.[30]

Ten years later, there was a series of admirably pointed limericks about politicians. One of the best among them pinpointed the great early weakness of the great Winston:

> If the gifted and young Mr. Churchill
> Is to stay on his eminent perch, he'll
>   Shed some of his side
>   Which is hard to abide –
> Yes, even in young Mr. Churchill.[31]

Another was this verse, featuring the Prime Minister (Lord Rosebery) and his rather cruelly nicknamed opponent, A.J. Balfour:

> A Premier of character canny,
> Who modestly bloomed in a cranny,
>   Though bland and urbane
>   Once was heard to complain
> He'd be blanked if he stood Pretty Fanny.[32]

Then, in 1904, the centuries-old and still recognisable characteristics of the Cecil family were amusingly recorded:

**A budding young poet of Kew
Wrote, "My inspiration is you,
Oh! crustless Diploma,
Your taste, your aroma,**

**Even editors
can't refuse you"**

TWO EXAMPLES OF LIMERICKS IN ADVERTISING

This and facing page – from unidentified cuttings pasted into C.B.'s copy of Langford Reed, 1924, *The Complete Limerick Book*.

Said a daring young male FIRE WATCHER

"Wolsey underwear's quite a TOPNOTCHER!

It's saved many chills for much water I spills

— for I say to incendiaries 'GOTCHER'!"

Wolsey

Coupons mean that what you buy must wear as ne'er before:
so wait for Wolsey (if you must), it's well worth waiting for!

The authors and illustrators of these two advertising limericks are unknown. The one above is certainly 1940 – 1945, and the one opposite is probably of about the same date.

> There was a lean lordling named Hugh,
> Who looked like a pious Hindoo;
>   But beneath that disguise
>   We could all recognise
> The chief of a cannibal crew.[33]

Also in 1904, the great cricketer 'Plum' Warner returned from Australia with his triumphant Test Match team:

> There once was a skipper named 'Plum',
> Whose team made the prophets all glum;
>   "It's bad through and through,"
>   They declared, "It won't do".
> But today all the prophets are dumb.[34]

And George Bernard Shaw lost his seat as a 'Moderate' Borough Councillor of St. Pancras:

> A Solon + Shakespeare named Shaw,
> Wished to practise St. Pancras's law;
>   He'd a Moderate mind
>   And to progress inclined,
> But St. Pancras resisted his jaw.[35]

When the first world war began, there appeared *The Book of William: with Apologies to Edward Lear*, in avowed imitation of *The Book of Nonsense* and consisting of a series of amusingly illustrated limericks about Kaiser Wilhelm of Germany. Limericks were certainly popular among the troops, but few of them seem to have been recorded – possibly because most of the favourites were unprintable. Fortunately, a complete set of one of the 'trench' newspapers, *The Wipers Times*, produced almost continuously by the 12th Battalion Sherwood Foresters despite all difficulties, has survived. The first issue, dated 31 July 1916, came off an abandoned press in a rat-infested cellar in Ypres (hence the title). The name was changed to *The New Church Times* when the battalion was transferred to Neuve Eglise, then successively to *The Kemmal Times, The Somme Times, The B.E.F. Times* and, as the war approached its end, *The Better Times*. It is surprising to note how few of the limericks printed were of a hun-hating nature. And, in view of the appalling squalor and physical degradation endured by the 'Tommies' in trench warfare, the wonderful good spirits of the verses are immensely creditable. Here are three examples:

> There was a fair Belgian of Locre,
> Who smothered herself with red ochre,

> When people asked why,
> She exclaimed with a sigh,
> "I've fallen in love with a stoker".

> The Kaiser once said at Peronne
> That the Army we'd got was 'no bon',
>   But between you and me
>   He didn't 'compris'
> The size of the job he had on.

> There was a young girl of the Somme,
> Who sat on a number five bomb,
>   She thought 'twas a dud 'un,
>   But it went off sudden –
> Her exit she made with aplomb![36]

Once the war was over, Mr. Punch returned to his rôle as history's handmaiden. Naturally enough, all sorts of stored-up resentments were now brought out. Against the Germans and their '*Allmächtig*' Kaiser:

> When the Bosches set fire to Louvain,
> It caused the All-Mightiest pain;
>   They say that the heart
>   Was the sensitive part,
> And I fear it is bleeding again.[37]

Against the Irish, seen as privileged but always complaining:

> There is a Green Isle of the West
> With abundance of provender blest;
>   Unconscripted and pampered,
>   By rations unhampered,
> Yet deeming herself most 'distressed'.[38]

Against conscientious objectors:

> There was an objector at Chirk
> Who was charged with an impulse to shirk;
>   But he answered, "All action
>   I love to distraction,
> But I loathe and abominate work".[39]

And a tribute to an impliedly exceptional hard-working worker:

> There was a young workman whose creed
> Was wholly untainted by greed;

> More work for more pay
> He considered fair play
> But nobody followed his lead.[40]

Then, as the armistice passed into the greater security of peace, it once more became emotionally possible to lampoon the nation's political leaders. Winston Churchill, Member of Parliament for Dundee, who had resigned from the Admiralty following the Dardanelles fiasco, was brought back into the Cabinet by Lloyd George and became Secretary of State for War and Air:

> There was a young man from Dundee,
> Who didn't succeed with the sea;
>   So they gave him command
>   Of the Air and the Land,
> Just to make it quite fair with all three.[41]

By 1920, really serious matters like cricket were being dealt with, especially in a series of 'Songs of an Ovalite'. These included the great batsman Jack Hobbs, the great bowler Percy Fender, and the great wicket-keeper Herbert Strudwick:

> There was a young man who said, "Hobbs
> Should never be tempted by lobs;
>   He would knock them about
>   Till the bowlers gave out
> And watered the pitch with their sobs".

> There's no one so dreadful as Fender
> For batsmen whose bodies are tender;
>   He gets on their nerves
>   With his murderous swerves,
> That insist on death or surrender.

> You should never be down in the dumps
> When Strudwick is guarding the stumps;
>   His opponents depart
>   One by one at the start
> But later, in twos and in clumps.[42]

And so *Punch* went on for the next five or six post-war years. There were the medical exploiters of the newly popular psychiatry:

> There was an old next-the-skin-flannelist,
> Who complained of the fees from his panel list;
>   But he grouses no more
>   Now the plate on his door
> Bears the lucrative lure 'Psycho-Analyst'.[43]

There once was a Man, Kaiser Will, who seldom, if ever, stood still;
He ran up and down with a horrible frown,
And his ideas of culture were *nil*.

AN ILLUSTRATED LIMERICK FROM THE FIRST WORLD WAR.

From the 1914 *The Book of William* . . . (author and artist unknown), London, Warne.

There was the new jazz music and its accompanying forms of dancing:

> There was an exuberant 'coon',
> Who invented a horrible tune
>> For a horrible dance,
>> Which suggested the prance
> Of a half-epileptic baboon.[44]

There was the eminent sculptor Epstein and his controversial 'Rima':

> There once was a sculptor of mark,
> Who was chosen to brighten Hyde Park;
>> Some thought his design
>> Most uncommonly fine,
> But more like it best in the dark.[45]

And the highly irritant (and equally irritable) H.G. Wells:

> Mr. Wells of the big cerebellum,
> Uses mountains of paper (or vellum);
>> When his temper gets bad,
>> And we ask, "Why go mad?",
> He replies, "They won't do as I tell 'em".[46]

And that generation's notion of 'permissive' literature:

> A novelist, wedded to scenes
> Disapproved of by orthodox deans,
>> Observed, "It is true
>> That my stories are blue;
> But they're told to the ultra-marines".[47]

Across the Atlantic, Susan Hale's *Nonsense Book: a Collection of Limericks* appeared in 1919. During the succeeding decade Randall Davies produced, under the *nom de plume* 'R.D.', a trio of unusually illustrated volumes. First, in 1923, came *A Little More Nonsense*, with woodcuts taken from a tome of 1862; in 1925, a re-issue of the 1912 *A Lyttel Book of Nonsense*, with woodcuts from the fifteenth and sixteenth centuries; finally, in 1927, *Less Eminent Victorians*, with woodcuts from 'improving' periodicals of that period. Limerick competitions on the grand scale seem to have reached their apogee in the U.S.A. rather later than in the U.K. But in 1925, when a public limerick contest was held in New York's Roosevelt Hotel, over two hundred competitors turned up to provide on the spot four completing lines to given first lines. The prizewinner met this difficult challenge thus:

There was an old Fellow of Shere,
Who was standing a little too near,
   When his tiresome daughter
   Who wouldn't drink water
Was opening a bottle of beer.

THE INGENIOUS MODERN USE OF OLD WOODCUTS.

From 'R.D.', 1927, *Less Eminent Victorians*, London, Peter Daines, in which each verse was illustrated by an amusingly selected woodcut from a nineteenth century periodical.

There was an old fellow named Bryan,
Whose voice was for ever more cryin'
    "Do you think that my shape
    Was derived from an ape?
Well, I think Charlie Darwin was lyin'."[48]

In 1930, the magazine *Liberty* ran a series of limerick contests, whose popularity was such as to make profitable K.R. Close's book *How to Write a Prize-Winning Limerick* – published by a University (that of Miami)! In 1937, the 'Old Gold' cigarette company conducted limerick competitions coast-to-coast. And then, as had earlier happened in England, the limerick 'craze' quite suddenly ran out of steam.

In 1925 Carolyn Wells (who had already produced *A Nonsense Anthology, A Parody Anthology, Folly for the Wise, A Satire Anthology, A Whimsey Anthology* and her great *Book of Humorous Verse*) brought out the *Book of American Limericks*. This contained 291 verses, about half of them from her own pen. Somewhat astringently, she remarked in her 'Foreword' that "A complete book of American Limericks would not only be impossible, but not at all desirable. Aside from the fact that a large proportion of the known Limericks are unfit for publication, a still greater majority are utterly worthless. The mere fact that a stanza follows the well-known five-line form, does not necessarily make it clever or witty"[49]. Would that all other anthologisers had been equally discriminating! Some of the limericks in this volume are worth noting for their peculiarly American place-names, as:

There's a lady in Kalamazoo
Who bites all her oysters in two;
    She has a misgiving,
    Should any be living,
They'd raise such a hullabaloo.[50]

while others cleverly exploit peculiarly American pronunciations, such as *Saynt Loo-is* for 'St. Louis':

A guy asked two jays at St. Louis
What kind of an Indian a Souis.
    They said "We're no en-
    Cyclopaedia, by hen!"
Said the guy: "If you fellows St. Whouis?"[51]

A few, by Clinton Burgess, are of great ingenuity in their unusual usage of mathematical (especially geometrical) themes:

Said Mrs. Isosceles Tri,
"That I'm sharp I've no wish to deny;
But I do not dare
To be perfectly square –
I'm sure if I did, I should die!"

Said Rev. Rectangular Square,
"To say that I'm lost is not fair;
For, though you have found
That I never am round,
You knew all the time I was there."[52]

Some others can most kindly be described as unintended master-pieces of bathos:

"A jug and a book and a dame,
And a nice shady nook for the same";
Said Omar Khayyam,
"And I don't give a damn
What you say, it's a great little game!"[53]

The really definitive volume of the 'twenties, however, was Langford Reed's 1924 *Complete Limerick Book*, announced in the 'Preamble' thus:

There was a young fellow named Reed,
Who said, "There's a need – a great need
For a Limerick Book".
So he wrote one, and look!
Here's the book that he wrote – now proceed.[54]

Reed's historical 'Introduction' was followed by some 388 selected verses, of which the first 6 were by Lear, then a miscellaneous 3, and then 7 by Rossetti. Next came 28 'Clerical Limericks', 12 of 'The Stock Exchange Variety', 16 'Literary Limericks', and 6 'Limericrit-ical Reviews'. A section not very accurately entitled 'The Tongue-twisting Variety' had 52 verses mainly depending for their effect upon spellings inconsonant with pronunciation, after which a 9-verse sequence told the tragic tale of a bridegroom too fat to get through the church door, while a 10-verse sequence dealt with a sadly frustrated romance between a centipede and a snail. Then came a miscellaneous dozen by Reed, another dozen chosen by different invited selectors as 'The Best Limerick of All', and Reed's own choice of 'The World's Worst Limerick'. There were 15 under the heading 'The Topical Limerick', 13 under 'The Limerick and Sport', and 15 'Limericks for the Epicure'. Next, Reed contributed 5 'Jungletown' limericks for children, which were followed by 116 'Old Favourites' and, finally, by 50 'New Ones'.

Reading this volume half a century later, one is struck by its catholicity of range, excepting only the coarsely vulgar and the positively obscene. Ingenious rhyming and last-line punch are exemplified by this verse of Charles Inge's:

> A certain young *gourmet* of Crediton
> Took some *pâte de fois gras* and spread it on
>   A chocolate biscuit,
>   Then murmured, "I'll risk it".
> His tomb bears the date that he said it on.[55]

and by this unattributed verse:

> Certain pairs, who had banns called, respectively,
> Were married at Whitsun, collectively;
>   Said the parson, in doubt,
>   "Let them sort themselves out".
> They are pondering now, retrospectively.[56]

But perhaps the cleverest in the whole collection (and one of the best limericks of all time) is Ronald Knox's 'Modernist prayer':

> O God, for as much as much as without Thee
> We are not enabled to doubt Thee,
>   Help us all by Thy grace
>   To convince the whole race
> It knows nothing whatever about Thee.[57]

It is interesting to note what was regarded in those days as somewhat 'daring':

> There was a young lady of Kent,
> Who said that she knew what it meant
>   When men asked her to dine,
>   Gave her cocktails and wine;
> She knew what it meant – but she went!

> There was a young lady of Joppa,
> Who came a society cropper.
>   She went to Ostend
>   With a gentleman friend;
> The rest of the story's improper.[58]

One or two of Reed's own 'Limericritical Reviews' were rather good. There was that period's most popular novelist of suburban

women readers, Ethel M. Dell; and, of course, the well-loved Marie
Corelli:

> A strong silent man on a ranch
> Thrashed a beautiful girl with a branch.
> > Cried she, "You are Hellish!
> > But deliciously Dellish,
> So take my affection, carte-blanche!"

> There was a maid fair to the sight,
> So stately, so pure – so – so White.
> > Being too good to live,
> > Fate, Corelli – tive,
> Made her poison herself in the night.[59]

Among the limericks categorised by Reed as 'tongue-twisting',
there were some cleverly based on pronunciation-spelling disparities, of which here are two:

> There was a mechalnwick of Alnwick,
> Whose opinions were anti-Germalnwick;
> > So when war had begun
> > He went off with a gun,
> The proportions of which were Titalnwick.

> A bald-headed judge called Beauclerk
> Fell in love with a maiden seau ferk
> > Residing at Bicester
> > Who said, when he kicester,
> "I won't wed a man without herk".[60]

Not unnaturally in 1924, one of the 'topical' limericks was scathing about the luxury hospitality provided at the Ritz hotel for a
German delegation visiting London in the hope of being freed from
war debts:

> Has our Government quite lost its wits
> In allotting such quarters to Fritz?
> > Would it not have looked better
> > While housing a debtor
> To alter its name to 'The Writs'?[61]

One is, however, rather surprised to note that, way back in those
early days, there was this open and quite friendly reference to the
great English pioneer of birth control:

> There was a young lady of Malta,
> When young was oft seen with a psalter,

But she's read Marie Stopes,
And now she just hopes
And prays to be took to the altar.[62]

Among the 'old favourites' there were, of course, some excellent verses, of which I especially like this one:

A tiger, by taste anthropophagous,
Felt a yearning inside his oesophagus;
He spied a fat Brahmin
And growled, "What's the harm in
A peripatetic sarcophagus?"[63]

For a century and a half in England, and over a century in America, the limerick has never really lost its lure. But, after the nineteen-twenties, its popularity diminished as other forms of light verse came into vogue and as the field of cash-prize competitions became dominated by crosswords, women's fashion choices, etc. In any case, Langford Reed's comprehensive collection seemed to have left little else for anybody else to do for a decade and more. And by then the second world war had turned people's minds to more terrible things.

VII

The Limerick's Range

"The themes . . . are so diverse that it does not seem to matter what they are . . . lively incidents and keenly drawn characters . . . wild extravagances . . . invitations to irresponsibility . . . illustrations of violence"[1]. So wrote the Opies about nursery rhymes, and one may say the same *a fortiori* about limericks. As Untermeyer has remarked, "After Lear, the limerick grew fantastically. It embraced every topic, territory and temperament; nothing was too sacred or too obscene for those five small lines. The limerick absorbed solemnities and absurdities, traditional legends and off-colour jokes, devout reflections and downright indecencies, without a quiver or the loss of a syllable"[2]. But perhaps the limerick's range has been best expressed by Brock: "Nothing human is excluded from its range. In politics, divinity, philosophy, philology, sociology, zoology; in botany, Latinity, relativity, revelry and ribaldry; it is equally at home. Geography is its happy hunting ground. Matters vegetable, animal and mineral are grist to its mill. Love, sacred and profane, is fair game. Bishops and tabby cats are equal targets. And the follies, foibles, fortunes, failures and fallacies to which our mortal flesh is heir, from the cradle to the grave, are the stuff to which its antics give the *coup de pied*"[3].

It came as something of a surprise to discover that the very first limerick to appear in *Punch*, as early as December 1845, was political. It concerned the Lord Chancellor, Henry Lord Brougham and Vaux, who had played an important part in promoting the Reform Act of 1832 (at which date the House of Commons still met in St. Stephen's chapel of the ancient Palace of Westminster):

> There was an old Broom of St. Stephen's,
> That set all at sixes and sevens;
>   And to sweep from the room
>   The convictions of Brougham
> Was the work of this Broom of St. Stephen's.[4]

But who the 'old Broom' – if another person and not merely a pun on

99

the common pronunciation of Brougham's name –was, I have quite
failed to elucidate, although this might just possibly have been a
reference to the legal writer Herbert Broom (1815-1882).

There was a revival of political limericks towards the end of the
nineteenth century, and again in the second and third decades of the
twentieth. In 1919 Joseph Kennedy, father of the future President
of the U.S.A., produced this comment on the 'reparations' controversy:

> Says the Frenchman, "You'll pay us for sure".
> Says the German, "We can't for we're poor".
> So Fritz with a whine
> Sings his 'Watch on the Rhine',
> But the poilu sings, 'Watch on the Ruhr' ".[5]

Others of the period were decidedly 'anti-red':

> Yelled a Communist, "Down with the Pope
> And all the crowned heads of Europe!
> 'Equal rights' is our creed,
> What more do we need?"
> Then somebody shouted out, "Soap".[6]

The specifically political limerick reappeared following the second
world war, one of them cleverly exploiting the Yalta conference
between Churchill, Roosevelt and Stalin:

> A canny old codger at Yalta
> Sent two statesmen back home and at Malta
> They talked quite a spell,
> And then they said, "Hell,
> He's just like the rock of Gibraltar".[7]

For some time after this, political limericks lay very much in
limbo, but they were revived by a Scottish *Sunday Post* competition
in 1974. In that year, when Britain was being torn apart by bitter
internal strife, the miners' communist vice-president had been
reported as proclaiming that their strike was intended not only to
secure higher wages but also to destroy the conservative government led by Edward Heath:

> Mick McGahey, or so it is said,
> Wants the crisis to scupper old Ted.
> Then he'll call in the troops
> From Moscow and – oops!
> Our union, Jack, will be red![8]

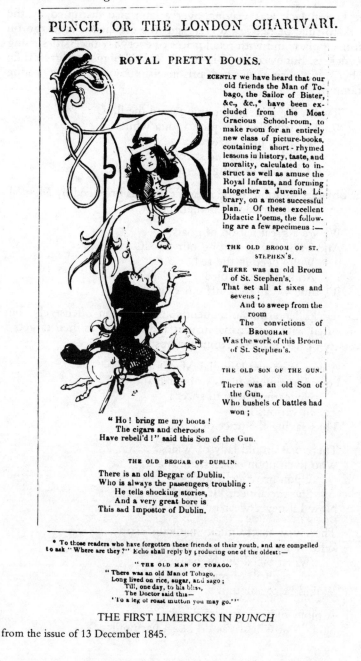

PUNCH, OR THE LONDON CHARIVARI.

ROYAL PRETTY BOOKS.

RECENTLY we have heard that our old friends the Man of Tobago, the Sailor of Bister, &c., &c.,* have been excluded from the Most Gracious School-room, to make room for an entirely new class of picture-books, containing short-rhymed lessons in history, taste, and morality, calculated to instruct as well as amuse the Royal Infants, and forming altogether a Juvenile Library, on a most successful plan. Of these excellent Didactic Poems, the following are a few specimens :—

THE OLD BROOM OF ST. STEPHEN'S.

THERE was an old Broom
of St. Stephen's,
That set all at sixes and
sevens ;
    And to sweep from the
    room
        The convictions of
        BROUGHAM
Was the work of this Broom
of St. Stephen's.

THE OLD SON OF THE GUN.

There was an old Son of
the Gun,
Who bushels of battles had
won ;
" Ho ! bring me my boots !
    The cigars and cheroots
Have rebell'd !" said this Son of the Gun.

THE OLD BEGGAR OF DUBLIN.

There is an old Beggar of Dublin,
Who is always the passengers troubling :
    He tells shocking stories,
    And a very great bore is
This sad Impostor of Dublin.

* To those readers who have forgotten these friends of their youth, and are compelled to ask " Where are they ?" Echo shall reply by producing one of the oldest :—

" THE OLD MAN OF TOBAGO.

" There was an old Man of Tobago,
    Long lived on rice, sugar, and sago ;
        Till, one day, to his bliss,
        The Doctor said this—
' To a leg of roast mutton you may go.' "

THE FIRST LIMERICKS IN *PUNCH*

from the issue of 13 December 1845.

The Union Jack was waving over a land also disrupted by the 'work-to-rule' of railway drivers and the oil sheiks' embargo on petrol supplies, and with retail prices of everyday necessities rising like rockets. But by contrast, in Brazil, Ronald Biggs (the 'great train robber') was being allowed prison-visits by his dusky young paramour:

> 'Tween the miners, the trains, and the ile
> We'll be troubled for quite a long while.
>> Wi' high prices tae meet
>> We'll be oot on the street.
> We'd be better like Biggs – in the jile.[9]

The obvious solution to the nation's ills was provided by Mrs. M. Pearson, a lively-minded centenarian:

> We are a great nation of goats,
> And *will* keep on cutting our throats.
>> We're deep in the red,
>> And still being bled.
> It's time we all took off our coats.[10]

Limericks have not infrequently (on occasion offensively, but more often with inoffensive insight and wit) had as their targets a diversity of national and ethnic groups:

> A bugler named Douglas MacDougal
> Found ingenious ways to be frugal.
>> He learned how to sneeze
>> In various keys,
> Thus saving the price of a bugle.[11]

> There was an old lady of Wales
> Who lived upon oysters and snails.
>> Upon growing a shell,
>> She exclaimed, "It is well,
> Now I'll never wear bonnets or veils".[12]

> There was an old micky named Cassidy
> Who was famed for impromptu mendacity.
>> When asked did he lie,
>> He replied: to reply
> Would be to impugn his veracity.[13]

> A pious old Jew from Salonika
> Said, "For Christmas I'd like a harmonica."

Yelled a Communist, " Down with the Pope,
And all the crowned heads of Eu-rope !
   ' Equal rights,' is our creed,
   What more do we need ? "
Then somebody shouted out, " Soap."

A POLITICAL LIMERICK OF THE 1920s

Author of verse unknown, illustration by H.M. Bateman, from Langford Reed,
1924, *The Complete Limerick Book*, Jarrolds, London.

> His wife, to annoy him,
> Said, "Feh! That's for *goyim*!"
And gave him a jews-harp for Chanukah.[14]

Limericks having been at one time very much the dons' delight, there is naturally a certain number of a collegiate nature, such as:

> There was a young fellow of Magdalen,
> Whose tutor accused him of dagdalen
> > And pledging his credit:
> > He wouldn't have said it
> Had the youth been a peer or a lagdalen.

> There was a professor of Caius
> Who measured six feet round the knaius;
> > He went down to Harwich
> > Nineteen in a carriage,
> And found it a terrible squaius.

> There was a young student of Queen's
> Who was fond of explosive machines.
> > He once blew up a door,
> > But he'll do it no more
> For it chanced that the door was the Dean's.[15]

American universities seem to have produced few institution-rhyming limericks with much literary virtue, and even fewer with any moral virtue. It is probably sociologically significant that, just as in England limericks tend to relate to the smaller collegiate rather than to the larger university units, so in America the better verses usually refer not to the really huge university campuses but to the more intimate communities of 'Ivy Leaf' colleges, or to chapter-organised fraternities and sororities:

> A distinguished professor from Swarthmore
> Had a date with a very young sophomore.
> > As quick as a glance
> > He stripped off his pants,
> But he found that the sophomore'd got off more.

> There once was a co-ed named Clapper,
> In psychology class, quite a napper –
> > But her Freudian dreams
> > Were so classic, it seems,
> That now she's a *Phi Beta Kappa*.[16]

There are also some quite decent (in both senses) limericks based on more general, non-institutional, features of higher education:

A maiden at college, named Breeze,
Weighed down by B.A.s and Litt. D.s,
   Collapsed from the strain.
   Said her doctor, " 'Tis plain
You are killing yourself – by degrees".[17]

There seem to have been comparatively few limericks relating to primary and secondary education; but during England's 1974 fuel crisis a nun (of all people!) contributed this admirable verse to *The Teachers' World*:

A junior school teacher once said
"One day I hope to be wed."
   Said Tommy, aged ten:
   "With oil short again
'Twill be warmer with two in the bed."[18]

A few years earlier, pupils at a pioneer comprehensive school in Kingston upon Hull had produced a number of clever limericks, including these two on a 'spiritual' theme:

There once was an unhappy spectre,
Who went by the first name of Hector.
   While haunting one night,
   He was given a fright,
And caught by our spirit detector.

There once was a ghost named Paul,
Who went to a fancy dress ball.
   To shock all the guests,
   He went quite undressed,
But the rest couldn't see him at all.[19]

And, much earlier still, the sudden departure to Madeira of a well-known county director of education, who was said to have left behind him a discrepancy of £2,767 in the official accounts, had been commemorated in a limerick:

A Bedfordshire man named Spooner,
Whom we shall see later or sooner,
   Said, "I'm off – goodbye all.
   I shan't hear if you call,
I'm taking a cruise on a schooner!"[20]

Literary figures have not infrequently come in for the limerick treatment:

A funny old person of Hylton,
When he read Robert Burns, put a kilt on;
    He dressed in a cope
    When reading from Pope,
And a nightshirt when reading from Milton.[21]

There lived on the banks of the Lune
A somewhat eccentric buffoon,
    For he asked De Vere Stacpoole
    To come down to Blackpool
And open a new brown lagoon.[22]

There was a young man of Moose Jaw,
Who wanted to meet Bernard Shaw;
    When they questioned him, "Why?"
    He made no reply,
But sharpened his circular saw.[23]

Charlotte Brontë said, "Wow, sister! What a man!
He laid me face down on the ottoman.
    Now don't you and Emily
    Go telling the femily,
But he smacked me upon my bare bottom, Anne!"[24]

That generous Dublin patron of the literary arts, Lady Gregory, was commemorated (with deliberately false stressing in the final word) by James Joyce:

There was a kind lady named Gregory
Said "Come to me, poets in beggary",
    But found her imprudence
    When thousands of students
Cried, "All we are in that category".[25]

And I like this inversion of the 'Bacon wrote Shakespeare' controversy:

Said Shakespeare, "I fear you're mistaken
If you think that my plays are by Bacon.
    I'm writing a book
    Proving Bacon's a crook
And his style's an obscure and opaque 'un".[26]

Within the field of mathematical studies, some limericks deal with the most elementary arithmetical incompetence:

There was a young lady of Lancashire,
Who once went to work as a bank cashier;

> But she scarcely knew
> 1 + 1 = 2,
> So they had to revert to a man cashier.[27]

And more recently, with school syllabuses moving towards so-called 'modern mathematics':

> There was a young student from Crewe,
> Who learnt how to count in base 2.
> > His sums were all done
> > With 0 and with 1,
> And he found it much simpler to do.[28]

Way back in 1872, if we may trust a verse of that date by A.C. Hilton, there would seem to have been some pretty gross algebraic incompetence at Cambridge:

> There was a young man of Sid. Sussex,
> Who insisted that $w + x$
> > Was the same as xw;
> > So they said, "Sir, we'll trouble you
> To confine that idea to Sid. Sussex."[29]

Fortunately, there have been other more effective algebrists:

> There once was a Fellow of Trinity,
> Who raised XYZ to infinity;
> > And then the old brute
> > Extracted the root.
> He afterwards took to divinity.[30]

While, at McGill, the late Leo Moser informed us:

> A quadratic function ambitious
> Said "It's not only wrong but it's vicious;
> > It's surely no sin
> > To have both *max* and *min* –
> To limit me so is malicious".

> There once was a function of x
> With deplorable notions of sex.
> > In a half-Baire condition
> > It attempted coition
> With a function weakly complex.[31]

So far as the early beginnings of geometry are concerned:

> In the Greek mathematical Forum
> Young Euclid was present to bore 'em.

He spent most of his time
Drawing circles sublime
And in crossing the *pons asinorum*.[32]

That mysterious factor *pi*, relating the radius of a circle to its circumference, has been provided with a usefully mnemonic limerick:

'Tis a favourite project of mine
A new value of π to assign.
I would fix it at 3,
For it's simpler, you see,
Than 3 point 14159.[33]

Nor has trigonometry escaped the limericker's net:

There was a young fellow called Dan,
Who knew about *sin*, *cos* and *tan*.
He talked rather big
Of his knowledge of trig –
He did seem a clever young man.[34]

Statistics, strangely enough, seems not yet to have attracted much attention, so when one of my sons told me that he was to give a light-hearted end-of-session lecture at St. Andrews, I presumed to proffer a hastily invented couple of verses for incorporation:

At St. Andrews, a quota-based sample
Of students gives evidence ample
That the men are such terrors
That their probable errors
Provide an improper example.

While, as for the women, their modes,
As judged by some strange episodes
Of avoiding repression
By means of regression,
Are such that their Warden explodes.

As we move from straightforward mathematics into the adjacent areas of theoretical physics and cosmogony, a number of conspicuously clever limericks appear. John St. Loe Strachey, a former editor of *The Spectator*, wrote this:

There was an old man who said, "Motion
A state is of comical notion;
It would seem to connote
That a single U-boat
Could be at two spots in the ocean".[35]

And, in 1923, a quite brilliant verse based on Einstein's theory of relativity was produced by a Manitoba professor of botany, A.H.R. Buller:

> There was a young lady named Bright,
> Whose speed was far faster than light;
>> She set out one day
>> In a relative way,
> And returned home the previous night.[36]

with a sequel in which (the physics purist might object) weight is confused with mass:

> To her friends said the Bright one in chatter,
> "I have learned something new about matter.
>> My speed was so great,
>> Much increased was my weight,
> Yet I failed to become any fatter!"[37]

No such minor theoretical flaw mars a later unknown author's illustration of the effect of very high speed upon longitudinal linear dimension:

> A fencing instructor named Fisk
> In duels was terribly brisk.
>> So fast was his action,
>> The Fitzgerald contraction
> Foreshortened his foil to a disk.[38]

The Doppler effect (of velocity upon sound-pitch) has been used in a contemporary *cri de coeur* which will appeal to all who live near airports:

> A scientist living at Staines
> Is searching with infinite pains
>> For a new type of sound
>> Which he hopes, when it's found,
> Will travel much faster than planes.[39]

Fairly recently, a B.B.C. investigation into the 'American way of life' produced a 'spin-off' in the form of some good colour-illustrated verses, by Peter Brookes, about famous inventors, of which I give three:

> Eli Whitney's prognosis was spot-on:
> He invented a gin to tease cotton.
>> His rivals quite blatant-
>> ly ignored his patent,
> And Eli was robbed something rotten.

Isaac Singer (you probably know)
Had a wish that his business should grow;
    But inventors before him
    A few grudges bore him,
And thought him a right sew-and-sew.

The Wright Brothers, dreaming of levity,
Made a flight of nonsensical brevity;
    The engine's bad shudder
    Was caused by the rudder,
And threatened the couple's longevity.[40]

Proceeding from physical science and technology to biology, there are some amusing verses at the zoological gardens level, such as these:

A cheerful old bear at the Zoo
Could always find something to do.
    When it bored him to go
    On a walk to and fro,
He reversed it and walked fro and to.

If you wish to descend from a camel,
That oddly superior mammal,
    You just have to jump
    From the hump on his rump:
He won't just stop dead like a tram'll.[41]

Other verses concern creatures more likely to be bred in the classroom, or to be kept as domestic pets:

It's easy to live with the djerbil:
His diet's exclusively herbal.
    He just munches and crunches
    Long vegetable lunches
And charms every ear with his burble.

A cat in despondency sighed
And resolved to commit suicide.
    She passed under the wheels
    Of eight automobiles
And after the ninth one she died.[42]

Just a few are a little more recondite, like these two, from proto-zoology and palaeontology respectively:

An amoeba named Sam, and his brother,
Were having a drink with each other;

> In the midst of their quaffing
> They split their sides laughing,
> And each of them now is a mother.[43]

> There once was a plesiosaurus
> Who lived when the earth was all porous.
> But it fainted with shame
> When it first heard its name,
> And departed long ages before us.[44]

And finally, here are two (whose scansion is more correct than their science) upon the genetics of skin pigmentation:

> There once was a maid from Japan,
> Who married a Hottentot man;
> The maid was pale yellow,
> Black as coal was the fellow,
> But their children were all black and tan.

> There was a young fellow named Starkie,
> Who had an affair with a darky;
> The result of his sins
> Was quadruplets, not twins –
> One black, one white and two khaki.[45]

If mathematics moves in one direction towards science, it moves in another towards philosophy, and in this area there have been some elegant productions. One of my favourites is this verse on determinism:

> There was a young man who said, "Damn!
> At last I've found out what I am:
> A creature that moves
> In determinate grooves –
> In fact, not a bus but a tram".[46]

Then there is Ashley-Montagu's presentation of philosophical idealism, good despite his mispronunciation (which is common enough) of the eighteenth century Irish bishop's name:

> A philosopher, one Bishop Berkeley,
> Remarked metaphysically, darkly,
> That what we don't see
> Cannot possibly be,
> And the rest is altogether unlarkly.[47]

C.E.M. Joad, one of the original members of the B.B.C's 'Brains

Trust' team, composed this clever comment on philosophical materialism:

> There was a professor of Beaulieu
> Who said mind was matter or ὕλη;
>   This contempt for the εἶδος
>   Though common at Cnidos,
> Distressed the New Forest unduly.[48]

There is an amusing verse invoking F.H. Bradley's views on the inadequacy of all cognition:

> As Bradley is said to have said,
> "If I think that I'm lying in bed
>   With this girl that I feel,
>   And can touch, is it real –
> Or just going on in my head?"[49]

And a similar philosophical problem has been posed in less pleasurable circumstances:

> There was a faith-healer of Deal
> Who said, "Although pain isn't real,
>   If I sit on a pin
>   And it punctures my skin,
> I dislike what I fancy I feel".[50]

Religion has been the subject of several extremely clever and sophisticated limericks, notably in the nineteentwenties by the Knox and Inge families and their connexions. A more recent stanza reflects the greater cynicism of today:

> God's plan made a hopeful beginning
> But man spoiled his chances by sinning.
>   We trust that the story
>   Will end in God's glory,
> But at present the other side's winning.[51]

Another deals with the sometimes bitter sectarian divisions between different branches of the church:

> There was a young lady named Alice
> Who peed in a Catholic chalice.
>   The Padre agreed
>   'Twas done out of need,
> And not out of Protestant malice.[52]

In the main, however, limericks lampoon the clergy (and especially the episcopate) rather than religion as such:

There were three young women of Birmingham,
And I know a sad story concerning 'em;
    They stuck needles and pins
    In the Right Rev'rend shins
Of the Bishop engaged in confirming 'em.[53]

There was an old Bishop of Chichester,
Who said thrice (the Latin for which is *ter*),
    "Avaunt and defiance,
    Foul spirit called Science,
And quit Mother Church, thou bewitchest her".[54]

The Bishop of Bath and Wells
Was wholly unconscious of smells;
    Throughout the whole diocese,
    No whiff was as high as his:
The odour of sanctity tells.[55]

Not that the lower ranks of the hierarchy have been altogether spared:

There was an Archdeacon of Bristol,
Who murdered his niece with a pistol;
    Said he, "I can't bear
    Your absurdly cropped hair
And your listening-in with a crystal".[56]

An indolent vicar of Bray
His roses allowed to decay;
    His wife, more alert,
    Brought a powerful squirt,
And said to her spouse, "Let us spray."[57]

There once was a pious young priest,
Who lived almost wholly on yeast;
    "For," he said, "it is plain
    We must all rise again,
And I want to get started, at least."[58]

But presumably they were limericks more piquant than these which led the Rev. Charles Inge, in acknowledging receipt of a batch from a relative, to write:

Your verses, dear Fred, I surmise,
Were not meant for clerical eyes.
    The Bishop and Dean
    Cannot think what they mean,
And the curate turns pink with surprise.[59]

Perhaps most remarkable, Reed informs us (although my most assiduous searching has failed to find a copy, or even to trace the Roman Catholic Society of St. Peter and St. Paul which is said to have published it), that in 1937 there actually appeared what can only be described as a 'Limerick Prayer Book', prefaced by its priest-author thus:

> These rhymes were designed by a priest,
> To affect your religion like yeast;
>   If they help it to grow,
>   Like the yeast in the dough,
> There'll be one better Christian at least.[60]

Whether psychiatry should in general be considered art, science, or pseudoscientific charlatanism may be much a matter of opinion, but this has not deterred limerickers from exercising their craft in this very inviting field:

> A young schizophrenic named Struther,
> When told of the death of his mother,
>   Said, "Yes, it's too bad,
>   But I can't feel too sad.
> After all, I still have each other".[61]

> Job's comforters now are emphatic
> That his illnesses – whether rheumatic,
>   Sclerotic, arthritic,
>   Myopic, paralytic –
> Were, quite simply, psychosomatic.[62]

> A lissom psychotic named Jane
> Once kissed every man on a train;
>   Said she: "Please don't panic;
>   I'm just nymphomanic –
> It wouldn't be fun were I sane".[63]

So far as sheer black-magic is concerned, W.S. Gilbert's 'Oh, my name is John Wellington Wells' was parodied in 1920 by Aleister Crowley, that fascinating and revolting character who claimed to be the wickedest man in the world:

> My name is Aleister Crowley,
> I'm a master of Magick unholy,
>   Of philtres and pentacles,
>   Covens, conventicles,
> Of basil, nepenthe and moly.[64]

Of the outdoor English sports, limericks have dealt with cricket:

> When people try googlies on Sandham,
> You can see he will soon understand 'em.
>> With a laugh at their slows,
>> He will murmur, "Here goes",
> And over the railings will land 'em.[65]

and with tennis:

> There was a young fellow of Ennis,
> Who was very effective at tennis;
>> The way he said "Love!"
>> Made each turtle-dove
> Think the racquet more mighty than pen is.[66]

and with golf:

> A young lady whose surname was Binks
> Went out for a walk on the Links;
>> When a young man cried, "Fore,"
>> She observed, "What a bore,
> To go home 'foursome' 'tee' when there's drinks".[67]

and with hunting ('Belvoir' being pronounced approximately *Beever*):

> My sister (if one can belelvoir)
> Created surprise with the Belvoir;
>> She thought one was bound
>> To furnish a hound,
> And had taken her big black retriever.[68]

To which I add this of my own for rowing:

> There once was a taciturn stroke,
> And rarely it was that he spoke,
>> But he called to the cox,
>> "You must care for your jocks
> If you value the power to poke".

Strangely enough, there have been scarcely any limericks dealing with that most popular of all team-games, soccer. Or perhaps it is not so strange: the composing (or, at least, the recording) of such verses has never been a particular pastime of the proletariat: their cultivation most commonly characterises the cultivated, who are not normally soccer enthusiasts.

So one could go on, illustrating theme after theme. There is the
legal system:

> The office of *Cestui que Trust*
> Is reserved for the learned and just.
>> Any villain you choose
>> May be *Cestui que Use*,
> But a Lawyer for *Cestui que Trust*.[69]

There is the railway system:

> There was a young fellow from Tyne
> Put his head on the South-Eastern line;
>> But he died of *ennui*
>> For the 5.53
> Didn't come till a quarter past nine.[70]

There is the automobile:

> Said the potentate gross and despotic,
> "My tastes are more rich than exotic.
>> I've always adored
>> Making love in a Ford
> Because I am auto-erotic".[71]

Architecture has been dealt with, in the person of Louis de Sois-
sons of Welwyn Garden City:

> A great architectural joss
> Who rejoiced in the name of De Swoss
>> Said "I'd like to embellish
>> My buildings with trellish
> And as many jazz colours as poss."[72]

and music:

> As Mozart composed a sonata,
> The maid bent to fasten her garter.
>> Without delay
>> He started to play
> *Un poco piu appassionata*.[73]

and dancing:

> In the backyard, a bold minx of Towton
> Danced the Charleston with nary a clout on;
>> Till her shocked mother spoke,
>> "You must put on your toque,
> I object to your dancing with nowt on."[74]

and drinking:

> There was a young fellow named Sydney,
> Who drank till he ruined his kidney.
>> It shrivelled and shrank
>> As he sat there and drank,
> But he had a good time at it, did'n' 'e?[75]

In 1913, there appeared in London a publication presenting limericks as an aid to the teaching of geography. In 1914, contemporary history was chronicled in a slim volume (which, interestingly, reverted to the three-line form of lay-out) containing verses such as this:

> There was a Bold Man of Germania, whose conduct grew stranger and strangia;
>> He turned all his sons into nothing but Huns,
>> That mistaken Bold Man of Germania.[76]

And, in 1945, an earlier period of history was made the subject of a book bemoaning the sad fates of the many wives of Henry VIII. What subject, indeed, has the limerick not dealt with?

In the preface to her *Faber Book of Children's Verse*, Janet Adam Smith wrote, "I have no patience with those who say that love and death are not proper subjects for children. Children can often respond to these large subjects . . . [and to] . . . the heroic, the quixotic, the stoical, the impossibly magnanimous . . . the variety of possible attitudes and moods . . . And if you do not learn what your powers of feeling are, and how to live with them and not be overwhelmed by them, then you will be easy game for those who wish to impose emotions on you for commercial or political ends"[77]. Much the same function may be served for adults by limericks. Wherever and whenever the limerick may have started, it has by now been almost everywhere and looks like going on for ever.

VIII

Some Masters of the Art

There are those who denigrate Edward Lear as a practitioner of the limerick art, sometimes on the grounds of his verse-structure, as in this comment by Legman: "Lear . . . invariably drops back, from the simple but dramatic resolution of the action in the final line, to the namby-pamby repetition of the first line . . . made to do double duty as the last line as well . . . The whole thing, and most particularly the invariably echoic last line, represents a clear failure of nerve, an inability . . . to resolve even the stated nursery situation in some satisfactory way"[1]. But Legman is demonstrably wrong on the simple facts of the situation. Lear's last line by no means invariably echoed the first: sometimes it was the second:

> There was an Old Man who said, "How
> Shall I flee from this horrible Cow?
> I will sit on this stile,
> And continue to smile,
> Which may soften the heart of that Cow".[2]

And sometimes there was no such echoing at all:

> There was an Old Man who supposed
> That the street door was partially closed;
> But some very large rats,
> Ate his coats and his hats,
> While that futile old gentleman dozed.[3]

And, much more important, Lear's critics seem not to have appreciated that for him the words and the illustrations formed a unity, with the latter at least as significant as the former. Nor do they seem to realise that young children (for whom, after all, Lear was writing) often actually enjoy verbal and situational repetition.

I suspect, moreover, that an unacknowledged factor in much of the modern denigration of Lear has been the preoccupation of so many critics today with 'permissiveness'. Instead of first assessing literary merit and then, if substantial merit is there, being prepared to accept relevant indecency, some of them tend to regard indecency almost as a necessary condition of literary merit. Here is a good example of this tendency almost to sneer at anything not salacious: "Except as the maidenly delight and silly delectation of a few elderly gentlemen . . . the clean limerick had never been of the slightest real interest to anyone, since the end of its brief fad in the 1860s"[4]. Legman even asserts, "The limerick is, and was originally, an indecent verse-form"[5]. There is evident confusion here of two quite different types of categorisation, the one socio-moral and the other metrico-structural: one might almost as logically say that honesty is an ungrammatical virtue. This, of course, is not to deny that some earlier limericks than Lear's were lewd. And, in common with folk-ballads and other related forms, they were in some cases detergised during Lear's lifetime. But, when it is claimed that "The 'clean' sort of limerick is an obviously [*sic*] palliation, its content insipid, it [*sic*] rhyming artificially ingenious, its whole pervaded with a frustrated nonsense that vents itself typically in explosive and aggressive violence"[6], one can only reply that this is patently special pleading. The content of Lear's limericks is usually amusing, their rhyming is often most natural and simple, their nonsense is not infrequently cathartic rather than frustrated, and the aggression which appears in some of them is far less explosive and violent than that in many unpleasantly pornographic modern productions. It is fairer to say, with Untermeyer, "Lear's limericks . . . revelled not only in peculiar rhymes but in warm good humour, wild whimsicality, and carefree nonsense. His absurdities are still delightful and sometimes uproarious; his 'plots' are breath-taking; his adjectives are strange but logical, his fantasies inexhaustible. The spell which they evoke is still potent"[7]. Edward Lear was unquestionably the first great master of the limerick art.

During Lear's lifetime the limerick stream bifurcated sharply. The nature of this bifurcation may be well exemplified by contrasting two closely contemporaneous writers, both scholarly and of high literary sensibility, but poles apart in their attitudes to linguistic propriety. Thomas Thorneley was born in 1855, Norman Douglas in 1868. They both lived to an advanced age, Thorneley dying in 1949 and Douglas in 1952. The former published, so far as I have been able to trace, only a single collection of his own limericks, consisting of a mere 61 verses. They are all nearly faultless in rhyme and rhythm, and without exception would be fully acceptable to the most respectable. The latter also published but one exclusively limerick collection, of 68 verses, several varied by him but probably only a few quite original. They are almost all bawdy.

Thomas Thorneley was born in Lancashire, went to Uppingham School and then to Cambridge, eventually becoming a University Lecturer in History, a Fellow of Trinity Hall and a Barrister-at-Law of the Inner Temple. Probably nobody today has any great interest in his *Collected Verse*, which he published in 1939 at the ripe old age of 84, or in his earlier *Whims and Moods* or his *Aganella and Other Poems*; but a fortunate few are familiar with his fascinating *Cambridge Memories*, published in 1936. In that same year, his *Provocative Verses and Libellous Limericks* appeared, with the 61 little jewels referred to above. From cover to cover, it is sheer joy to read, most of his limericks combining linguistic ingenuity with drily satisfying academic wit, and often conveying an acute sense of the human condition. His themes range impartially among cosmogony, philosophy and religion; they explore aspects of aesthetics and natural science; and there are occasional illuminating incursions into political and social affairs. But not one of them contains a single crude word or even a crude thought.

Thorneley's alliterative skill is often striking on retrospective analysis, and yet sufficiently subdued to pass almost unnoticed on initial reading:

> There was a young Man from the West,
> Who was seldom, if ever, impressed.
>> He would watch with a yawn
>> The millenium dawn,
> And be bored by the bliss of the blest.[8]

In a verse gently chiding non-naturalistic painting, he even manages as many as six initial sibilants without over-doing things:

> The figure is not anatomical –
> Said a Sitter – the attitude's comical;
>> Said the Painter – Quite true,
>> But when looked at askew,
> Both are seen to be sweetly symbolical.[9]

One may possibly deplore his aesthetic conservatism, but always we must admire his metrical perfection:

> An old-fashioned artist observes –
> These Modernists get on my nerves,
>> They eliminate grace
>> From both figure and face
> And substitute angles for curves.[10]

In these days, as profitable pornography becomes increasingly

pervasive, one can even enjoy his attack on exaggeratedly erotic
aestheticism:

> A morbid and decadent Youth
> Says – Beauty is greater than Truth,
> > But by Beauty I mean
> > The obscure, the obscene,
> The diseased, the decayed, the uncouth.[11]

And one certainly relishes this tilt at charlatanism in the world of art:

> A Painter, unencumbered with cash,
> Said – It's time to be making a splash.
> > I can paint, if I care,
> > Things to startle and scare,
> Though I'm fully aware they are trash.[12]

We cannot be quite sure that Thorneley had H.G. Wells in mind
for this chastening of intellectual arrogance:

> A Novelist, flushed with success,
> Said – The World's in a horrible mess
> > With its quarrels; it needs
> > The new morals and creeds
> I shall shortly be sending to press.[13]

but it is a fair guess that in the next two verses he was thinking, at
least partially, either of Wells or of G.B. Shaw:

> The World, some are saying, began
> Without any purpose or plan,
> > Nature never was led,
> > But just blundered ahead,
> And reasoned things out as she ran.

> The Life-Force, afflicted with doubt
> As to what it was bringing about,
> > Cried – Alas, I am blind,
> > But I'm making a Mind,
> Which may possibly puzzle it out.[14]

It is worth comparing carefully these last two limericks. They are
equally faultless in rhyme and scansion, and there is little to choose
between them in point of assonance, alliteration or verbal dexterity.
Why, then, is the second so much the superior? Because in the first,
the 'World' is merely an impersonal assemblage of phenomena,
while in the second one can almost see lines of puzzlement on the

features of a personalised 'Life-Force'. The 'World' just began and continued intransitively; the 'Life-Force' speaks and fabricates, it performs transitive actions, it even specifies a scarcely-to-be-expected solution to a clearly posed problem. This comparison helps us to identify certain canons of limerick criticism: given two verses of equal point and prosodic merit, the better is that which is the more sharply characterised, the more decisively transitive, and the more surprising (or incongruous or paradoxical).

With his deep understanding of human nature, Thorneley was able repeatedly to use this simple five-line form not just for fun, still less as a mere means of neurotic release, but for the epigrammatic expression of philosophical fundamentals. Here is his view of the logical outcome of lack of teleological conviction:

> A Cynic says – Now that we know
> Life's a futile, inconsequent flow,
>   And there's really no knowing
>   The way it is going,
> I am going to let myself go.[15]

Here, of sophism:

> There was an old Sophist, whose soul
> Felt an urge towards the Infinite Whole.
>   He said – It is grand
>   That the soul should expand
> While the body subsists on the dole.[16]

Here, of the perennial problem of determinism and free will:

> Determinists say that the Will
> Is, in point of initiative, Nil.
>   If we say – We are free!
>   They cry – Fiddle-de-dee!
> Yet they hold us responsible still.[17]

And here of the weakness of philosophical punditry in the face of physical reality:

> Said a Stoic, tormented by gout –
> There are times when I'm tempted to doubt
>   Our pose about pain,
>   And disposed to maintain
> It is something we're better without.[18]

Thorneley also understood how (contrary to common delusion) the creative scientist really works:

A candid Professor confesses
That the secret of half his success is,
    Not his science, as such,
    Nor its marvels so much
As his bright irresponsible guesses.[19]

He was aware of the need to ask deeper questions than those which
the physical science of his day had been so remarkably successful in
answering:

A Physicist readily shows
From the rate at which radiance grows
    That matter, one day,
    Will have fizzled away.
But the puzzle is how it arose.[20]

He punctured impartially the pretensions of hypocritical communist
and power-craving capitalist alike:

A Man, who had lately declared
That property ought to be shared,
    Thought it going too far
    When they called for his car,
And a list of exceptions prepared.

A Millionaire, filled with elation
At his newspaper's wide circulation,
    Said – With murders, divorces,
    And hints about horses,
I am moulding the mind of the Nation.[21]

And, as might be expected of any liberally minded man in the 1930s,
he had nothing but loathing for authoritarian fascism:

A Fascist, erect and irate,
With the pose of implacable Fate,
    Said – Our triumph has been
    Making man a machine
To be worked by the will of the Great.

There was a great German Grammarian
Whose grandmother wasn't an Aryan,
    So his books have been burned,
    And his person interned,
And his doctrine denounced as barbarian.[22]

Even when dealing with so apparently trivial a matter as the

untidiness of day-trippers, Thorneley looked below the surface of
things into the inherently self-defeating nature of their behaviour:

> Said a Tripper – O joy to have found
> Such glories of sight and of sound!
> How our heart strings were stirred
> By the song of a bird,
> As we scattered our litter around![23]

Despite his comparatively small output of published limericks,
Thorneley was undoubtedly a master of the art.

A little limerick master of quite a different sort was George
Norman Douglas. He also, strangely enough, was educated at
Uppingham, going later into the Diplomatic Service, in which he
was posted first to St. Petersburg and later to Naples. It was not until
1901 that his first book appeared – *Unprofessional Tales*, written
jointly with his wife. Then, with each succeeding publication, it
became increasingly clear that his was an important new pen of
discernment and distinction. To describe his *Siren Land*, his *Fountain
in the Sand* and his *Old Calabria* simply as 'travel books' would be far
less than justice: they are amalgams of topographical description,
antiquarian expertise, sociological insight, and critical self-
perception, the whole expressed in an elegant and sometimes limpid
literary style. But it was Douglas's 1917 book, *South Wind*, which
really established his reputation as a novelist. Set in the mythical
mediterranean island of 'Nepenthe' (pretty clearly based on Capri),
the story dealt with the ways in which the interacting seductions of
warm sunshine and a hedonist expatriate society gradually so eroded
the moral values of a visiting anglican bishop as eventually to let him
condone a cold-blooded murder. And, tinctured throughout as it is
with its author's marvellously polymathic erudition, the novel is a
delight to read. Norman Douglas produced a number of other
works, including *Goodbye to Western Culture* and (privately printed in
Florence) *Paneros: Some Words on Aphrodisiacs and the Like*. His last
publication, *Footnote on Capri*, came in the year of his death.

Here, our concern is with *Some Limericks: Collected for the use of
Students and Ensplendour'd with Introduction, Geographical Index, and
with Notes Explanatory and Critical*, which Douglas had privately
printed in 1928 by Orioli in Florence, in an edition of only 110
copies. It was several times reprinted *sub rosa* in the U.S.A., and in
1939 an edition emerged from the Obelisk Press in Paris. Eventually,
in 1967, it was published openly in New York, with a London
edition following in 1969 under the title of *The Norman Douglas
Limerick Book*. Douglas was the first person with the courage to put

his own name to a wholly indecent limerick publication – a step in which Legman has been one of the very few to follow. This open signature, however, has not prevented unprincipled and unacknowledged plagiarising by any number of anthologisers, most of them lacking alike in Douglas's literary skill and in his encyclopaedic scholarship. The book was dedicated 'To the Unknown Poet' – but one might well wish to know not only the author but also the complete verse of this promising opening couplet:

> There were three young ladies of Grimsby,
> Who asked: "Of what use can our quims be . . ."[24]

Douglas's editing of this slight volume is masterly, with an introduction and many mock-scholarly footnotes which add a touch of distinction to what might otherwise have become just another Customs-confiscated continental paper-back. For example, while many others have printed various variants of this verse:

> The young things who attend picture-palaces
> Have no use for this psycho-analysis;
>> And, although Dr. Freud
>> Is distinctly annoyed,
> They cling to their long-standing fallacies.[25]

Norman Douglas also provided a marvellously pedantic pseudo-scholarly accompanying dissertation on its 'Freudian' significance, with appropriate play upon the homophones 'fallacies' and 'phalluses'. Similarly, for this verse appearing on page 77 of the book:

> There was a young lady of Louth,
> Who returned from a trip in the South.
>> Her father said: "Nelly,
>> There's more in your belly
> Than ever went in at your mouth".[26]

the 'Geographical Index' gives the mock-serious reference, 'Louth, a blunt old resident of, 77'. Those with a wide knowledge of bawdy limericks will be able to guess the verses to which the following Index entries, selected almost at random, refer: 'Buckingham, justifiable retort by local ecclesiastic, 59'; 'Devizes, birth-place of prize-winner, 43'; 'Lucknow, not so dull as Cawnpore, 26'; 'Nantucket, enviable accomplishments of a resident, 33'; and 'Siberia, monastic discipline in, 35'. (At least one critic, however, has found Douglas's notes tedious rather than amusing – *de gustibus* . . .).

If Douglas had confined his collection to such as these, and to sheer lustiness like this:

> There was a young woman who lay
> With her legs wide apart in the hay.
>   Then, calling a ploughman,
>   She said: "Do it now, man!
> Don't wait till your hair has turned grey!"[27]

one might have been inclined to sympathise with him in his complaint, "I may be abused on the ground that the pieces are coarse, obscene, and so forth"[28]. Unfortunately, so many of his selections are so morbidly preoccupied with perversion and scatology that any normal person would be bound to find them altogether revolting; and not even my devotion to scholarship can persuade me to give them wider currency by quoting them here. It is to me quite mystifying that one of such exquisite literary sensitivity as Norman Douglas could possibly be so utterly insensitive in this respect. Still, despite this, one cannot deny that in the field of deliberately and delightfully spurious limerick 'scholarship' he has been our one and only master.

Six years before Norman Douglas was born, the little town of Rahway in New Jersey saw in 1862 the birth of Carolyn Wells. Deaf from infancy as a result of scarlet fever, she nevertheless managed to distinguish herself at school, went on to study Shakespeare under William J. Rolfe at Amherst, became a librarian, and pursued a literary career of immense productivity. Her first book, *At the Sign of the Sphinx* (a collection of charades and other puzzles), appeared in 1896, to be followed during the next three decades by a continuous stream of limerick, nonsense and satire anthologies, which culminated in her outstanding 1920 *Book of Humorous Verse*. Betweentimes, she managed to write some seventy-odd detective stories, and in 1937 (five years before her death) there came her fascinating autobiography, *The Rest of My Life*. All told, she ended up with about 170 volumes to her credit, of which it is the 1925 *Carolyn Wells's Book of American Limericks* that chiefly concerns us here.

It started with a selection of verses from the 1864 publications by the Sanitary Commission in aid of Civil War sufferers. Many of these are not much more than mediocre, but some, such as this, have the true tang of satire:

> There was a discreet Brigadier,
> Very fond of Four Thousand a-year;
>   Who, when he heard the guns rattle,
>   Fiercely cried – "Ha! the battle!" –
> Then complacently slid to the rear.[29]

Next came forty 'Credited Limericks' (mostly of such quality as not in fact to do their composers much credit), followed by a couple of hundred 'Anonymous Limericks' (many of them far better). Unfortunately, although Miss Wells stated in her Preface that generally speaking throughout the book about half the verses were from her own pen, she did not identify these.

The collection included five verses from Anthony Euwer's *Limeratomy*, of which I give here two (the first being such a favourite of Woodrow Wilson's that he was commonly but incorrectly thought to have been its originator):

> For beauty I am not a star,
> There are others more handsome by far;
> > But my face I don't mind it,
> > For I am behind it,
> It's the people in front that I jar.

> The ankle's chief end is exposiery
> Of the latest designs in silk hosiery;
> > Also I suspect
> > It was made to connect
> The part called the calf with the toesiery.[30]

A fair number of the limericks are pretty certainly of British rather than American authorship. For example (read 'Beauchamp' as *Beech-em*):

> A pretty young school-mistress named Beauchamp,
> Said, "These awful boys, how shall I teauchamp?
> > For they will not behave
> > Although I look grave
> And with tears in my eyes I beseauchamp."[31]

Many, on the other hand, are by pronunciation or idiom quite unmistakeably American in origin:

> There was a young lady named Hannah,
> Who slipped on a peel of banana.
> > More stars she espied
> > As she lay on her side
> Than are found in the Star Spangled Banner.

> There was an old man who said, "Gee!
> I can't multiply seven by three!
> > Though fourteen seems plenty.
> > It might come to twenty –
> I haven't the slightest idee!"[32]

The final section of the book consisted of 'A Limerick Alphabet', which I feel almost certain was by Carolyn Wells herself, and from which I give three verses taken almost at random:

> A is for affable Annie,
> Who is younger, they say, than her granny.
>> Now that I can't tell,
>> As I don't know her well,
> But, anyhow, A is for Annie.

> G is for gay, giddy Gertie,
> Who will not acknowledge she's thirty;
>> She was twenty, I know,
>> Seventeen years ago;
> But, gee! I guess G is for Gertie.

> V is vivacious Viola,
> Who plays on an old pianola;
>> My thoughts at this time
>> Are not fit for rhyme,
> But I've verified V for Viola.[33]

All twentysix stanzas suffer technically from the name-repetition at the end of the last line – but, after all, this is unlikely to have marred the pleasure of the little girls for whom they were primarily written.

In some other cases, the authorship of Carolyn Wells is unambiguous, and she was something of a specialist in 'tongue twisters' such as these two – of which the first, I surmise, was inspired by Basil Hood's lyric (in Edward German's 1902/3 *Merrie England*) which begins, 'Oh! here's a to-do to die today, At a minute or two to two! A thing distinctly hard to say, And harder still to do!':

> There was a young man of Typhoo
> Who wanted to catch the 2.02,
>> But his friend said, "Don't hurry
>> Or worry or flurry,
> It's a minute or two to 2.02".

> A canner, exceedingly canny,
> One morning remarked to his granny:
>> "A canner can can
>> Anything that he can,
> But a canner can't can a can, can he?"[34]

All in all, it is the name of Carolyn Wells which stands out as the great pioneer populariser of limericks in America. Perhaps her own

Said a Cat to his sons, "I should deem
This blithe Picture-Book Boy carried cream."
 "Let us give him a scare,
 "So he'll leave it right there"—
This will show the success of the scheme.

—J. G. FRANCIS.

AN EARLY AMERICAN ILLUSTRATED LIMERICK FOR CHILDREN.

Verse and illustration by J.G. Francis (reproduced in Carolyn Wells, 1925, *Book of American Limericks*, New York, Knickerbocker Press).

productions are scarcely of sufficiently sustained high quality to qualify her for the title of master (or mistress) of the art, but her place in its history must be an honoured one.

The world's first really serious student of the limerick art was Herbert Langford Reed, described by J.M. Cohen as "the limerick's only historian and principal anthologist"[35]. This was an over-statement, but not very much so. Born in 1889 to a comfortably-off family, educated at Clapham Collegiate School and Hove College, he had a happy childhood and (like Edward Lear) embodied those 'middle-class values' at which today's trendies find it so fashionable to sneer. He spent most of his life as a hard-working journalist, but also lectured frequently on literary subjects, wrote many screenplays including some for Charlie Chaplin, and founded the yearbook, *Who's Who in Filmland*. During the first world war he served for a time in France, but was soon brought back to England to help in the production of official films. After the war, he returned to a busy life of writing (and to the pursuit of his hobbies of painting and music), soon following up his 1917 *The Chronicles of Charlie Chaplin* with a whole string of limerick books, some of them anthologies but others entirely of his own invention. He also wrote *The Life of Lewis Carroll* and edited *The Complete Rhyming Dictionary*.

Reed's first major collection came in 1924, *The Complete Limerick Book: the Origin, History and Achievements of the Limerick, with about 350 Selected Examples*. As to the origin of the name of this form of verse, he may or may not have been right, but there is no doubt about either the thoroughness of his anthologising or the excellence of many of his own verses. They are generally full of fun and sometimes (as with Lear himself) rather ruthless, as in this stanza:

> Said a foolish young lady of Wales,
> "A smell of escaped gas prevails."
>   Then she searched, with a light,
>   And later that night
> Was collected – in seventeen pails![36]

He had no sort of obsession with obscenity – indeed, he could perfectly justly be described as prim. This was about the most 'daring' verse in the whole collection:

> There was a young girl of Australia,
> Who went to a dance as a dahlia.
>   When the petals uncurled
>   It revealed to the world
> That the dress, as a dress, was a fail-ia![37]

There was an Old Person of Anerley,
Whose conduct was strange and unmannerly;
He rushed down the Strand, with a Pig in each hand,
But returned in the evening to Anerley.

A RARE IMPROVEMENT ON A LEAR ILLUSTRATION.

Above – from Edward Lear's 1846 *Book of Nonsense.*
Below – illustration by H.M. Bateman (from Langford Reed, 1924, *The Complete Limerick Book*, London, Jarrolds) which much better captures the conception of 'He rushed'.

The book had some good tongue-twisters and a number of classical examples of what has been called 'coordinated orthography':

> There was an old dame of Dunbar,
> Who took the 4.4 to Forfar;
>> But went on to Dundee,
>> So she travelled, you see,
> Too far by 4.4 from Forfar.

> There was a young lady of Warwick,
> Who lived in a castle histarwick;
>> On the damp castle mould
>> She contracted a could,
> And the doctor prescribed paregarwick.[38]

Also included were Mary Kernahan's nine-verse 'A Tale of Tragedy' (about the vicissitudes of an unbelievably fat man) and Reed's own ten-verse sequence, 'The Irony of Fate' (chronicling the courtship misadventures of the sweet centipede Abigail and Horace the prosperous snail). There was a section of topical limericks, exemplified by this one about the first invasion of the Palace of Westminster by female parliamentarians:

> Lady Astor, M.P. for Sobriety,
> Mrs. Wintringham – she's for Propriety.
>> Now Berwick-on-Tweed
>> With all speed has decreed
> Mrs. Phillipson wins – for Variety.[39]

There were limericks about the church and churchmen, about games and sports, about epicures (and otherwise), and about literary figures. Among these last, I specially like this one:

> An author who laid down the law,
> Though fed upon lentils and straw,
>> Lived in the Adelphi
>> And piling up pelf, he
> Was pleased with himself, to B. Shaw.[40]

Reed also gave his personal choice of 'the world's worst limerick' (which had been submitted for a *Tit-Bits* competition):

> I met a smart damsel at Copenhagen,
> With her pretty face I was very much taken
>> "What!" she said, "Turned-up trousers – a London man!
>> Fall in love with a crank I never can".
> She turned-up her nose and away she ran.[41]

In 1925 Reed produced *Nonsense Verses: an Anthology*; the next year, *A Book of Nonsense Verses*; the year after, *Sausages and Sundials: a Book of Nonsense Ballads*. Then, in 1928, his second substantial collection of limericks (all by himself) appeared in *The Indiscreet Limerick Book: 200 New Examples*. Certainly none of these new examples was noticeably indiscreet by the standards of today, and one almost envies the innocence of an age when that epithet could be applied to such innocuous compositions as this:

> Said an angry old man of Amritsar,
> "Have the goodness to mind where you spit sir!
>   That last shot of yours
>   Has besmirched my plus fours,
> You really aren't careful a bit sir:"[42]

Believing as he rightly did that "just as the Geographical Limerick is the Limerick in its purest and most traditional form, so those examples which are based on imaginary place-names . . . are outrages upon Limerickal art"[43], Reed confined the locations of his two hundred characters to real places.

Many of these verses had a delightfully Lear-like sense of the absurd:

> There was a young fellow of Graney,
> Incredibly clever and brainy,
>   When he put up his gamp,
>   If he found it was damp,
> He could tell that the weather was rainy!

> There was a young wife of Kilrush,
> Who went out in pants of red plush,
>   When they asked her, "Why crimson?"
>   She replied, "I've got Jim's on,
> Their colour goes well with my blush".[44]

There was also an almost Victorian addiction to punning:

> There was a young fellow of Acre,
> Who took off his hat to a Quaker;
>   When the worthy man said,
>   "You are very well bred",
> He replied, "Well, you see, I'm a baker".

> There was an old girl of Uganda,
> Renowned for her coolness and candour,
>   When, during abuse,
>   Her spouse yelled, "You goose!"
> She quickly retorted, "Uganda!"[45]

And some of these limericks had that not always mild degree of masocho-sadism, camouflaged by comicality, which is also to be found in Lear's nonsense:

> A curious old person of Hythe,
> Amputated his nose with a scythe,
>   That he might ascertain
>   If he'd writhe with the pain,
> Then yelled, "I undoubtedly writhe".

> An epicure living at Gratz,
> Was exceedingly partial to cats;
>   He relished them toasted,
>   Or boiled, baked, or roasted,
> Or thoroughly stewed in old hats.[46]

In this book Reed also provided several good new examples of 'coordinated orthography' (requiring for their appreciation some knowledge of English county-name abbreviations):

> There was a young fellow of Hertfordshire,
> Who dallied about with the Ertfordshire;
>   But was no good at any,
>   So lost every penny,
> And the poor chap is now driving certfordshire.

> A clever young fellow of Huntingdon,
> Could perform some remarkable stuntingdon;
>   He would skate on his nose,
>   Brush his hair with his toes,
> And pole at one time seven puntingdon.

> There was an old Croesus of Nottinghamshire,
> Of money he simply had pottinghamshire;
>   He'd his own private train,
>   And a large aeroplane,
> And many magnificent yottinghamshire.[47]

All in all, these 200 original verses by Reed were of admirable quality and unambiguously established him as a limericker of high talent.

In 1932 there came *The Child's Own Limerick Book*, followed a year later by *Limericks for the Beach, Bathroom and Boudoir: 120 Examples*. Meanwhile, Reed had been ploughing assiduously through more than 180 volumes of *Punch*, from which he disinterred some 500-odd limericks and reprinted 167 of them. As he put it at the front of his 1934 *Mr. Punch's Limerick Book*:

> An author there was with a 'hunch'
> To examine the pages of *Punch*,
> And prepare an anthology
> Of Limerickology,
> To be read and enjoyed after lunch.[48]

The anthology included 11 'Political Limericks', 26 'Literary Limericks', 12 'Limericks and the Great War', 5 'Clerical Limericks', 18 on 'Music and Jazz', 8 about railways, and 8 'Seaside Limericks'. Next came 12 'Limericks and Sport', 5 'Zoo-illogical Limericks', and 5 'Nomenclatory Limericks'. These were followed by a 12-stanza satirical sequence entitled 'The Limerick in Bohemia' and, last of all, 45 'Limericks in General'. This final section covered a very wide variety of subjects, ranging from the young lady of Bute who was so dreadfully cute, through the builder of Kent who purchased a load of cement, to the Victorian *roué* who was a follower of Coué. And not one of these 167 verses would have brought a blush even to the cheeks of the vain little lady of Pisa who thought she was like Mona Lisa. The volume is one to which the reader is tempted to return time and again, for few others so crystallise the everyday essence of the nine-tenths of a century which Reed's *Punch* selections spanned.

In 1937 there followed *The New Limerick Book*, devoted entirely to the coronation of that year, but many of the verses, though technically good, seem to me excessively sentimental. On the other hand, *My Limerick Book*, published in that same year especially for children and containing some 300 verses, each (with just a few exceptions) based on a child's name, is quite a *tour de force*. Many of these limericks have just that touch of absurdity, or of fairly mild catastrophe or irreverence, or of rather 'corny' humour, which children love so much. Introducing the first section, 'Limericks for the Naughty', Reed remarked that "There is this to be said for naughty people. If they did not exist, how could those of us who are not naughty – at least, not naughty enough to get into print – know that we were good? So that naughtiness in others – that is to say, in a few others – is absolutely indispensable to the goodness and pleasure of the majority"[49]. Here are two of the limericks for naughty children:

> An inexact lad, ALEXANDER,
> Once called an old lady a gander;
> Said she, "You mean 'goose',
> I'll not stand such abuse,"
> And took out a summons for slander.

A larkish young lady named LILLIAN,
Protruded her tongue at a Chilean;
    Her mother said, pleading,
    "Remember your breeding,
That trick is distinctly reptilian".[50]

Reed's 'Limericks for the Good' were preceded by the advice "But don't be too good, for that's bad. Angels upon earth are highly-objectionable creatures. Be sufficiently naughty, at wide intervals, for people to know that you are usually very good – by comparison"[51]. Since the absolutely perfect are rarely quite so interesting as the slightly peccant, a single stanza will here suffice:

There once was a paragon, PEARL,
My word, what an exquisite girl!
    Her acquaintances said,
    "When she's grown-up she'll wed
A prosperous duke or an earl!"[52]

The next section, 'A Course of Food Limericks', is on the whole not very exciting, but every limerick is clever:

Consider fastidious TONY,
He couldn't abide Macaroni;
    This may appear petty
    For he relished spaghetti
And loved a nice podgy polony.[53]

Some of the 'Zoo(il)logical Limericks' are pleasantly pedantic:

"Oh, teacher, please tell me," cried DORIS,
"What kind of a beast is the loris?"
    Said her teacher, from Braemar,
    "It's the Indian lemur,
I fancy it's mentioned in Horace".[54]

'Limericks and Sport' has amusing verses such as this:

There was a young fisher named OLGA,
Who angled one morning for tolga;
    These fish are like kippers
    With red carpet slippers,
And chiefly inhabit the Volga.[55]

'Limericks and Art' and 'Some Educational Limericks' tend to be weaker, but several of the 'Avuncular Limericks' are loveably Learish:

> There was a young lady named JOSIE,
> Whose uncle's proboscis was rosy;
>> When she said to him, "Uncle,
>> Is that a carbuncle?"
> He tersely replied, "Don't be nosy".[56]

And the section 'Limericks and Music' included some very clever verses, of which this is an example:

> A musical student named RALPH
> Delighted in music, by Balfe;
>> Of his brothers, young Hubert
>> Enthused about Schubert,
> While Wagner appealed more to Alf.[57]

When the second world war came along, Langford Reed enlisted in the R.A.F. at the age of 50. His last volume, *King of the Jesters*, appeared in 1952, and he died in 1954. His merit as a master of the limerick art will live on.

With limericks, as with any other art form, critical assessment cannot but be subjective, and what to one reader seems masterly may to another appear mediocre. Baring-Gould, for example, thinks highly of Oliver Herford (1863-1935), Gelett Burgess (1866-1951), Morris Bishop (1893-1973) and Ogden Nash (1902-1971). To me, although each of these has a deservedly high reputation in other respects and each has produced some admirable limericks, most of their output in this particular *genre* seems not especially outstanding. I should rank Bennett Cerf (1898-1971) a good deal higher, while the American mycologist A.H.R. Buller (1874-1944) has produced some limericks of sheer brilliance. The same may be said of several members of the Inge and Knox families in England. Among those men of letters who are still active today, Paul Jennings has recently published in limerick form some splendidly acerbic comments on the literary scene, while Gershon Legman has performed invaluable service to limerick scholarship. But there can be little doubt that the names which for one reason or another stand out most conspicuously as masters of the limerick art are those of Edward Lear, Thomas Thorneley, Carolyn Wells, Norman Douglas and Langford Reed.

IX

The Risqué, the Ribald and the Rancid

Many *literati* and pretenders to that title seem to take the view that limericks are almost necessarily indecent. Arnold Bennett wrote, "All I have to say about limericks is that the best ones are entirely unprintable"[1]. G.B. Shaw was so conditioned to this view that, evidently without taking a fair sample of those that Rossetti wrote, he delivered himself of this judgement: "There are several personal limericks by D.G. Rossetti . . . but . . . they are mostly unfit for publication"[2]. A.P. Herbert commented, "The most memorable limericks, I suspect, were the work of gifted amateurs on the Stock Exchange"[3]. A reviewer in *Sporting Life* judged that "The best limericks are lewd. Somehow or other it is not an art form which lends itself to innocence"[4]. Gershon Legman wrote, "The 'clean' sort of limerick is an obvious palliation, its content insipid, its rhyming artificially ingenious, its whole permeated with a frustrated nonsense"[5]. The idea is still being perpetuated in the 'quality' press as represented by *The Guardian*: "That's the trouble with nearly all limericks. They're either not funny or else they are unrepeatable"[6]. And, although J.M. Cohen acknowledged that there have been many perfectly pure specimens of the form, he believed that in more recent times "Its hold remains strong only on the bluer portions of its former empire"[7]. There is thus a good deal of support for the view that:

> The limerick packs laughs anatomical
> Into space that is quite economical:
> > But the good ones I've seen
> > So seldom are clean,
> And the clean ones so seldom are comical.[8]

and its analogue:

> The limerick is furtive and mean;
> You must keep it in close quarantine,
> > Or it sneaks to the slums
> > And promptly becomes
> Disorderly, drunk and obscene.[9]

138

For my part, I feel rather sorry for anyone so fixated on feculence as to be incapable of enjoying limericks whose quality lies entirely in their wit, epigrammatic precision, linguistic elegance, metrical or rhyming ingenuities, simple jolly fun, or sheer absurdity. Yet undoubtedly there seems to be something about the limerick that tends to attract turpitude, and this was apparently as true a century ago as it is today. Not only people of admitted sexual peculiarity like Swinburne, but others of the highest public repute like Alfred Lord Tennyson, are known to have composed indecent limericks (although most of the latter's were destroyed after his death). The published erotica and pornographia of that and of later periods have been meticulously documented by Legman, who acquired an unrivalled knowledge of this field during his years as bibliographer to Kinsey's sexual research institute in Kansas. *Cythera's Hymnal* was mainly compiled by Edward Sellon, notorious as a writer of pornographic novels, and George Augustus Sala, who indulged in flagellational writing. This turbid stream has never stopped flowing underground, semi-surfacing occasionally and more recently emerging right out into the open on both sides of the Atlantic. Following the 1928 limited edition of Norman Douglas's *Some Limericks* issued by Orioli in Florence, the Erotica Biblion Society had *Heated Limericks* privately printed in 1933 (statedly in Paris but in fact probably in Havana). Other publications of this sort include *Forbidden Limericks* (San Francisco), *The Bagman's Book of Limericks* (Paris), *A Book of Anglo-Saxon Verse* ('Printed on the Concavo-Convex Press' in Oakland, California), *Lusty Limericks & Bawdy Ballads* (by 'Harde, Dick', with no indicated place of publication), *Peter Pauper's Limerick Book* (New York), *Cleopatra's Scrapbook* ('Blue Grass, Kentucky'), and *A Bouquet of Choice Limericks* (Palmetto Press, New Jersey). In about 1941, *Pornographia Literaria* was printed somewhere in the U.S.A., while in 1945 some members of the U.S. Army of Occupation managed to print *From Bed to Verse* surreptitiously in Wiesbaden. In 1953 came the first printing (in Paris) of Legman's massive volume, *The Limerick: 1,700 Examples, with Notes, Variants and Index*; and, two years later in the same city, *The Book of Limericks*, by 'Count Palmo Vicarion' (whom several have suspected to be the poet Christopher Logue – a suspicion which Logue himself has personally confirmed to me). There are also mimeographed collections of this sort, including those produced at the University of Michigan, at Yale, and at the California Institute of Technology. Finally, there are substantial manuscript collections at Ann Arbor and in the Library of Congress, while the university library at Berkeley houses a comprehensive card-index collection, the so-called *Index Limericus*. The vigour with which this rather rank undergrowth has lately flourished in the U.S.A. must surely say something about the increasingly foetid cultural climate of that over-affluent land.

Although the existence of all these publications and collections is established, I have succeeded in inspecting only a few of them. To be quite honest, my efforts in this direction have not been particularly persistent. The British Museum's cataloguing system does not make things easy. So far as its British Library printed works are concerned, the first Subject Index volume to give 'Limericks' as a separate main heading was that of 1926-30, but this heading seems to have disappeared again in 1946. Its enormous collection of manuscript material is most inadequately catalogued. Its many erotica are largely locked away in the 'Private Case', whose contents are examinable only by rather tedious and time-consuming procedures. If it had seemed worth the effort, I could, no doubt, have dug out a good deal, both in Bloomsbury and in the major American libraries. But, while willing to wade knee-deep in manure if that prove necessary to retrieve real treasure, I see no special point in doing so just to savour the stink.

Dirtyness does not lie in any particular word or words: everything depends upon the manner and context in which the words are used. Consider, for example, an indecent limerick of Swinburne's:

> There was a young girl of Aberystwith,
> Who took grain to the mill to get grist with;
>   The miller's son, Jack,
>   Laid her flat on her back
> And united the organs they pissed with.[10]

The penultimate word is admittedly not used (or, at least, was not until very recently) in polite society, but it was good enough for Shakespeare and it has long been in common semi-private usage. What many may well find offensive, however, is not the word, but the linking of the idea of making love with the idea of making water. For myself, I cannot see how any particular combination of letters can ever be in itself indecent or obscene: it would be absurd to hold that a graeco-latin vocabulary is somehow inherently more innocent than an anglo-saxon one. Thus, in principle, there cannot be any logical moral objection to impolite words such as 'balls' or 'cock' or 'prick'; not even to the much more vetoed 'quim' and 'cunt' and 'fuck'. But verbal communication is not just a simple matter of abstract ethical principle: it is part of the complex reality of human relations, in which the gratuitous giving of offence is wherever possible to be avoided. The decent citizen, therefore, will always consider not only the general cultural climate of his period and society, but also that of any microsocial group concerned.

Grose spelled out in full the last of these four-letter words in his great 1785 *Dictionary of the Vulgar Tongue*, while in 1933 the *Oxford English Dictionary* (perhaps too timidly) did not do so. For a couple of centuries, the word has been taboo in most reputable company; but it has continued in public use on the lips of louts, and at work among mainly manual labourers, and in private between lovers as part of the language of intimate endearment. Today, it may once again appear in print without fear of prosecution, and it is not impossible that it may eventually achieve such common currency as no longer to be considered especially offensive. In considering limericks containing such words, therefore, it is always necessary to ask a few pertinent questions. For what sort of company was the verse composed, and to whom may it be communicated without offending their susceptibilities? Are the words used gloatingly, or as a self-conscious signal of pseudo-emancipation, or as a lazy means of avoiding the search for more appropriate words? Or are they used with real ingenuity and wit, to produce a particularly powerful rhyming effect or to provide an unexpected and amusing 'twist' to the verse? Or is no other single word strongly enough transitive, or as capable of avoiding verbosity or pedestrian periphrasis? In these latter cases, the 'indecent' word may indeed be the *bon mot*. But manners still makyth man, and retailers of limericks should still shew consideration for the feelings of others. It is well, therefore, to bear in mind a sentiment, originally applied to very different subject-matter, from Lewis Carroll's 'Poeta Fit, Non Nascitur':

> Such epithets, like pepper,
> Give zest to what you write;
> And, if you strew them sparely,
> They whet the appetite:
> But if you lay them on too thick,
> You spoil the matter quite![11]

The descent from complete propriety to utter obscenity is a continuum, with the slightly risqué somewhere near the top, the ribald about half-way down, and at the bottom what I can only describe as the thoroughly rancid. But down the declivity there are many routes, some traceable in terms of vocabulary, others in terms of explicit story-line, and yet others in terms of implicit attitudes. The word 'risqué', not very widely used today, has overtones of social refinement and cultivated wit, without which its relatively mild degree of taboo-defiance is perhaps better described as 'daring'.

'Indelicate' is a word rather more redolent of what might offend a maiden aunt, while the 'impure' would perhaps be more likely to earn reproof from a perpetual curate. 'Ribald' is not easily differentiated from 'bawdy', but somehow has about it a higher degree of irreverence and maybe a larger measure of merriment. When a verse is described as 'coarse', the imputation is more likely to refer to language than to meaning, while 'smutty' generally relates mainly to meaning, and 'gross' to either of these impartially. 'Salacious' seems to indicate not merely a taste of, but an altogether excessive, sexual flavouring; 'lewd' has about it a touch of the leering; 'lubricious' more than a touch. Then there are four epithets – 'foul', 'filthy', 'obscene' and 'pornographic' – all of which denote degrees of dirtyness, the last two also tending to imply a sexual or sadistic content and perhaps a corrupting influence. 'Erotic', however, is a term of very different and much wider connotation than any of these. It may apply equally to one verse of verbal elegance and delicate wit, to another heavily loaded with gutter-words, and to yet another whose whole purport would be rejected by most readers as immoral and even degrading. Thus, the evaluation of indecent limericks is a complex and far from easy matter.

Langford Reed never soiled the pages of his collections by taboo tetragrams, but he printed several limericks best categorised as ever-so-slightly-risqué, such as this one:

> There once was a sculptor named Phidias,
> Who had a distaste for the hideous,
>> So he sculped Aphrodite
>> Without any nightie,
> And shocked all the ultra-fastidious![12]

Untermeyer's collection similarly contains a number of verses which he aptly described as "pleasing and provocative in their very casualness; they are nimble, a little naughty, sometimes bold but never really brazen"[13]. Three specimens must suffice:

> A much-worried mother once said,
> "My dear, you've been kissing young Fred
>> Since six; it's now ten.
>> Do it just once again,
> And then think of going to bed".

> There was a young poet of Thusis,
> Who took twilight walks with the Muses.
>> But these nymphs of the air
>> Are not quite what they were,
> And the practice has led to abuses.

> Said a pretty young student named Smith,
> Whose virtue was largely a myth,
>> "Try hard as I can
>> I can't find a man
> Who it's fun to be virtuous with".[14]

At something like the same level of mild impropriety are any number of other limericks, each with its own particular point of merit. There is a rather clever last-word ambiguity of meaning:

> A publisher once went to France
> In search of a tale of romance;
>> A Parisian lady
>> Told a story so shady
> That he instantly made an advance.[15]

And a final-line denial of expectation:

> A bather whose clothing was strewed
> By winds that had left her quite nude,
>> Saw a man come along –
>> And, unless we are wrong,
> You thought the next line would be lewd.[16]

And a witty use of French words and phrases:

> There was a plump girl from Bryn Mawr
> Who committed a dreadful *faux pas*;
>> She loosened a stay
>> On her *décolleté*
> Thus exposing her *je ne sais quois*.[17]

And there are two verses ending rather cleverly with Latin tags of respectively mathematical and legal usage:

> Some gels – and I don't understand 'em –
> Will strip off their clothing at random
>> Without any qualms
>> To exhibit their charms:
> In short – *quod erat demonstrandum*.

> There was a young lawyer called Rex,
> Who was sadly deficient in sex;
>> When had up for exposure,
>> He said with composure,
> "*De minimis non curat lex*".[18]

A housewife called out with a frown
When surprised by some callers from town,
    "In a minute or less
    I'll slip on a dress"—
But she slipped on the stairs and came down.

THE SOMEWHAT 'RISQUÉ' OF THE EARLY 1960s.

This and facing page – from Louis Untermeyer, 1963, *The Pan Book of Limericks*
(illustrated by R. Taylor), originally published 1962, London, W.H. Allen.

There was a young lady of Tottenham,
Her manners—she'd wholly forgotten 'em.
    While at tea at the Vicar's,
    She took off her knickers,
Explaining she felt much too hot in 'em.

Some verses can be best appreciated by those with at least a little knowledge of the persons or places or activities which inspired them. For those knowing something of art, here are two of my variants upon already established themes:

> Said the Duchess of Alba to Goya,
> "Do some pictures to hang in my foyer";
>   So he painted her twice –
>   In the nude to look nice,
> And then in her clothes to annoy 'er.

> While Titian was mixing rose madder,
> His model leaned over a ladder;
>   The position, to Titian,
>   Suggested coition,
> So he rose from his madder, and 'ad 'er.[19]

For those familiar with the love-affairs of former monarchs:

> Have you heard of Madame Lupescu,
> Who came to Rumania's rescue?
>   It's a wonderful thing
>   To serve under a King:
> Is anything better? I esk you![20]

> Said Queen Isabella of Spain,
> "I like it just now and again;
>   But I wish to explain
>   That by 'Now and again'
> I mean *now* and *again* and *again*".[21]

And for those with Cambridge connexions:

> A Magdalene don in Divinity
> Had a daughter who kept her virginity;
>   The young men of Magdalene
>   Must have been dawdlin' –
> It couldn't have happened at Trinity.[22]

Going slightly beyond this sort of generally sexual allusiveness, and becoming more specifically anatomical, there are any number of amusing limericks, such as this:

> A signora who strolled down the Corso
> Displayed quite a lot of her torso.
>   A crowd soon collected
>   And no one objected,
> Though some were in favour of more so.[23]

to which I add four of my own variants of themes long in oral circulation:

> A young bathing beauty at Bude
> Paraded the prom in the nude;
>> She really had got a m–
>> agnificent bottom,
> And thought it deserved to be viewed.

> On the bust of a barmaid in Hale
> Were tattooed current prices of ale –
>> While on her behind
>> (For the sake of the blind)
> Were all the same prices in Braille.

> There was a young dentist called Trevor,
> Whose technique was deplorably clever:
>> Since, out of depravity,
>> He filled the wrong cavity,
> He's more women patients than ever.

> There was a young lady of Norway,
> Swung on a trapeze in a doorway;
>> With her legs opened wide,
>> To her lover she cried,
> "I think I've discovered one more way".

And one which I once produced simply to prove that even a most unlikely English place-name was limerickable:

> A workman who dwelt in Wyre Piddle
> Met a maiden and posed her a riddle:
>> "I find I'm afire
>> With carnal desire;
> My poker is hot – is your griddle?"

In recent years, so many limericks in the median range of ribaldry have been put into print that it would be pointless to reproduce many here. Some of them eschew any really crude word, although employing a very minor terminological impropriety:

> To his bride said the lynx-eyed detective,
> "Can it be that my eyesight's defective?
>> Has your east tit the least bit
>> The best of the west tit?
> Or is it a trick of perspective?"[24]

A Classical Master of Arts
Told his wife he was still keen on tarts.
Said she: 'That's just dandy,
To think you're still randy:
You still know your principal parts.'

THE SLIGHTLY 'DARING' OF THE EARLY 1970s.

This and facing page – from John Letts, 1973, *A Little Treasury of Limericks Fair and Foul*
(illustrated by Ralph Steadman), London, Pan Books.

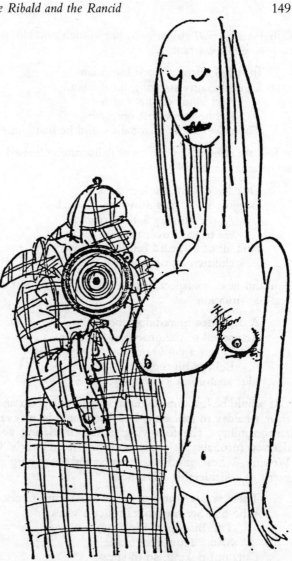

To his bride said the lynx-eyed detective:
'Can it be that my eyesight's defective?
Has your east tit the least bit
The best of the west tit?
Or is it a trick of perspective?'

Others use verbal vulgarisms, but in such suitable circumstances as to give good warrant:

> In the Garden of Eden lay Adam,
> Complacently stroking his madam,
>   And loud was his mirth
>   For he knew that on earth
> There were only two balls – and he had 'em.[25]

A few are effective by means of deliberately devised denial of final-word anticipation:

> Our Vicar's an absolute duck –
> But just now, he's down on his luck.
>   At the Sunday School treat
>   He tripped over his feet,
> And all of us heard him say "Now
>   children let us stand up and say Grace".[26]

And this next, I suspect, may reflect a possibly not too uncommon real-life situation:

> A delighted incredulous bride
> Remarked to the groom at her side:
>   "I never could quite
>   Believe till tonight
> Our anatomies *would* coincide".[27]

It would be less unpleasant to stop at this point and not move on from ribaldry to rancidity, but that would be an evasion of critical responsibility. The following orally circulating verse, obviously derived (probably at many removes) from Lear's 'Old Person of Woking, Whose mind was perverse and provoking', at least has the merit of considerable cleverness:

> There was a young woman of Barking Creek
> Who had her monthlies twice a week.
>   The Bishop of Woking
>   Said, "How provoking!
> Cuts out poking, so to speak".[28]

But it is difficult to credit that Oliver Herford, who has been described as the 'Number One' wit of the (American) Players Club, could have produced this poor crudity:

> There was a young lady of Twickenham
> Whose shoes were too tight to walk quick in 'em.

> She came back from a walk
> Looking whiter than chalk
> And took 'em both off and was sick in 'em.[29]

or that Paul Jennings could actually consider this anonymous effort to be an especially good limerick:

> There was a young lady of Spain
> Who was dreadfully sick in a train,
> > Not once, but again
> > And again, and again,
> And again and again and again.[30]

or that Conrad Aiken was responsible for this:

> There once was a wonderful wizzard
> who got a fierce pain in his gizzard
> > so he drank wind and snow
> > at fifty below
> and farted a forty-day blizzard.[31]

Only those who regard both promiscuity and venereal infection as funny could possibly enjoy the following verse, which according to Frank Harris was recited to him in Monte Carlo by the Prince of Wales (the future King Edward VII) in 1889:

> There was a young lady at sea
> Who said – "God, how it hurts me to pee".
> > "I see", said the Mate,
> > "That accounts for the state
> Of the Captain, the Purser and me".[32]

Nor could any one, to whom the mere idea of homosexuality is not in some sick way hilarious, find much to laugh at in this one:

> There once was a Fellow of Wadham,
> Who approved of the folkways of Sodom.
> > For a man might, he said,
> > Have a very poor head
> But be a fine fellow at bottom.[33]

Surprisingly, it seems to be well attested that the great American Judge of Appeal, Learned Hand, once entertained Chief Justice Oliver Wendell Holmes and the famous legal theorist Felix Frankfurter by singing a long (and, to me, disgusting) ballad in limerick form, beginning thus:

> The good ship's name was *Venus*,
> Her mast a towering penis,
>> Her figure-head
>> A whore in bed –
> A pretty sight, by Jesus![34]

That three such men, all of international eminence and each of elegant wit, should find such stuff amusing, seems scarcely credible. But this, perhaps, makes it less surprising that distinguished academics in London should have retailed the following unendearing combination of necrophilia, prostitution, scatology and parsimony:

> There was a young man of Belgrave,
> Who kept a dead whore in a cave;
>> He said, "I admit
>> I'm a bit of a shit –
> But think of the money I save!"[35]

It has been widely generalised that most women loathe limericks, but in my experience thay are as capable as men of enjoying them – with one proviso. The proviso is that, even in today's 'anything goes' atmosphere, many women (to their credit) still retain a distaste for mere dirt, and some still have sufficient moral courage to say so. But there is more to this matter than a greater degree of delicacy on the distaff side. I suspect that one important reason for the common aversion of women from some of the most widely circulated limericks lies in the fourth line of this verse:

> The limerick's an art form complex
> Whose contents run chiefly to sex;
>> It's famous for virgins
>> And masculine urgin's
> And vulgar erotic effects.[36]

That is to say, the vulgar erotic effects are usually presented from an exclusively male point of view. If I were a woman, I also should find such verses offensive. This has nothing to do with narrow-mindedness: it expresses a perfectly justifiable female resentment at being presented as mere sex objects for men.

Some idea of the sheer nastiness of many limericks in Legman's 1974 collection may be gained by a glance at his section headings, which include: 'Organs', 'Strange Intercourse', 'Oral Irregularity', 'Buggery', 'Abuses of the Clergy', 'Zoophily', 'Excrement', 'Prostitution', 'Diseases', 'Sex Substitutes', and 'Chamber of Horrors'.

No consideration, not even a deep commitment to the objectivity of research, could persuade me to give most of these verses a wider circulation. Clifton Fadiman (for many years book review editor of *The New Yorker*) likewise felt it better not to quote some limericks from Edward Gorey's 1954 *The Listing Attic*. As he put it, "Mr. Gorey thinks nothing of wrapping up such material as infanticide, simple murder, algolagnia, human vivisection, and the lynching of sexual deviants in a verse form traditionally consecrated to the innocent enjoyments of the nursery"[37]. There is nothing new about such literary perversions. What is relatively new, is the scale on which they are now openly printed and commercially promoted. If one expresses any scintilla of doubt about the desirability of totally uninhibited freedom of the press, there are immediate accusations of illiberality, and loudly indignant invocations against any form of censorship. But the question is not a simple one, and I am no longer convinced that certain very limited forms of social control of publication may not in some circumstances be justified. One of these circumstances might well be that highly profitable pandering to the prurience of a deliberately manufactured mass-market which has in recent years become so prevalent.

There is much truth in this comment on the limerick by Don Marquis:

> It needn't have ribaldry's taint
> Or strive to make everyone faint.
> There's a type that's demure
> And perfectly pure –
> Though it helps quite a lot if it ain't.[38]

But, like Quiller-Couch forty years ago, "I am at a loss what to do with a fashion of morose disparagement; of sneering at things long by catholic consent accounted beautiful; of . . . hanging up (without benefit of laundry) our common humanity as a rag on a clothesline"[39]. And I associate myself with W.H. Auden in his pithy protest against excessive preoccupation with the unpleasant:

> The Marquis de Sade and Genet
> Are most highly thought of today;
> But torture and treachery
> Are not my sort of lechery,
> So I've given my copies away.[40]

So far as limericks in general are concerned, they can provide so much pleasure of a passing sort that to give one's copies away would be simply foolish. But so far as that wide and complex category of

the 'indecent' is concerned, I may perhaps best summarise my own
feelings thus:

> The risqué verse has its attraction;
> The ribald may give satisfaction;
>   But I never have fancied
>   The nastily rancid
> Or verses of sick putrefaction.

X

Variants

No limerick-lover can fail to be struck by the manner in which so many old favourites may be met in a wide range of variants (a common characteristic of any literary form usually transmitted orally). Limericks have been adapted to the differing circumstances of different localities, to secular swings in social climate or literary fashion, to different age-groups, and to miscellaneous microcultures within the larger society. Moreover, being so often a recreation of intellectuals, they are particularly prone to 'improvement' for purposes of metrical amusement, rhyming ingenuity, and sheer one-up-man-ship. But, like the Opies in their *Oxford Dictionary of Nursery Rhymes*, "We have not thought it necessary to set down endless variants of a rhyme unless these variations, in themselves, have a particular interest"[1].

A good example is the 'Tobago' verse which first set Edward Lear upon the limerick trail. Langford Reed claimed (without producing any evidence) that the original went back three hundred years, but its earliest known appearance in print was in the 1822 *Anecdotes and Adventures of Fifteen Gentlemen*. Reed gives the following as the version by which Lear was inspired:

> There was an old man of Tobago,
> Long lived on rice, gruel and sago;
>   Till one day, to his bliss,
>   His physician said this,
> "To a leg of roast mutton you may go".[2]

The change from the original hyphenated 'rice-gruel' to 'rice, gruel' was presumably effected by somebody incognisant that the former was once a popular prescription for sufferers from 'tender stomachs', while other minor changes (including that from 'sick' to 'old') were probably mere accidents of imperfect transmission. At any rate, whether sick or old, the celebrated Tobagan turned up again in 1865 in Charles Dickens's *Our Mutual Friend*. A corpse, believed to have been thrown overboard from a vessel recently arrived from across the Atlantic, had been hauled out of the Thames. " 'Now, Mortimer', says Lady Tippins . . . , 'I insist upon your telling all that is to be told about the man from Jamaica.' 'Give you my honour I never heard of any man from Jamaica . . .', replies Mortimer. 'Tobago, then'. 'Nor yet from Tobago'. 'Except,' Eugene strikes in . . . 'except our friend who long lived on rice-pudding and isinglass, till at length to his something or other, his physician said something else, and a leg of mutton somehow ended in daygo'."[3].

The apparently meaningless last word of this passage must indicate that the version which eventually appeared in *Punch* in 1926 had already been at least partially evolved by 1865:

> There was a dyspeptic old Dago
> Who lived on hot water and sago;
>   When people asked why,
>   He made this reply,
> "Well, it's better than chronic lumbago".[4]

By 1932, the dago had been changed to General Mago – possibly, I suggest, by some classicist aware of the celebrated Carthaginian military man of that name:

> The eminent General Mago
> Was a martyr to chronic lumbago,
>   But gained some relief
>   From underdone beef
> Washed down by hot water and sago.[5]

Meanwhile, Reed had in one version changed the pronunciation of the place-name:

> There was an old man of Tobago,
> Whose Limerick jokes did too far go;
>   Till a kick on the seat
>   Made him much more discreet.
> He wonders now, "When will the scar go!"[6]

and in another had changed the sex of the sufferer:

> A violent old girl of Tobago
> Was known as a vicious virago;
>   When they said to her, "Why?"
>   She screamed in reply,
> "It's through this 'ere plaguey lumbago!"[7]

A similar distinct and extensive set of variants is based upon Lear's 'Calcutta' verse:

> There was an Old Man of Calcutta,
> Who perpetually ate bread and butter;
> Till a great bit of muffin, on which he was stuffing,
> Choked that horrid old man of Calcutta.[8]

In 1924 an anonymous version was printed:

> There was an old man of Calcutta,
> Who doted on muffins and butta,
> He went out to tea
> And ate seventy-three,
> And was carried home 'bust' on a shutta.[9]

and a considerable improvement by Ogden Nash came later:

> There was an old man of Calcutta,
> Who coated his tonsils with butta,
> Thus converting his snore
> From a thunderous roar
> To a soft, oleaginous mutta.[10]

Normally, one would reluct at any limerick exploiting physical handicap, but this one is amusing and not particularly offensive:

> There was an old man of Calcutta
> Who had an unfortunate stutter,
> "I would like,' he said,
> "Some bub-bub-bub-bread
> And some bub-bub-bub-bub-bub-bub-butter".[11]

I should scarcely say the same of this extension of the exploitation:

> An unfortunate lad from Calcutta
> Vibrated all through with his stutter;
> To eat, walk or speak
> He would shake for a week,
> But he *was* rather good as a rutter![12]

Gone all quite kindly metrical use of the stutter, and in its place a gross exaggeration of its corporeal effects. And to what end? Simply to permit the introduction of a not at all funny reference to coition. Nor, although it is in no way offensive, do I think over-much of this transfer to the golf links:

> There was a plus-four of Calcutta,
> Whose thoughts were too pungent to utter
> When his wife, as he found
> Ere commencing a round,
> Was whisking the eggs with his putter.[13]

A sad decline through a series of variants befell the 'pious old woman of Leeds' who had appeared in the 1820 *History of Sixteen Wonderful Old Woman*. It is difficult to weigh piety against cranial infestation, but Lear did not particularly improve the lady:

> There was an Old Person of Leeds,
> Whose head was infested with beads;
> She sat on a stool, and ate gooseberry fool,
> Which agreed with that person of Leeds.[14]

By the early 1920s, the infestation was no longer trichological, but had become horticultural:

> There was a young seedsman of Leeds,
> Rashly swallowed six packets of seeds;
>   In a month, silly ass,
>   He was covered with grass,
> And he couldn't sit down for the weeds.[15]

And eventually someone (apparently with an avidity for the anal) converted the 'ass' from its mildly affectionate quadrupedal meaning to an unpleasantly scatological sense:

> A doughty old person of Leeds
> Rashly swallowed a packet of seeds.
>   In a month his poor ass
>   Was all covered with grass
> And he couldn't sit down for the weeds.[16]

A perceptive reviewer in *The Times Literary Supplement* once applied to limericks the concept of degradation in an almost thermo-dynamic manner. "A line", he remarked, "seems in the course of transmission to meet the loss or deformation of its best tropes"[17]. But, more often, any plotting of the metrical merits of a secular series of variants would tend to resemble a feverish patient's up-and-down temperature chart rather than a continuous entropic trend in one direction. Certainly this can be said of the Ryde-Hyde-Bryde-Clyde cluster, which apparently derives from an inter-penetration of two of Lear's verses. First, in 1846, he produced a young lady of Ryde:

> There was a Young Lady of Ryde,
> Whose shoe-strings were seldom untied;
> She purchased some clogs, and some small spotty dogs,
> And frequently walked about Ryde.[18]

Then, in 1872, he produced an old person of Hyde:

> There was an old person of Hyde,
> Who walked by the shore with his bride,
> Till a Crab who came near, fill'd their bosoms with fear,
> And they said, "Would we'd never left Hyde!"[19]

By 1908 the young lady of Ryde had appeared in *London Opinion* with her locks consid'rably dyed. By 1924 she had appropriated the status of bride originally applying to Hyde:

> There was a young lady of Ryde,
> Who was longing to be someone's bride,
>> So she walked out of doors,
>> Gaily clad in 'Plus Fours',
> And her wishes were soon gratified.[20]

The Ryde bride has also appeared in a most mystifying variant in a verse illustrated by an old plate reproduced in 'R.D.' 's *Less Eminent Victorians*:

> There was a young Fellow of Ryde
> Who was terribly shocked at his bride,
>> She said she was reading
>> A book on 'Good Breeding' –
> Which proved to be really 'Bell's Guide'.[21]

Many hours of library work have failed to produce elucidation. The book could conceivably have been Thomas Bell's 1837 *The Beadle's, Headborough's and Constable's Guide*, with the bridegroom's shock being brought about by fearful anticipation of perhaps sinister implication in the latter part of its title, *as to their Duty in respect to Coroner's Inquests*. But, if so, what was the connexion with 'Good Breeding'? One faint but fascinating possibility is that the reference may have been to another book by Bell, published in 1821 with the intriguing title, *Kalogynomia, or the Laws of Female Beauty: being the Elementary Principles of that Science*, which is mentioned in Norman Himes's scholarly *Medical History of Contraception*. Or was there perhaps some Bell's guide to racehorse breeding? It would be nice to know for certain what the young lady was reading. At a later date, the bride became a fat lady, and changed the spelling of her former status, which became a place-name. But she reverted to her original trouble with her footwear:

> There was a fat lady of Bryde,
> Whose shoe-laces once came untied;
>> She didn't dare stoop,
>> For fear she would poop,
> So she cried and she cried and she cried.[22]

In yet another variant, she moved from Bryde to Clyde, where the short-line couplet became:

> She feared that to bend
> Would display her rear end.[23]

Once established in her new domicile, she became a good deal less respectable:

> There was a young harlot of Clyde
> Whose doctor cut open her hide.
> > He misplaced her stitches
> > And closed the wrong niches;
> She now does her work on the side.[24]

but we do not know whether she met there this irresponsible and mean young man:

> There was a young fellow from Clyde
> Who once at a funeral was spied.
> > When asked who was dead,
> > He smilingly said,
> "I don't know, I just came for the ride".[25]

Yet another example of the subsequent intermingling of earlier distinct locations and activities begins with these three Lear originals:

> There was an old person of Hove,
> Who frequented the depths of a grove,
> Where he studied his books, with the wrens and the rooks,
> That tranquil old person of Hove.

> There was an Old Man of Peru,
> Who watched his wife making a stew;
> But once by mistake, in a stove she did bake
> That unfortunate Man of Peru.

> There was a young lady of Tyre,
> Who swept the loud chords of a lyre;
> At the sound of each sweep, she enraptured the deep,
> And enchanted the city of Tyre.[26]

A later anonymous hand made the Hoveian into a female, who maladroitly misused the Peruvian stove:

> There was a young lady of Hove
> Who sat down by mistake on a stove;
> > When they asked, "Is it hot?"
> > She replied, "It is not".
> They said, "She's a tough one, by Jove!"[27]

In 1924 the Tyrean was male and the stove became a fire:

> There was an old fellow of Tyre,
> Who constantly sat on the fire.
>> When asked, "Is it hot?"
>> He replied, "No, it's not;
> I'm James Winterbottom, Esquire".[28]

And, later still, he became an Irishman (who could not even properly pronounce the name of his own country):

> There was an old fellow of Eire
> Who perpetually sat on the fire.
>> When they asked, "Are you hot?"
>> He declared, "No, I am not,
> I am Pat Winterbottom, Esquire".[29]

So one might go on. There are several variants upon:

> There was a young woman of Wantage
> Of whom the Town Clerk took advantage.
>> Said the Borough Surveyor,
>> "Of course, you must pay her.
> You've altered the line of her frontage".[30]

but none of them nearly so neat as this version. Not surprisingly, many verses, mainly anonymous, have been set in the great railway junction of Crewe:

> A railway official at Crewe
> Met an engine one day that he knew.
>> Tho' he smiled and he bowed,
>> That engine was proud,
> It cut him – it cut him in two![31]

One, possibly from the pen of Cosmo Monkhouse, was located in the Crewe dining room:

> An epicure, dining at Crewe,
> Found quite a large mouse in his stew.
>> Said the waiter, "Don't shout,
>> And don't wave it about,
> Or the rest will be wanting one too".[32]

Reed did not really improve things with this dentural accident:

> There was an old lady of Crewe,
> Who dropped her false teeth in the stew.

> Said the sensitive waiter,
> "It's horrid to cater
> For careless old females like you".[33]

Nor has this more recent variant much to commend it:

> A lady while dining at Crewe
> Found an elephant's whang in her stew.
> Said the waiter, "Don't shout,
> Or wave it about,
> Or the others will all want one too".[34]

Similarly, and in this case evidently developed from Lear's 1846 'Young Lady whose eyes were unique as to colour and size', by 1863 *Punch* had informed its readers:

> There was an old girl of Devizes,
> Her *forte* was in little surprises;
> She let you come near,
> And cried, "Bless us, my dear,
> Your eyes are of quite different sizes".[35]

Later, it was the Devizes girl herself (no longer specified as old) who had the unequal eyes:

> An odd-looking girl from Devizes
> Had eyes of two different sizes.
> The one was so small
> It was no use at all;
> But the other took several prizes.[36]

And from time to time, in other variants, the prize-winning organs have become virtually everything, ranging from ears through breasts to balls, of which either womankind or mankind may possess a pair.

The young lady of Gloucester whose friends quite thought they had lost her, and the young lady of Ealing who walked upside down on the ceiling, have through the years been so subjected to mixed limerickal acrobatics (often of Kama Sutral sexuality) that no new combination of 'Gloucester', 'Ealing', 'tossed her' and 'right up to the ceiling' could possibly come as a surprise. One is only astonished that Lear's 'young bird in this bush' seems never after all this time to have become a human 'bird' and been taken in a rush; that his 'Young Lady of Portugal' has not yet been asked 'ought you, gal?'; that the 'old person of Dover' has not become a young lady and been asked 'please turn over'. There seems, indeed, to be virtually no limit to the variant potential of the simple five-line limerick form.

XI

Sequences

The limerick is, almost of its very nature, a single-stanza one-off form of verse. Being usually either a light-hearted little piece of nonsense, or a bit of bawdy, or cleverly epigrammatic, or wittily terse, or linguistically ingenious, it scarcely lends itself to sequential narrative. There have been a few quite brilliant examples of coupled stanzas, the second in response to the first or complementary to it. There are even a few good triplets and quadruplets. But rarely has anything much longer than this been attempted, and still more rarely been successful. Nevertheless, it is worth looking at a few such cases.

The Pearl of February 1880 had a nine-verse sequence, in the section titled 'Lady Pokingham, or They all do it', to be sung to the tune of 'A Man's a Man for a' that' and possibly going back to an origin in Robert Burns's *Merry Muses of Caledonia*. Four of these verses follow (with the refrain):

> The grit folk an' the puir do'it,
> The blyte folk an' the sour do't,
>   The black, the white,
>   Rude an' polite,
> Baith autocrat an' boor do't.
>
> > *For they a' do't – they a' do't,*
> > *The beggars an' the braw do't,*
> > *Folk that ance were,*
> > *An' folk that are –*
> > *The folk that come will a' do't.*
>
> The licensed by the law do't,
> Forbidden folk an' a' do't,
>   An' priest an' nun
>   Enjoy the fun,
> An' never ance say n' to't
>
> The boars an' kangaroos do't,
> The titlins an' cuckoos do't,

> While sparrows sma'
> An' rabbits a'
> In countless swarms an' crews do't.
>
> The midges, fleas an' bees do't,
> The mawkes an' mites in cheese do't,
>   An' cauld earthworms
>   Crawl up in swarms,
> An' underneath the trees do't.[1]

Interestingly enough, a much bowdlerised derivative of this was still being sung in the streets by Liverpool children in the 1920s; and a completely detergised and semi-americanised version, with a sentimental refrain, 'Let's do it, let's fall in love', has been repeatedly broadcast in Britain.

A sequence of an unusual sort, not from one pen but by a succession of mainly anonymous authors, was developed early in this century from the original 'Old Man of Nantucket' verse. This original (from *The Princeton Tiger*), with two of the best of those later produced (from *The Chicago Tribune* and *The New York Press* respectively) follow:

> There was an Old Man of Nantucket,
> Who kept all his cash in a bucket;
>   His daughter, named Nan,
>   Ran away with a man –
> And, as for the bucket, Nantucket.
>
> Pa followed the pair to Pawtucket
> (The man and the girl with the bucket)
>   And he said to the man,
>   "You're welcome to Nan",
> But as for the bucket, Pawtucket.
>
> Then the pair followed Pa to Manhasset,
> Where he still held the cash as an asset;
>   And Nan and the man
>   Stole the money and ran,
> And as for the bucket, Manhasset.[2]

And, perhaps significantly, this consecutive composition made up of individual verses by different hands turned out a good deal more terse than most sequences produced at one sitting by a single writer.

In 1924 Langford Reed published his 'Limerick Drama in Ten Spasms', entitled 'The Irony of Fate; or Why She was Jilted', of which four verses ran:

Oh, list to the dolorous tale
Of unfortunate fair Abigail,
    A centipede sweet,
    Engaged to discreet
Young Horace, a prosperous snail.

His 'best man' was Sidney, the spider,
An excellent fellow as guider,
    In four pairs of new pants,
    With a bunch of choice plants
For the bride, a bouquet to provide her.

But, alack and alas! – Where's the bride?
Is she ill? Is she shy? Does she hide?
    Thus queried the guests
    When, in spite of all quests,
No sign of Miss C. could be spied.

When the groom heard the news, loudly sniffed he,
"The wedding is off, I'm too thrifty
    To give my life's care
    To a partner who'll wear
Not one pair of shoes, sir, but fifty!"[3]

And in the same collection he printed Mary Kernahan's 'A Tale of
Tragedy' in nine verses, of which the first two were:

There was an old person who cried:
He was so exceedingly wide,
    When they took him to church
    He was left in the lurch,
For he could not get in, though he tried.

So the whole congregation, politely,
Adjourned to his house Sunday-nightly;
    The choir-boys in pairs
    Arranged on the stairs,
Where they fitted exceedingly tightly.[4]

Both these sequences were certainly successful with the age-ranges
of children for which they were presumably intended.

Carolyn Wells's 1925 'Limerick Alphabet', each of its stanzas
based on a girl's name, can perhaps scarcely be counted as a sequence
and is not in my view very successful, but here is the last of the
twentysix:

Z is for zealous Zenobia,
Who says there is no hydrophobia.

> She'll argue all day
> In her pretty fool way,
> And Z stands staunchly for Zenobia.[5]

Immensely more impressive was a twelve-verse sequence, 'I will be a Bohemian – I will', which appeared in *Punch* in 1926. A few selected stanzas will convey the gay debunking irreverence of its unknown author:

> And I will be Bohemian, I will!
> I'll talk about Art till I'm ill;
>   On my stomach I'll lie,
>   And discuss Roger Fry,
> I will be Bohemian, I will!
>
> And Olga Popolga's divine,
> And if she decline to be mine
>   I'll try to look Tchekov
>   And shatter the neck of
> A bottle of strawberry wine.
>
> And if you paint eyelashes green,
> I'll murmur, "I see what you mean",
>   And express no surprise
>   At triangular thighs,
> I WILL be Bohemian, old bean!
>
> Turn on the gramophone, boys!
> I'm rapidly losing my poise;
>   Try to avoid
>   The subject of Freud,
> And let's make a terrible noise.
>
> I will be Bohemian, I swear!
> But I should like a little fresh air;
>   I should not presume
>   To suggest there's a gloom,
> But are we as gay as we were?[6]

Euwer's 1927 'Literatomy' sequence has been much quoted; but when I read his introductory explanatory stanza:

> As I lay in my bed on the flat o' me
> I was shocked at the sight of the fat o' me,
>   So to keep my nerves steady
>   I concocted and edi-
> ted this liminous, lim'rick anatomy.[7]

my inclination is to reply:

> A limericker, Anthony Euwer,
> Displeases the present reviewer.
> > No doubt there are worse
> > Examples of verse,
> But I wish that he'd written far fewer.

In his 1937 *My Limerick Book*, Reed returned to Carolyn Wells's idea of a sequence (better, a series) based on children's names, but without her exclusively female concentration, without her last-line repetition of the child's name, and on a vastly larger scale running to about three hundred verses. I rather like 'Clive' and 'Vivian':

> There was a young apiarist, CLIVE,
> Who took a queen bee for a drive;
> > When asked, "Does she sting?"
> > He said, "No such thing,
> She's always been known to beehive".

> There was a young fellow named VIVIAN
> Who had a dear friend, a Bolivian,
> > Who dropped his cigar
> > In a gunpowder jar –
> His spirit is now in oblivion. [8]

That same year, Reed's *New Limerick Book* was devoted entirely to the coronation of King George VI and consisted of ninetysix verses – the longest sequence of limericks ever written or ever likely to be written. This heroic effort included stanzas ranging from the splendidly patriotic to the sloppily sentimental, straying *en route* perilously close at times to the jingoistic and even (in just a few verses) to the xenophobic. But, in general, it was a *tour de force*:

> There are Persians patrolling the Strand,
> And folks from the States and the Rand,
> > Serbs, Germans and Greeks,
> > And Arabian sheiks
> And Chinamen, smiling and bland.

> There are Britons from over the seas,
> Too long have they been absentees;
> > They are bone of our bone
> > And their King is our own,
> So a thrice-double welcome to these.

Said a miserly peer at the Abbey,
" I fear I shall look rather shabby,
    For I've replaced my ermine,
    Infested with vermin,
With the fur of my dear defunct tabby."

TWO VERSES FROM AN ILLUSTRATED SEQUENCE

from Langford Reed, 1937, *The New Limerick Book* (illustrated by 'Batchelor'),
London, Herbert Jenkins.

There was a young fellow from Brest,
Who strolled about town half undressed;
   When folks cried : " How skittish ! "
   He replied : " I'm pro-British,
Observe the Royal Arms on my chest."

This and facing page – selected from ninetysix verses commemorating the coronation of George VI – the longest limerick sequence ever written.

Oh hark at the clapping and cheers,
As the King to his subjects appears;
    The crowds in the street
    Show gladness, complete,
But the folks in the stands are in tiers!

No wonder His Majesty's Guards,
Prompt paeans from poets and bards;
    What style and what rhythm,
    I'd love to march with 'em
If only my height were two yards.

When Ma saw her son in the Show,
She cried: "I would much like to know,
    Why they choose raw recruits
    To march on these routes,
They're all out of step except Joe!"

A patriot, living at Ewell,
Found his bonfire wanted more fuel;
    So they threw Uncle James
    To heighten the flames,
A measure effective though cruel.

Good news for the bards of the nation,
Who pant to pay loyal adulation;
    Two thousand words rhyme
    With that very subline
And popular word, 'Coronation'.[9]

About a year later (the precise date is not quite certain) there was produced at Ann Arbor, Michigan, a manuscript collection entitled *Lapses in Limerick* which included not only indecent verses from earlier 'private' publications, but also over three hundred from oral circulation. Among them was a technically brilliant twentyeight verse sequence entitled 'The Misfortunes of Fyfe', but I find only two of these sufficiently this side of the simply revolting for me to wish to quote them here:

There was a young fellow named Fyfe
Who married the pride of his life,
    But imagine his pain
    When he struggled in vain,
And just couldn't get into his wife.

But his efforts to poke her assiduous,
Met a dense growth of hair most prodigious

> Well, he thought he might dint her
> By waiting till winter,
> But he found that she wasn't deciduous.[10]

Then, in 1940, Hilaire Belloc's *Selected Cautionary Verses* had a witty and occasionally hilarious sequence, chronicling a land-and-buildings case in the law courts, with some limerickally if not legally admirable *obiter dicta* from the Judge on the Bench and some marvellously meretricious forensic forays by Sir Henry Waffle, K.C.:

> A strip to the South of the Strand
> Is a good situation for land.
>   It is healthy and dry
>   And sufficiently high
> And convenient on every hand.
>
> I have often been credibly told
> That when people are awfully old
>   Though cigars are a curse
>   And strong waters are worse
> There is nothing so fatal as cold.
>
> Your Lordship is sound to the core,
> It is nearly a quarter to four.
>   We've had quite enough
>   Of this horrible stuff
> And we don't want to hear any more![11]

But Britain was by then facing far more terrible trials of a different sort, and the great trade union leader Ernest Bevin was brought into Churchill's national government, where he set about persuading non-conscripted citizens to volunteer for work of national importance. The people responded magnificently, and it is not just blind patriotism which enables one to assert that they did so without allowing their deep sense of duty to destroy their characteristically British sense of the ridiculous or their impatience with bureaucratic bungling. There was therefore a good reception in 1943 for Quentin Crisp's forty-verse limerick sequence, *All This and Bevin Too*. It told the tale of a patriotic kangaroo, who had hitherto done nothing much more serious than playing hop-scotch:

> But that was before he had heeded
> the wireless announcement that pleaded,
>   or read in the press
>   the distressed S.O.S.
> saying 'KANGAROOS URGENTLY NEEDED'.

It was clear to him what he must do.
He must offer himself to the Zoo.
    But the moment he tried
    the committee replied,
"We've already got plenty of you."

So our hero returned to his room,
(O Bloomsbury, where is thy bloom?)
    and he lit in an attic
    to make it dramatic
a candle to lighten the gloom.

And he sat there and tried not to snivel
while wading through pages of drivel
    compiled in verbose
    and ambiguous prose
by the servants that some have called civil.

But week after week after week
drifted by, either sunny or bleak,
    before, less out of pity
    than pique, the committee
could deign or be bothered to speak.

When it did, it was hardly to state,
but more nearly to hint at, a date
    when an interview might,
    if the weather be bright,
be arranged for deciding his fate.

And he said to me, "Though I've succeeded
in finding out how we're impeded,
    it *does* puzzle me
    that the posters I see
still say, 'KANGAROOS URGENTLY NEEDED' ".[12]

In 1943 the U.S.A., although it had at last belatedly entered the
war, still knew nothing at first hand of bombing or rationing or
other real hardship. Its outstanding limerick sequence of that period
appeared in the Los Angeles 'Bidet Press' publication, *Unexpurgated*.
In this, there was a fifteen-verse sequence, 'Socially Conscious Pornography', which, whilst being rather bawdy, was quite free from
sadistic violence or sick rancidity. Four stanzas will give a good idea
of the quality of the whole:

We've socially conscious biography,
Esthetics, and social geography.

AN ANTIPODEAN FRUSTRATED BY BUREAUCRACY.

From Quentin Crisp's 1943 *All This and Bevin Too*, London, Nicholson & Watson (artist, Mervyn Peake).

Today every field
Boasts its Marxian yield,
So now there's class-conscious pornography.

Miss de Vaughan was a maker of panties
For all girls from sub-debs to grand-aunties.
　　Her very best ad
　　Was herself, lightly clad
In her three-ninetyfive silken scanties.

Now our Joe was the first proletarian
Who had filled with his sperm the ovarian
　　Recess of de Vaughan
　　Which had sheltered the spawn
Of unnumbered Fascists, all Aryan.

So after nine months, to the day,
The employer in labor pains lay.
　　As the boy hove in sight
　　He yelled, "WORKERS UNITE!"
And the doctors all fainted away.[13]

Nearly three decades seem then to have elapsed before any other substantial sequence worthy of critical notice appeared. This was by the Rt. Rev. Sydney Cyril Bulley, the (since then retired) Bishop of Carlisle and formerly Chaplain to the Queen, who paused in his pastoral duties to enter (and worthily win) a limerick competition conducted by the London *Daily Mail* in 1971. Its seven stanzas satirised Prime Minister Harold Wilson's sudden change of attitude when he unexpectedly lost a general election and found himself relegated to the Opposition benches against the new Premier, Edward Heath. Among the other *dramatis personae* were General de Gaulle, George Brown, Shirley Williams and Roy Jenkins; and the Bishop's effort was noble enough to re-establish the earlier eminence of the clergy in the limerick art. The first four verses run:

"Common Market?" said Harold, "Of course
I'll plead with De Gaulle till I'm hoarse,
　　We'll go on a spree –
　　Just Georgie and me,
We'll pull off a real *tour de force*".

"*Non, non*", said de Gaulle with a shout,
"I'm determined to keep Britain out!"
　　Harold puffed at his pipe,
　　Said "The moment's not ripe –
But the cause is quite right, I've no doubt".

But suddenly Harold was sacked
And strange to relate – though 'tis fact –
    When Ted came along,
    Harold's 'right' became 'wrong' –
He abandoned the cause he had backed.

"Naughty! Naughty!" said Shirley and Roy,
"Let's restrain this obstreperous boy –
    His hatred of Ted
    Must have gone to his head
Or he would not these tactics employ".[14]

Two years later, my old Liverpool schoolmate Arthur Tattersall, who had been Academic Registrar to the University of London and in 1973 was Secretary to University College, London, similarly re-established Cambridge alumni to their former limericking distinction. He found himself faced with a resolution from his college's branch of the Association of University Teachers, demanding 'paternity leave' for any member of staff on every occasion of his becoming a father. He wisely and wittily replied to it as if it were a joke (as, indeed, in an earlier generation it could only have been), with a six-stanza limerick sequence, 'Ode of Thanksgiving to the A.U.T.', in *The University of London Bulletin*:

The whole academic fraternity
Can relax in the joys of paternity,
    Since he, she or it,
    In sin or legit,
Can now go on leave till eternity.

No need any more for Sabbatical,
We have a solution more practical;
    Have a kid every year
    And there's nothing to fear –
Your leave comes around mathematical!

So sing we a hymn to virility.
Let's breed to our greatest ability.
    It's not for the College
    To propagate knowledge
But only to worship fertility.

This College produced Marie Stopes,
Ah, what has become of her hopes?
    Away with that book,
    Start learning to cook –
It's surprising how soon a man copes.

What's all this about Education?
What matters is more population.
    You can't beat a nappy
    To keep a dad happy –
Add zest to your dull copulation!

So God bless our great A.U.T.,
Which sets us from lecturing free:
    As we hop into bed
    Let it ever be said
'It's The Organisation for me!'[15]

If any sequences belie the general rule that limericks do not lend themselves to multi-verse sagas, they must be these last two.

XII

Lines in Lesser Tongues

Here and there already in this text there have appeared a few verses including foreign phrases, but Untermeyer was justified in his fairly recent remark that the limerick seemed "as English as cricket, Big Ben, afternoon tea and crumpets"[1] (although it has also taken firm root and flourished in the U.S.A.). Or, as Norman Douglas wrote half-tongue-in-cheek many years ago, "Limericks are as English as roast beef . . . it is limericks that keep the flag flying, that fill you with a breath of old England in strange lands, and constitute one of the strongest sentimental links binding our colonies to the mother-country," and "Whatever one may think of American achievements in other fields, it must be admitted that in this one she is a worthy competitor with the old country . . . . Not for nothing did the *Mayflower* sail"[2].

The longer one studies limericks, the more strongly one is struck by their overwhelmingly strong affiliation with the English tongue. In native French literature there are an odd few specimens such as *Digerie, digerie, doge* and *On s'étonne ici que Caliste*, but nothing remotely approaching the vast wealth to be found in our own language. There is very little in German, apart from occasional brave efforts by Englishmen and a handful of translations from English originals. Several assertions about the existence of limericks in Italian and Latin and Greek literature turned out, on investigation, to be most dubious if not downright erroneous. Other language-groups, such as Slavonic or African or Asian, could only be explored by men more multilingual than me, but native speakers from these areas have been unable to provide me with authentic examples. And my inquiries through *The Times Literary Supplement* and *The New York Times Book Review* produced not a single specimen from the wide and varied readership of those periodicals.

Why there should be so marked an anglo-orientation of this particular verse-form is an interesting (and probably a complex) question. It is sometimes assumed that limericks flourished merely as a manifestation of some peculiarly English streak of nonsensicali-

177

ty, but I doubt if the explanation is quite so simple. There is also the fact that the English are (or, at least, were until quite recently) a people inclined to relish the raw edge of sharply personalised and sometimes cruelly penetrating wit: where else may one find any real equivalent of *The Dunciad*? Nor may we safely ignore technological, commercial and social considerations. It was in England that steam-power was first widely applied to printing, with an almost immediate proliferation of semi-popular dailies and weeklies abounding in acrostics, epigrams, quips and brief humorous verses. Later, fierce competition among the new breed of newspaper millionaires provided rich rewards by way of prizes for the common man who could combine a certain measure of metrical skill with some degree of wit. In these islands, moreover, and notably during the nineteenth century, whimsical and even extraordinarily eccentric men were accepted in positions of importance from which they would elsewhere probably have been debarred by reason of apparent lack of *gravitas*. But I strongly suspect that certain features of the language itself have also played an important part. Its great economy allows the compression of complete statements into very short lines. Its characteristically strong stressing is suited to the oral repetition of humorous or satirical verse. Its marvellously rich and varied vocabulary facilitates the task of any versifier struggling for a third-rhyme ending to the limerick's fifth and final line. All these factors may have been involved, and perhaps others also. At any rate, so vigorously prolific has been the production of limericks in the English language, that one can appreciate the point of this verse:

> The limerick, peculiar to English,
> Is a verse form that's hard to extinguish.
>> Once Congress in session
>> Decreed its supression,
> But people got round it by writing the last
>> line without any rhyme or rhythm.[3]

One is presumably not intended to take too seriously a specimen, supposedly in 'Early English', printed by Carolyn Wells in her *Nonsense Anthology*:

> When that Saint George hadde sleyne ye draggon,
> He sat him down furninst a flaggon;
>> And, wit ye well,
>> Within a spell
> He had a bien plaisant jag on.[4]

Nor does it need an orientalist to be amusedly sceptical of her *Book of*

Humorous Verse's 'quotation' of this next one as coming from the lips of a Chinese child (especially when one reads the averred translation):

> If – itty – teshi mow Jays
> Haddes ny up-plo-now-shi-buh nays;
>> He lote im aw dow,
>> Witty motti-fy flow;
> A – flew-ty ho-lot-itty-flays.
>
> Infinitesimal James
> Had nine unpronounceable names;
>> He wrote them all down,
>> With a mortified frown,
> And threw the whole lot in the flames.[5]

So far as French is concerned, one may wonder why the limerick failed to flourish in what might seem to have been quite favourable soil. The Provençal troubadours of the thirteenth and fourteenth centuries produced many complex types of *rondeaux*, which were further developed during the fifteenth century by Charles d'Orleans and François Villon, and during the seventeenth by Voiture. Voiture's type consisted of thirteen lines, each usually of eight syllables, distributed between three stanzas (the first of five lines rhyming *aabba*, the second of three lines rhyming *aab* (plus a refrain), and the third of five lines rhyming *aabba* (also plus refrain). Thus, the two longer stanzas each contained the limerick rhyming-scheme, and required only minor changes of scansion to form actual limericks. Interestingly enough, during the nineteenth century a group of English poets, including Austin Dobson and Edmund Gosse, experimented with a variety of complex verse-patterns derived from the French, and produced some frivolous triolets which very nearly included limericks within them. But why did native French versifiers not simplify *rondeaux* into limericks?

I have, however, managed to spot several near-limerick verse-sequences in the original Italian of Boccaccio's *Decameron*. This is one of them, appearing as part of a song sung by Dioneo to the Queen and her assembled company:

> e quanto fosse grande il tuo velore,
> il bel viso di lei mi fe' palese,
>> il quale immaginando,
>> mi sentii gir legando
> ogni virtú a sottoporlo a lei.[6]

Deliberately eschewing exact literal translation, I proffer the follow-

ing as conveying the general spirit of the verse in English limerick
form:

> Your Majesty, humble your servant!
> And yet of her charms I'm observant;
>   When I think of the same,
>   I'm set all a-flame,
> And to her I would be subservient.

The five original Italian lines form part of what is technically called a
ballata or *canzone a ballo* or *canzonetta*, and such a *ballata* has a refrain
(as, in convivial circumstances, limerick-singing sometimes has in
England). Part of each complete nine-line stanza (the *sirma*) is of
variable rhyme-pattern and, I am informed by a knowledgeable
friend, "Theoretically there is no reason why the 'sirma' . . . should
not . . . be in limerick form"[7]. But my friend cannot recall ever
having actually come across a genuine limerick in Italian literature.
    Intriguingly enough, in the old Latin missal used until fairly
recently by Roman Catholic priests, there is to be found a prayer by
St. Thomas Aquinas which includes (although not set out, as I have
done here, in five separate lines) the following passage:

> *Sic vitiorum meorum evacuatio*
> *Concupiscentiae et libidinis exterminatio,*
>   *Caritatis et patientiae,*
>   *Humilitatis et obedientiae,*
> *Omniumque virtutum augmentatio.*[8]

Moreover, Aquinas wrote many short hymns and religious verses in
various prosodic forms, so possibly the limerick-like rhyming and
scansion are not just accidental. But neither I, nor several latinist
scholars of whom I have inquired, know of anything in classical
Latin literature which could properly be so called. In Greek, and
especially in Aristophanes, there are verses which are very limerick-
like in spirit if not in prosody. *The Wasps* includes a number of
'Sybaritics', which are "short, snappy stories of 5 or 6 lines apiece"
with "a central figure . . . a man or woman of Sybaris" and having
"wit and no moral"[9]. The author's intent and the audience's reactions must have been almost identical with what they are today when
satirical and bawdy limericks are recited. But the analogy can be
pushed no further, for my expert informant has never met an actual
limerick in Greek (apart from a translation from English by an
Englishman).
    The average Englishman is so inordinately proud of whatever few
foreign phrases he may possess that there are a fair number of

limericks in which such slight possessions have been paraded. And, as might be expected of a nation which has also produced some of the world's best linguists, there are a few examples displaying the most exquisite linguistic ingenuity. I refrain from providing translations for the verses which follow, since I would not deprive my readers of the pleasure of themselves making out their meanings with whatever dictionary aid they may find necessary.

Some of the earlier cases of frenchification emerged from – or made friendly fun of – the efforts of 'Tommy Atkins', during the first world war, to acquire a smattering of the language of his *poilu* allies. These are fairly typical examples:

> There was a young soldier called Joe
> With a *penchant* for whisky and *eau*;
> > When they asked him to halve
> > A bottle of Graves,
> He answered, "Not *demi, quel* ho!"[10]

> There was a young man from Bordeaux,
> Whose English was not *comme il faut*;
> > When asked if he'd drink,
> > He replied with a wink:
> "Not *demi, quel* jolly well ho!"[11]

> There was a young maid of Tralee,
> Whose knowledge of French was "*Oui, oui*":
> > When they said, "*Parlez vous?*"
> > She replied, "Same to you!"
> She was famed for her bright repartee.[12]

In 1924, Reed quoted a limerick entirely in French:

> *Il était une jeune fille de Tours*
> *Un peu vite, qui portait toujours*
> > *Un chapeau billy-coque,*
> > *Un manteau peau-de-phoque,*
> *Et des p'tits pantalons en velours.*[13]

And, in the following year, Carolyn Wells published this translation of a variant of the 'young lady of Riga':

> *Il y avait une demoiselle de Nigre,*
> *Qui souriait en se promenant à tigre;*
> > *De la course en rentrant*
> > *Voilà la dame en dedans,*
> *Et le sourire à la gueule du tigre.*[14]

Quite the most successful limericker in French has been the artist George du Maurier (himself of gallic extraction) who, together with his actor son Sir Gerald, was thus celebrated in a *Punch* verse of 1925:

> *L'Artiste du* Punch, *feu Du Maurier,*
> *Moissonait un beau tas de lauriers;*
> > *Et, de nos jours, son fils*
> > *Dans les rangs de Thespis*
> *S'est établi au front, et encore y est.* [15]

The following amusing invention has been attributed (I feel sure, correctly) to du Maurier *père*, who was completely bilingual, and Dame Daphne tells me that it is absolutely typical of his sense of humour:

> *Il était un homme de Madère*
> *Qui frappait le nez à son père;*
> > *On demandait, "Pourquoi?"*
> > *Il répondait, "Ma foi!*
> *Vous n'avez pas connu mon père!"* [16]

And one could scarcely speak too highly of a set of six produced by George du Maurier under the general heading, '*Vers Nonsensiques*':

> *À Potsdam, les totaux absteneurs,*
> *Comme tant d'autres titotalleurs,*
> > *Sont gloutons, omnivores,*
> > *Nasorubicolores,*
> *Grands manchons et terribles duffeurs.*

> *Un vieux Duc (le meilleur des époux)*
> *Demandait, en lui tâtant les pouls,*
> > *À sa vieille Duchesse*
> > *(Qu'un vieux catarrhe oppresse):-*
> *"Et ton thé, t'a-t-il até ta toux?"*

> *Il nagit près de Choisy-le-Roi;*
> *Le Latin lui causit de l'effroi;*
> > *Et les Mathématiques*
> > *Lui donnait des coliques,*
> *Et le Grec l'enrhumait. Ce fut moi.*

> *Il était un gendarme, à Nanteuil,*
> *Qui n'avait qu'une dent et qu'un oeil;*
> > *Mais cet oeil solitaire*
> > *Était plein de mystère;*
> *Cette dent, d'importance et d'orgueil.*

> "*Cassez-vous, cassez-vous, cassez-vous,*
> *O mer, sur vos froids gris cailloux!*"
> > *Ainsi traduisit Laure*
> > *Au profit d'Isadore*
> (*Beau jeune homme, et son futur époux*).

> *Un marin naufragé (de Doncastre)*
> *Pour prière, au milieu du désastre,*
> > *Répétait à genoux*
> > *Ces mots simples et doux:-*
> "*Scintillez, scintillez, petit astre!*"[17]

There are scarcely any limericks using German phrases, but this one is amusing enough to quote:

> There was a young charmer named Sheba
> Whose pet was a darling amoeba.
> > This queer blob of jelly
> > Would lie on her belly
> And blissfully murmur, "*Ich liebe*".[18]

As for the use of Italian words, my music master of fifty years ago, Dr. J.E. Wallace, once fabricated the following, to the great amusement of the boys in the school choir:

> There once was a tenor *vibrato*,
> Who sang an extensive *rubato*;
> > The start was *staccato*,
> > The middle, *legato*,
> The finish – a rotten tomato.[19]

An anonymous rhymester has provided another verse using Italian musical terms:

> There was a young lady of Rio,
> Who tried to play Mendelssohn's *Trio*;
> > Her knowledge was scanty,
> > She played it *Andante*
> Instead of *Allegro con Brio*.[20]

which, improving (I hope) upon some slightly improper but also slightly irregular variants, I have finally put into this form:

> A concert conductor in Rio
> Once loved a young lady called Cleo;
> > As she took off her panties,
> > He said, "No *andante*s;
> I want you *allegro con brio*."

Many Latin tags and phrases have crept into common English usage, and as young sixth-formers in Liverpool we used to greet with great guffaws any lavatory-based limerick ending with *vox et praeterea nihil*. But it is disappointing to discover that so distinguished a writer as James Joyce was responsible for so weak an effort as this:

> There was a young priest named Delaney,
> Who said to the girls, "*Nota bene*,
>   'Twould tempt the archbishop
>   The way that you swish up
> Your skirts when the weather is rainy."[21]

Some other verses, of unidentified authorship, are a good deal better:

> There was a young lady of Bandon,
> Whose feet were too narrow to stand on;
>   So she stood on her head,
>   "For my motto," she said,
> "Has always been *Nil desperandum*."[22]

> There was an old man of Saxmundham,
> *Qui habuit ventrem rotundum.*
>   He borrowed five pounds
>   From the master of hounds,
> And refused with an oath to refund 'em.[23]

In about 1924, there appeared in Cambridge an amusingly mixed Latin-with-English verse:

> *Erat Romanorum* dictator,
> *Qui* hated his *uxoris mater*;
>   *Cum leo* her *edit*,
>   A holla he *dedit*,
> *Et dixit*, "*Vale*, Ma, till later".[24]

The famous 'young lady of Riga, 'who went for a ride on a tiger' has been latinised by an unknown hand:

> *Puella Rigensis ridebat,*
> *Quam tigris in tergo vehebat;*
>   *Externa profecta*
>   *Interna revecta,*
> *Sed risus cum tigre manebat.*[25]

And, of course, there have been some immensely clever classical-tongue limericks by Ronald Knox. He once, between breakfast and 10 a.m., did a 'Devizes' variant into both Latin and Greek versions:

There was a young man of Devizes,
Whose ears were of different sizes;
⁣ The one that was small
⁣ Was no use at all,
But the other won several prizes.

Visas erat: huic geminarum
Dispar modus auricularum:
⁣ *Minor haec nihili:*
⁣ *Palma triplici*
Jam fecerat altera clarum.

Κλυτὸς ἦν τις ἀνὴρ ἀπὸ Φίσης
ὤτων ποσοτῆτος ἀνίσης.
⁣ Τὸ μὲν οὖν ὀλίγον,
⁣ Τὸ δ᾽ ἀεθλοφόρον
Νεμέας πάρα καὶ παρὰ Πίσης.[26]

There is even a multilingual verse, once recited by Sir Osbert Lancaster, which went as follows:

There once was a black cat of Truro,
Qui cantabat nocte in muro,
⁣ *On dit que ce chat*
⁣ *Ein schwartz Teufel war*[27]

– but Sir Osbert had forgotten the last line, which was in Greek.
For my own part, I have not often essayed limericks in languages other than my own. But one day in 1972, at luncheon in Hexham, when my wife looked through the window at the driving rain outside and, just as I was starting on some rather inferior Stilton, exclaimed rather dolefully, "*Quel dommage!*", I replied:

Un jeune homme, qui aimait fromage,
Se récriait, "O! Quel dommage!
⁣ *Ce fromage très cher,*
⁣ *Malgré que c'est bleu,*
N'a pas le goût de son âge".

And, during a holiday the following year in Tunisia, I amused myself by composing (and my wife by reciting) these three verses – which commemorate, in a manner of speaking, the fact that we first met as undergraduates at Cambridge where she was a member of Girton and I of Queens':

In the shade of a palm tree at Sousse
He said, "*J'aime tes deux pamplemousses*";

With languorous sigh
She murmured reply,
"Je pense que ta banane est douce".

The Queens' man, somewhere near Zaighen,
Asked, *"Liebling, wollst du dich legen?*
 Dann, erste den Kampf
 Und nächste den Krampf,
Geschlechtliche Wolluste pflegen".

The Girton girl, just outside Gabes,
Said, *"Membrum virilem habes;*
 Cunnum habeo:
 Animo meo
Nunc conjunctemus per labies."

Visas erat : huic geminarum
Dispar modus auricularum :
  Minor haec nihili ;
  Palma triplici
Jam fecerat altera clarum.

Κλυτὸς ἦν τις ἀνὴρ ἀπὸ Φίσης
ὤτων ποσοτῆτος ἀνίσης.
  Τὸ μὲν οὖν ὀλίγον,
  Τὸ δ' ἀεθλοφόρον
Νεμέας πάρα καὶ παρὰ Πίσης:

LIMERICKS IN LATIN AND GREEK

Verses by Ronald Knox, illustration by H.M. Bateman, from Langford Reed, 1924,
The Complete Limerick Book, London, Jarrolds.

XIII

Ingenious Typographics

In most cases, limericks fall more compellingly upon the ear than on the eye, but there are two sorts which are exceptions to this general rule. The first sort consists of those verses which the genius of an artist has indissolubly linked to their accompanying illustrations. The second sort I call 'ingenious typographics', and they achieve their special effects by rigidly imposing typographical uniformities upon those strange disparities between spelling and pronunciation to which the English language is so prone. A few such ingenious typographics have already appeared in earlier chapters, but the class is worthy of systematic examination as a whole.

Some of the earliest examples – perhaps the first – appeared in *Punch* in 1896, and depended upon the idiosyncrasies of pronunciation of certain aristocratic English patronyms. Here are a couple, both from unknown pens:

There was a young chappie named Cholmondeley,*Chum-lee*
Who always at dinner sat dolmondeley;
 His fair partner said,
 As he crumbled his bread,
"Dear me! you behave very rolmondeley!"

A fine old landowner named Marjoribanks *March-banks*
Found the summer heat dry paths and parjoribanks;
 So about his estate,
 To protect his old pate,
He arranged fine plantations and larjoribanks.[1]

Then, in 1904, Major C.K. Phillips provided *Punch* with a limerick employing this same ploy in the short-lined couplet also:

A charming young lady called Geoghegan, *Gay-gan*
(Whose Christian names are peoghegan)
 Will be Mrs. Knollys   *Noals*
 Very soon at All Ksollys';
But the date is at present a veogheg 'un.[2]

Soon, of course, variants upon these early versions began to appear:

> There lived a young lady named Geoghegan,
> The name is apparently peoghegan;
>> She'll be changing it soon
>> For that of Colquhoun,   *Co-houn*
> But the date is at present a veoghegan.[3]

And some clever completely new ones:

> There was a young lady named Menzies,   *Min-gis*
> Who said, "Do you know what this thenzies?"
>> Said her aunt, with a gasp,
>> "Why, my dear, that's a wasp!
> And you're holding the end where the stinzies".[4]

Sometimes, as with the following verse by P.L. Mannock, there is a peculiarly appealing ingenuity which is fully appreciable only after a second or two of cerebration:

> An author, by name Gilbert St. John,   *Sin-jun*
> Remarked to me once, "Honest t. John,
>> You really can't quote
>> That story I wrote;
> My copyright you are infrt. John."[5]

Other limericks of this sort, by contrast, are pretty mediocre specimens, with nothing bizarre about them, no special surprise of pronunciation, only the mere mechanics of the thing:

> There was a young lady named Psyche,
> Who was heard to ejaculate, "Pcryche!"
>> For, when riding her pbych,
>> She ran over a ptych,
> And fell on some rails that were pspyche.[6]

But, it must be admitted, the number of surnames amenable to really effective treatment of their aphonetic spellings is somewhat limited.

Topographic nomenclature, on the other hand, offers almost endless possibilities of exploitation. Vyvyan Holland printed (but plain, with the ordinary spelling of each word) this example, which I have revised into coordinated orthography so as to demonstrate what can be done:

> There was a young servant of Drogheda,   *Droy-da*
> Whose mistress had deeply annogheda;

> She proceeded to swear
> In language so rare
> That afterwards no one emplogheda.[7]

Reed's 1924 collection included some fine gems from this new vein; among them, the following verse:

> There was a young fellow of Beaulieu,   *Bew-lee*
> Who loved a fair maiden most treaulieu;
>   He said, "Do be mine",
>   And she didn't decline,
> So the wedding was solemnised deaulieu.[8]

He also printed (but plain) this one, which he stated to be by Dr. Blomfield, the late Bishop of St. Albans, and to have been composed as an aid to the traditional pronunciation of the town that it refers to:

> There was a young lady of Cirencester,   *Si-si-ter*
> Who went to consult her solicitor;
>   When he asked for her fee,
>   She said, "Fiddle-de-dee!
> I only dropped in as a visitor".[9]

Yet a not too arduous search in *Crockford* reveals that from its foundation that diocese has never had a bishop of that name, so this seems to be just one more example of the slackness of scholarship which has characterised so many of those who have written about limericks. (There was, however, a nineteenth century Bishop Blomfield, first of Chester and then of London, and he is presumably the prelate referred to.) A variant of this verse was later produced by E.V. Knox ('Evoe' of *Punch*) with its orthography coordinated:

> There was a young lady of Cirencester,
> Whose fiancé went down to virencester
>   By the Great Western line,
>   Which he swore was divine,
> And he couldn't have been much explirencester.[10]

Among the other English towns which have attracted attention of this type are Welwyn, Leicester and Gloucester. Unidentified hands produced these felicitous efforts:

> There was a young woman of Welwyn,   *Well-in*
> Loved a barman, who served in the 'Belwyn'.
>   But the 'Belwyn', oh dear!
>   Had a welwyn the rear;
> So they never got wed, for they felwyn.

An obstinate lady of Leicester   *Less–ter*
Wouldn't marry her swain, though he preicester;
    For his income, I fear,
    Was a hundred a year,
On which he could never have dreicester.

There was a young fellow of Gloucester,   *Gloss–ter*
Whose wife ran away with a coucester;
    He traced her to Leicester,
    And tried to arreicester,
But in spite of his efforts he loucester. [11]

And somebody, with more ingenuity than respect for public library rules, has written into the Kingston upon Hull copy of *The Indiscreet Limerick Book* a most dexterous (but plain and unpunctuated) doubling-up of these last two place names. I print the verse here after effecting orthographic coordination:

An innocent maiden of Gloucester
Fell in love with a coucester named Foucester;
    She met him in Leicester –
    He merely careister,
Then the hard-hearted coucester just loucester. [12]

Ever inventive, 'Evoe' provided *Punch* in 1928 with a limerick cleverly utilising the archaic form of an English place-name:

There was an old Sultan of Salisbury,   *Ser–rum*
Who wanted some wives for his halisbury;
    So he had them sent down
    By a fast train from town,
For he thought that his motor would scalisbury. [13]

which little jewel has been reshaped by some unascertained artificer to shine even brighter:

There was a young curate of Salisbury
Whose manners were Halisbury-scalisbury.
    He wandered round Hampshire   *Hants.*
    Without any pampshire
Till his Vicar compelled him to Walisbury. [14]

Another innominate innovator has contrasted the considerable formality of the Bicester hunt in Oxfordshire with the rather easier-going Fernie hunt of Leicestershire:

They're a disciplined lot are the Bicester,   *Biss–ter*
And the Huntsman is always called 'Micester';

> When a girl from the Fernie
> Addressed him as 'Ernie',
> They all gathered round her and hicester.[15]

Within a decade of the appearance of the pioneer 'Beauchamp', 'Cholmondeley' and 'Marjoribanks' verses in England, Carolyn Wells was printing efforts of similar sort on the other side of the Atlantic. Her 1906 *A Whimsey Anthology* included a set of five stanzas about musicians, and some based upon English topography, but none of these were very scintillating. Here are two of them:

> Another composer, named Haydn,   *Hie-d'n*
> The field of Sonata would waydn;
>   He wrote the 'Creation',
>   Which made a sensation,
> And this was the work that he daydn.

> A lady who lived by the Thames   *Tems*
> Had a gorgeous collection of ghames.
>   She had them reset
>   In a large coronet
> And a number of small diadhames.[16]

Much more successfully, she blazed a peculiarly American trail with a limerick sequence capitalising on the inconsonance of spelling and pronunciation of a well-known Red Indian tribe. The second and third verses are reprinted here:

> When out on the war-path, the Siouxs   *Soo*(s)
> March single file – never by tiouxs –
>   And by 'blazing' the trees
>   Can return at their ease,
> And their way through the forest ne'er liouxs.

> All new-fashioned boats he eschiouxs,
> And uses the birch-bark caniouxs;
>   They are handy and light,
>   And, inverted at night,
> Give shelter from storms and from dyiouxs.[17]

This rich wide range of tribal nomenclature has remained strangely unexplored, but considerable use has been made of the names of States in the U.S.A. Sometimes, as with this effort by Ogden Nash, there has been only a rather routine (though clever) following of fairly well-worn paths:

> There was a brave girl of Connecticut   *Conn-et-i-c't*
> Who signalled the train with her pecticut,

> Which the papers defined
> As presence of mind,
> But deplorable absence of ecticut.[18]

In some other verses, like the next one, abbreviations of State names have been used, but are to be pronounced precisely as printed:

> Endeavoured a lady of No. Dak.   *North Dakota*
> To picture a bear with a Kodak.
> The button she pressed,
> And the bear did the rest –
> The lady stopped running in So. Dak.[19]   *South Dakota*

More frequently, however, such abbreviated forms have been printed for full pronunciation, producing in some cases an admirable effect:

> A lady from Atlanta, Ga.   *Georgia*
> Became quite a notable fa.
> But she faded from view
> With a quaint I.O.U.
> That she signed, "Mrs. Lucrezia Ba."

> A handsome young gent down in Fla.   *Florida*
> Collapsed in a hospital ca.
> A young nurse from Me.   *Maine*
> Sought to banish his pe.
> And shot him. Now what could be ha.?

> There was a young lady from Del.   *Delaware*
> Who was most undoubtedly wel.
> That to dress for a masque
> Wasn't much of a tasque,
> But she cried, "What the heck will my fel.?"

> There are plenty of people in Md.   *Maryland*
> Who think that their state is a fd.
> It seems odd to find
> That they don't really mind
> That Wis., not Md., is Dd.[20]   *Wisconsin*

Incidentally, in 1948, Kenneth Cornish produced a collection of limericks based upon queer-sounding South African place-names. Other originators have developed ingenious typographics based upon quite different sorts of common abbreviations. For example:

> When you think of the hosts without No.   *Number*
> Who are slain by the deadly cuco.,

It's quite a mistake
Of such food to partake;
It results in a permanent slo.[21]

A girl who weighs many an Oz.   *Ounce*
Used language I will not pronoz.
    Her brother, one day,
    Pulled her chair right away;
He wanted to see if she'd boz.[22]

As he filled up his order book pp.   *Pages*
He decided, "I want higher ww."
    So he struck for more pay,
    But, alas, they now say,
He is sweeping out elephants' cc.[23]

The sermon our Pastor Rt. Rev.   *Right Reverend*
Began, may have had a rt. clev.,
    But his talk, though consistent,
    Kept the end so far distant
That we left since we felt he mt. nev.[24]

And the following awful exaggeration of Australian speech pillories the painful deformations which our antipodean descendants have inflicted upon what used to be standard English:

There was once an eccentric Strine   *Australian*
Whose speech was so sesquipedine,
    And his vowels so refined
    That their patience got strined,
And they treated him just like an ine.[25]

There are evident opportunities for similar 'send ups', caricaturing the characteristics of what are sometimes euphemistically called 'zonally evolved varieties' of our tongue, and ranging from Pakistan to Port of Spain.

My own rather few efforts in the field of patronymic limericks are perhaps not very impressive – possibly, I try to persuade myself, because most of the best names have long ago been pre-empted by earlier authors. However, here are two of them, the first printed plain (just try analysing the pronunciation of 'Featherstonehaugh' at the same time phonetically and syllabically!) and the second with coordinated orthography:

"Today," said the Hon. Freddie Featherstonehaugh,   *Fan-shor*
"If you take your yacht over to France, you're

With plebs all the way
From Nice to Gris Nez –
The whole coast is one long artisan shore."

The Honourable Winifred Wemyss   *Weems*
Saw styli and snakes in her dremyss –
    And these she enjeud
    Until she heard Freud
Say, "Nothing is quite what it semyss."

So far as well-known place-names are concerned, there is still some scope for new inventions, as in this verse of mine:

There was an inn-keeper of Towcester,   *Toe-ster*
Who was quite an inveterate bowcester;
    He claimed that Queen Bess
    Had left her impress
When she slept in his famous four-powcester.

But it is in the remoter retreats of the north country that there remain any number of neglected odd place-names, many of which I have from time to time played about with when their pronunciations happened to intrigue me. I offer the reader this selected posy of seven such peculiarities:

A spinster, who lived outside Slaithwaite,   *Sloo-et*
Made puddings all soggy with saithwaite;
    She said that the trick
    To avoid being sick
Was liberal use of the craithwaite.

A monastery mason at Meaux   *Mewss*
Said, "This site is a sink of abeaux;
    And, as for the Prior,
    He'll fry in hell-fire:
His sins are not scarlet, they're peaux."

A gardener, living at Barnoldswick   *Bar-lik*
Once wanted to water his garnoldswick.
    It was futile to try,
    For the summer was dry
And the one pump he had was hydrarnoldswick.

A modest young maiden of Glamys,   *Glarms*
Whilst bathing was bothered by quamys
    Lest curious shrimps
    Might catch a brief glimpse
Of all her most intimate chamys.

There once was an *amant* from Atwick   *At–ik*
Who suffered from spasms rheumatwick;
    So whether each thrust
    Was lumbago or lust
Seemed always a bit problematwick.

An addle-pate farmer of Appletreewick   *Ap–trik*
Habitually had a madcapple treewick;
    He piled up his hay
    In the damp to decay
Instead of upon the most applet reewick.

A Skavieman, marooned in Milngavie,   *Mul–guy*
Became a most pityfiln gavie;
    He said to his wife,
    "This is no sort of life,
To the island of Skavie we must havie."

Perhaps I may add, as a sort of trefoil decoration in my posy, a linked trio of inter-penetrating verses:

A 'black' Benedictine from Prinknash   *Prin–ach*
Had such an aversion from spinknash
    That soon he was sated
    By that which he hated,
And gorged on green gherkins from Grinknash.

A gastronome, dining at Greenwich,   *Grin–ich*
Had such a strong yearning for speenwich
    That, later that night,
    He booked for a flight
And jumped from the plane over Preenwich.

A shipload of second-crop spinach
Was freighted from Prinach to Grinich;
    But, needless to say,
    It decayed on the way
And was sent back from Grinich to Prinach.

Here, too, is my quintet of counties, spelled out in full but to be pronounced as commonly abbreviated:

A cottager, living in Oxfordshire,   *Oxon.*
Made a pile of fine earth with old croxfordshire;
    When people asked, "Why?",
    She gave this reply,
"That there's what I grow hollyhoxfordshire".

A lad who dyed cotton in Lancashire   *Lancs.*
Was always engaging in prancashire;
    One day, sad to say,
    He tripped in his play
And died in his own dyeing tancashire.

A bolshevik, boarding in Bedfordshire,   *Beds.*
Said, "I'll see that, when my son wedfordshire,
    His bride's not in white
    Like a pre-Raphaelite,
But robed in the reddest of redfordshire."

A teetotal rector in Gloucestershire   *Glos.*
To his bibulous cousin said, "Coucestershire,
    I don't think it right
    That you should get tight
And climb up that fine reredoucestershire."

Along the slow rivers of Huntingdonshire,   *Hunts.*
Young couples make love in their puntingdonshire;
    Beneath weeping willows
    They lie on their pillows
And murmur their gratified gruntingdonshire.

By way of contrast, I submit also three stanzas with the key-word printed in its commonly abbreviated form but to be read as if spelled out:

In the dark dismal days of Dec.   *December*
It is always a joy to rem.
    That, come Christmas Day,
    You'll have (hip hooray!)
A turkey trussed up to dism.

There was a poor pliant Prof.   *Professor*
Who, faced with a student transgr.,
    Sank down on his knees
    And begged, "If you please,
Treat me as your cruel oppr."

There once was a devious Dr.,   *Doctor*
Of lies was a chronic concr.;
    But he found his divorce
    Was devoid of all force
When he came up against the Queen's Prr.

Nor are the possibilities of devising other sub-types of ingenious typographics as yet exhausted. One could make use of the recognised abbreviations of the many orders of aristocracy and nobility, as in these two experiments of mine:

> Sir Simon Sartorius, Kt.,   *Knight*
> Said, "We Tories are dining tokt.;
>> And therefore, I think,
>> I'll wear not a pink,
> But a beautiful blue acokt."

> Sir Gadwin de Gambleby, Bt.,   *Baronet*
> Makes a thousand a week playing f(t.
>> Of all taxes);
>> And so he relaxes,
> With paeans of praise on his clt.

Or one could utilise symbols commonly used by authors and compositors, as in the next two:

> An amorous writer of *vv*.   *Verses*
> Was specially enamoured of *nn*.;
>> But he found each advance
>> In pursuit of romance
> Met only with starchy re*vv*.

> You don't show suspenders (or { })   *braces*
> When dressed up for Jockey Clu{ };
>> But items like these
>> May drop to your knees
> While engaging in loving em{ }.

Or one might use symbols from the physical and biological sciences:

> All persons of higher °   *degree*
> Are proud of a long pe°;
>> And even the masses
>> Of inferior classes,
> Unless they are misle°.

> Whether you are ♀ or ♂,   *female; male*
> If ever your spirits should fail,
>> You can cheer yourself up
>> By a good claret cup
> Or even by supping so ♂.

As yet, moreover, versifiers have not even begun to explore the virtually virgin territory of modern industrial and technological terminology. Why not, for example, a little imaginative limerick-making along such lines as these?:

> A tailor, by name Terry Lean,   *terylene*
> Said, "My suits have a beautiful sheen;
> > They wear very well,
> > In cut they excel,
> And they either drip-dry or dry-clean".

> A student of 'stinks', Polly Ester,   *polyester*
> Was quite an ingenious jester;
> > One day, from old waste,
> > She made a foul taste
> To mix with her tutor's ingesta.

> "Please give me a roll, Anna Glipta",   *anaglypta*
> Her gaffer said, as he unzipped her;
> > "I can't decorate
> > With so lovely a mate";
> The next thing she knew, he had stripped her.

And, for that matter, why neglect the almost innumerable products of the present-day craze for acronymics?:

> A congress convened by UNESCO   *United*
> Broke up in a fight *re* a fresco: *Nations*
> > Was it Slav, was it Spanish,   *Educational*
> > Was it Greek, or Romanische, *Scientific and*
> Was it French or was it Tedesco?   *Cultural*
>   *Organisation*

> How jurors must yearn for an ERNIE   *Electronic*
> To take on their court-of-law journey; *Random*
> > And there analyse   *Number*
> > The half-truths and lies   *Indicator*
> That issue from each slick attorney! *Equipment*

> When nine nations set out on a JET,   *Joint*
> Their leaders should never forget *European*
> > That nuclear fusion   *Torus*
> > Is but a collusion
> At the world's most wicked thing yet.

But, if I go on like this, my intended slight posy of personally produced typographical ingenuities will end up as a ponderous wholesale lorry load. Enough is enough. I hope that it has not already become too much.

XIV

The 'Prose' Limerick

The very idea of a prose limerick may superficially seem to be a contradiction in terms, but it is not necessarily so. Much depends upon the definitions of words. Prose is often regarded as the antithesis to poetry, which was once rather shrewdly (but here, not very helpfully) identified as that which is lost in translation. Poetry has also been characterised as the expression of beautiful thought in appropriate language containing a rhythmical element and metrical form – but that all depends upon precisely what is meant by metrical form. And some high-quality poetry expresses thought which, far from being beautiful, is in itself most unpleasant and is palliated only by its poetic expression. As for prose, Coleridge once defined it as proper words in their proper places – but that description would seem to be equally applicable to poetry.

Here, however, I antithesise 'prose' not to 'poetry' (which is a high and recondite concept), but to 'versification' (which is a fairly mundane matter of metre, rhyme, rhythm and line lay-out). In this sense, limericks are typically five-line versifications, with rhyme-scheme *aabba*, and with the three *a* lines each usually of three feet and the two *b* lines each usually of two feet. By any such simple definition, there could certainly be no such thing as a prose limerick.

But limericks are also intended to be vehicles of fun. And might it not be rather fun if one were able to 'take in' the unwary reader by presenting a limerick in what appeared at first sight to be simply an ordinary prose passage (in effect, the ultimate in ingenious typographics)? And especially so if the deluded reader were a person in a responsible position, who did not even realise that he had been taken in until he had put the prose limerick into print? It is said – although I have not succeeded in tracing the original newspaper appearance – that the ever-inventive Ronald Knox once succeeded in slipping this 'small ad.' past the unsuspecting eye of the advertisement manager of *The Times*:

> An Anglican curate in want of a
> second-hand portable font would exchange

for the same a portrait (in frame) of
the Bishop-elect of Vermont. [1]

Certainly the following 'gossip' item of unknown authorship
appeared in print, for a cutting containing it was found pasted into
my second-hand copy of *Mr. Punch's Limerick Book*:

At <u>the Theatre</u>

A GENTLEMAN home from
Malay was taken one night
to a play. He said, "I don't
mind if their accent's refined,
but I wish I could hear what
they say". [2]

But, since I suspect from its type-fount that the cutting itself is from
Punch, perhaps this hardly counts.

It has long seemed to me that the well-known admirable response
to Ronald Knox's limerick on philosophical idealism could have
been given a special savour had it been printed in the form of a letter,
thus:

Dear Sir,
   Your astonishment's odd. I'm always
about in the quad. And that's why the
tree continues to be, since observed by,
      Yours faithfully,
                              God.

Following up this line of thought, I have produced, and here present,
as from a range of differing social situations, half a dozen limericks in
'letter' form:

Dear Pater,
   (And Mater, and Kid). Please
could you send me ten quid? My
tuckshop account requires that
amount to clear it.
      Yours hopefully,
                              Syd.

Dear Doctor,
   Please look at young Millie. I hope
she's not done nothing silly. She's been
staying out late, and she's putting on
weight.
      Yours faithfully,
                              (Mrs.) O'Killey.

Dear Commodore,
   Will you say when I may take
firmer steps with the men?
   The whole lower-deck looks like
an old wreck.
                      I. Whippem
                              Lieutenant, R.N.

Dear Mam
   I am lernin to spel I hoap
you an dad are boath well this
skool is kwite nice but Ive run
away twyss
                   With luv from yor dorter
                                        yung Nell

Dear Prof.,
   In reply to your note, we find you
are far too remote. To cut out conject-
ures, we're cutting your lectures.
               The Class
                      (by unanimous vote).

Dear Vicar,
   So glad you can speak ('Young Wives'
on next Saturday week).
   Our film show tomorrow is 'Games
in Gomorrah'.
               Good wishes
                      from
                  Marian Meek.

There also seem to be possibilities in imaginary memoranda
couched in administrators' 'officialese', for which I offer three
prototypes:

   Town Clerk to F. & G.P.: Since spending
   has been far too free, it's clear that we're
   fated to be higher rated, so save on all
   servants but me.

   From the Clerk of the Joint River Board.
   Employees should note that the Lord of the
   Manor of Mews has not paid his dues. His
   flooding should thus be ignored.

Admin. Memorandum to Staff. I regret
an unfortunate gaffe by which every
tutor received from computer an in-
comprehensible graph.

As a third possible category for the exploitation of this suggested
new limerick form, there is the vast field of notices posted by those in
various positions of authority. One might start with a couple from a
garage proprietor, the first in the forecourt to delude the customers
and the second in the workshop to indicate to the employees the
reality of the situation:

When cars are left here for repair, our charges are
modest and fair. And owners may rest quite content
that we test all work that is done with great care.

In the shed at the end of the mews there's a bucket
of old bolts and screws, and right at the back you will
see a large stack of old junk that perhaps you can use.

Then there could be a couple for railway stations, one for the
passenger concourse and the other for the refreshment room:

The train that was due to depart at 8.10. is not
likely to start. We're working to rule: you'd
best get a mule or a bike or a horse and a cart.

Please note the new list of prices. All sand-
wiches, rolls and cream slices are up 10%, and we
cannot prevent an increase in prices of ices.

And how about two from a university? One from the Students'
Union, the other from the Vice-Chancellor:

By bare (and disputed) majority we must now give
united priority to support of each faction that takes
direct action against all established authority.

In future, by Senate decree, I shall greet Student
Reps. on one knee. This is not lack of guts (which
Senate rebuts) but a sign of our wish to agree.

Next, from a travel agent's brochure and an airport's departure
lounge:

If, when you have travelled by jet and been by
our courier met, the sands are black silt and the
hotel's not yet built, we trust you will not be upset.

All flights that are leaving today may well be
hi-jacked on the way – but don't lose your nerve, for
we shall still serve a pleasant cold meal on a tray.

And finally, to bring much-needed encouragement to the twin
bastions of our national way of life, a couple of suggestions are here
provided, the first for the parliamentary daily 'order' paper and the
second for the entrance porch of a 'progressive' church:

That this House asks for a freeze on prices
and wages and fees, and points out the need for
action with speed to double the pay of M.P.s.

The Vicar much hopes that you'll sing and make the
hymns go with a swing; but – needless to say – when you
kneel down to pray, you needn't believe in a thing.

A few years ago, I decided to put to the test the possibility of
slipping a crypto-limerick letter past the eye, not just of the adver-
tisements manager of a daily newspaper, but of the editor of a
pedagogical journal. At the time, those directly engaged in the
professional preparation of teachers were getting a little tired of
pompous pretensions to expertise in that task by people who had no
experience whatever of it, so I duly devised and despatched the
following:

SIR – How strange that so many
head teachers make statements
whose dominant features imply
that they must have the deepest
distrust of all but head-teacherly
creatures. Engaged as I am in a
college of education I don't claim
the knowledge to tell every head
how to make his own bed and this
I most fully acknowledge. But how
I should welcome some sign that
those who so strongly opine on a
job they've not tried could modestly
hide their omniscience quasi-divine.
                                CYRIL BIBBY[3]

The ploy succeeded: my sequence of three 'prose' limericks was
printed in the correspondence columns of the official organ of the
National Union of Teachers. Perhaps some slight gratification at
having out-knoxed Knox by three verses to one may be excused.

XV

The Latter-Day Revival

Following the ending of the second world war, it was not very long before the U.S.A. saw a substantial revival of interest in the limerick art. One form it took was the running of a nation-wide limerick competition by the Mark Twain Society, resulting in over 3,000 entries. The general standard does not seem to have been very high, but a Mrs. Burgess of Nebraska managed to win a prize with this effort:

> Mark Twain was a mop-headed male,
> Whose narratives sparkled like ale;
>   And this Prince of the Grin
>   Who once fathered Huck Finn
> Can still hold the world by the tale![1]

It was also at about this time, in November 1946, that the magazine section of *The New York Times* carried H.I. Brock's article entitled 'A Century of Limericks', which elicited from readers a vast number of such verses, many of them published during the following month in a special 'Limerick Addenda'. Two other signs of the revival were the founding during the 1940s of the 'Fifth Line Society' in Chicago and of the 'American Limerick Society' in Berkeley, California.

It was also in the U.S.A. that the first volumes of post-war limerick collections appeared in print. In 1945 there was Witherspoon's *Glimerick Book*; two years later there came Brock's *Little Book of Limericks*; in 1954 Edward Gorey's *Listing Attic*. The following year, the 'Peter Pauper Press', run by the late Peter Beilensen, brought out its *Little Limerick Book (An Uncensored Collection)*, followed in 1960 by its *Laundered Limericks*. In that year also the veteran humorist Bennett Cerf (chairman of the highly reputable publishing company, Random House) produced his *Out on a Limerick: A Collection of over 300 of the World's Best Printable Limericks: Assembled, Revised, Dry-cleaned and Annotated by Mister Cerf*. Louis Untermeyer soon followed with his *Lots of Limericks: Light, Lusty, and Lasting*; in 1963 Gordon and Eisenberg's *Limericks for the John* was published for

loo-sitting perusal; in 1964 there came Nick Urda's *Eighty-eight Best
Limericks*; and then, in 1966 in Texas, *Grand Prix Limerix: 1,001 New
Limericks You Never Saw Before!* (reputedly produced by a wealthy
San Francisco advertising executive, John Coulthard).

Far too large a part of this post-war American output was of a not
simply bawdy, but of a sadly sickly, nature. However, there were
also many very proper productions, such as the winning entry to a
competition conducted in 1965 by *Business News* (which, instead of
requiring a fifth line to a given first four, required a first four to a
given fifth):

> If it's management men you pursue
> Don't hunt every beast in the zoo –
>   Just look for the signs,
>   That say: 'Tigers and Lions'.
> It isn't how many – it's who.[2]

One may think that the prize – a transatlantic round trip, with a
'medieval feast' in Bunratty Castle, a stay in the city of Limerick,
and a visit to the Blarney stone, was fairly easily won.

In Britain, where the war had been long and weary, and where
rationing continued for several years after its conclusion (owing to
the almost immediate cutting-off of American aid), it was not until
the late 1960s that the post-war limerick revival began to get really
into stride. One of its early indications was a characteristically vulgar
seaside postcard, prominently displayed in 1969 in the bar-parlour of
a public house in Thirsk. Instead of the usual type of printed comment capable of a double meaning, the text at its foot was this verse:

> A lovely young lady named Sally
> Stripped at the working men's Palais.
>   She got lots of applause
>   When she took off her drawers,
> 'Cos the hairs on her head didn't tally.[3]

The nature of the coloured illustration above the verse may easily be
imagined!

Soon signs of renewed interest began to appear in England's
newspapers, with competitions somewhat reminiscent (except for
the much smaller scale, the comparative modesty of the prizes
offered, and the much greater freedom in expression) of the great
limerick 'boom' in the first two decades of the century. In the August
of 1971, the *Eastern Evening News* ran a contest for verses based upon
East Anglian place-names. It was in the same month that, in a
London *Daily Mail* competition, the then Bishop of Carlisle was

awarded a meagre £5 for an admirable entry. Four of its seven stanzas, celebrating the contorted course of the early negotiations for Britain's entry into the European Economic Community, have already been quoted, and the remaining three are too good to be left hidden away in library newspaper files:

> Good George, he spoke up like a man,
> Saying, "Ted's terms are the same as our plan.
> > He's not a bad bloke
> > Who can at a stroke
> Wipe the floor with the General's ban."

> Harold James leaves the course in a huff,
> Edward George sails along through the rough.
> > "Ship ahoy! Harold dear,
> > I'll be soon in the clear,
> I'm so sorry you've made such a muff ".

> "Just meet me in Brussels, dear man,
> For a drink to the E.E.C. plan,
> > Bring Jenkins and George,
> > New friendships to forge,
> You've muffed it, *c'a ne fait rien!*"[4]

And here, one must at least recall Arthur Tattersall's impressive six-stanza sequence (already fully quoted in an earlier chapter) about the demand of the London branch of the Association of University Teachers for 'paternity allowances'.

In the October of that same year, 1971, the Wine Correspondent of *The Sunday Times* conducted a limerick competition, under the heading 'the Great New Beaujolais Race', offering to each of the hundred best entrants a free visit to the declaration of the 'Beaujolais Nouveau', with a bonus of a quarter of a hogshead of the best new vintage for whichever one won a 'race' to the wine. The average quality of the winning entries is pretty fairly represented by this verse:

> There was a young man from Beaujolais
> Who in restaurants was given to folly.
> > When sated with Fleurie
> > His speech became slurry
> And he sped round the room on a trolley.[5]

We must hope that the quarter-hogshead was of higher merit.

Then, in December, the official organ of the National Union of Teachers printed two prize-winning entries, from a twelve-year-old

girl in Southampton and a thirteen-year-old girl in Chelmsford
(who were awarded the not too extravagant sum of £2 each), for a
limerick competition sponsored by the National Society of Non-
Smokers:

> Lighting up, the girl started to cough.
> Her boyfriend exclaimed: "I'm off.
>   What, marry a wife
>   Who does that all her life?
> I'll look somewhere else: that's enough".[6]

> Gasped the girl as she lighted a fag,
> "I really must have a quick drag".
>   Her boyfriend said: "Dear,
>   We can't marry, I fear.
> You'll soon be a stinking old hag."[7]

It seems a pity, in an age when cancer-causing tobacco sales are so
profitabley promoted by highly paid publicity men, often managing

> There was an Old Man at a Junction,
> Whose feelings were wrung with compunction;
>   When they said 'The Train's gone!'
>   He exclaimed 'How forlorn!'
> But remained on the rails of the Junction.

A LEAR LIMERICK ADAPTED TO MODERN POLITICAL SATIRE.

Above – from Edward Lear's 1872 *More Nonsense* . . .
Facing page – Cartoon by 'Garland', from *Daily Telegraph*, 5 July 1971. The train has
been marked 'Common Market Express' and provided with a driver (Edward Heath)
and an advance-runner holding Union 'Jack'. The by-stander has become Roy Jenkins
and the 'forlorn' 'Old Man' is clearly Harold Wilson.

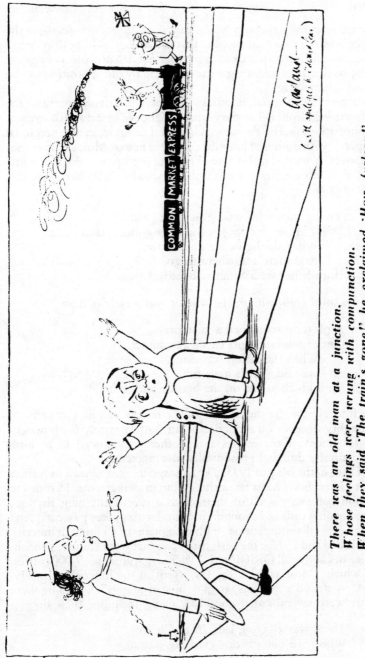

There was an old man at a junction.
Whose feelings were wrung with compunction.
When they said 'The train's gone!' he exclaimed 'How forlorn!'
But remained on the rails of the junction.

subtly to convey the impression that their clients' products are the open sesames to sexual success, that the advocates of healthy living do not make more use of such inexpensive talent from youngsters who so clearly consider cigarette-smoking by the opposite sex to be most unattractive.

Before 1972 was out, limericks were back in Britain once more for advertising alcohol. The purveyors of Salignac brandy ran a series of competitions in *The Yorkshire Post* (and, I imagine, in other regional papers), with bottles of branded cognac as prizes. Most of the entries were pretty mediocre, but one or two are perhaps worthy of reprinting. A Scarborough woman's fifth line won her first place in the first competition:

> Young men who woo girls with candy
> Don't know that there's something more handy;
> When the lights are down low,
> And there's nowhere to go,
> Beguile her with Salignac brandy.[8]

In the third competition, the winner was a Halifax man:

> A playboy renowned as a sinner
> Once took out a girl friend for dinner;
> When the eating was done,
> He said, "Let's have fun,"
> With his thoughts on the brandy within her![9]

Fortunately for the moral tone of the nation, not all competitors' thoughts were set on seduction – but, unfortunately for limerick-lovers, most of the entries along other lines tended to be both thematically dull and prosodically incompetent.

Then, in the May of 1973, *The Sunday Mirror* reminded its readers that "Everybody has a favourite – from drawing room decorous to saloon bar saucy – all of them with a special rhyming rhythm, playing on words and pronunciation and with a jokey pay-off". And it announced a competition, with cash prizes of £5 for each limerick published and £50 for the best, for verses that were "funny, publishable, and above all ORIGINAL."[10]. There were some 7,000 entries, of which "Most were in the true spirit of the limerick – bawdy, irreverent, and with transparent double meanings"[11]. Among them there were several rather good specimens, including these three:

> There was a young lady from Cheam,
> Who tried out a breast-growing cream;

She woke in the night
With a terrible fright –
Another had grown in between. [12]

A lady I know – rather merry,
Spilt a glass of Babycham perry.
    It made quite a mess
    Down the front of her dress,
But what fun as I looked for the cherry![13]

A surgeon of some imprecision
Decided on self-circumcision.
    A slip of the knife –
    "Oh, dear," said his wife,
"Our sex-life will need some revision". [14]

And, I was glad to see, a Hull reader submitted one so simply and innocently absurd that it might almost have been penned by Edward Lear himself:

There was a young man from Kent,
Whose nose was terribly bent.
    One day, I suppose,
    He could follow his nose,
And no one would know where he went. [15]

During the early autumn of 1973, the *Daily Mirror* offered ten prizes, each of £10, for a 'Holiday Limerick' competition in which the first line was given. One of the winners was:

The Holiday Mirror is best . . .
It fills an old man with new zest.
    The girlies with curves
    Have done more for my nerves
Than the whole of the medicine chest. [16]

In November, the *Daily Mail* offered bottles of champagne as prizes, the two co-equal prize-winners being these:

A nasty old vampire named Dracula,
Had habits really spectacula;
    He drank by the keg,
    But 'twas pure rhesus neg
– Red Barrel, to use the vernacula. [17]

When they catch a chinchilla in Chile,
They cut off its beard, willy-nilly,

> With a small razor blade,
> Just to say that they've made
> A Chilean chinchilla's chin chilly. [18]

One of the 'runners-up' was also rather clever:

> There was a small dog of Pirbright,
> Who would play at the organ all night;
>   And in this shrewd way
>   It kept burglars at bay,
> For its Bach was much worse than its bite. [19]

Just three months later, and the Scottish *Sunday Post* entered the latter-day limerick stakes, with the not very princely prize of £5 for the best verse each week, plus 'consolation' prizes for all others published. During that dreadful winter and early spring of 1973-74, Britain seemed to lurch from crisis to crisis, with the oil sheikhs withholding petroleum supplies, the miners on strike for a massive pay increase, the two big railway unions at loggerheads with each other and the general public being ground between them, the national balance of payments getting worse each month, and prices soaring almost daily in the most rampant inflationary spiral in the nation's history. Clearly – a perhaps peculiarly British reaction – the times demanded the injection of some light-hearted humour. There were many thousands of entries, including the following:

> "Dear Mither", wrote wee Jimmy Broon,
> "I've dug a hole twenty feet doon.
>   I'll dig and I'll toil,
>   Until I've struck oil".
> So she sent him a card, "Get well soon!" [20]

> An angry young driver named Mac,
> Sent a telegram off to Iraq.
>   He said, "Tell King Feisal
>   To stuff all his diesel –
> I've traded my car for a yak". [21]

> A wife wi' a stutter frae Dyce
> Wiz aye caught by the rise in the price.
>   By the time that she panted
>   Oot just whit she wanted,
> The cost o' the stuff went up twice. [22]

> McGahey and Daly will soon
> Be checking for mines on the moon.

> If there's men at the face,
> Oot there in space,
> They'll have them on strike before June.[23]

During the autumn of 1975, with inflation still raging unchecked, there were still more limericks on this theme. They ranged in subject from the housewife out shopping to the suburban male on the golf links, to the nobility in their historic homes, and even to the Queen herself in Buckingham Palace:

> An angry young housewife from Kent
> Said, "I'm broke, I haven't a cent.
>   I just made two stops
>   In a couple of shops –
> And I'm dashed if I know where it went".[24]

> A golfer, who sought to survive
> With grit, dedication and drive,
>   'Inflation," he'd claim,
>   "Is affecting my game,
> I used to shout 'fore' – now it's 'five'."[25]

> The Duchess and Duke of McPhail
> Went doon the Clyde for a sail;
>   After high teas and dinner,
>   With purses much thinner,
> A wing of their castle's for sale.[26]

> Inflation, it's sad to relate,
> Has now reached the head of the state.
>   There's no sentry to pass,
>   Just marquees on the grass,
> And a big 'B-and-B' on the gate.[27]

Thank goodness for such evidence of resilience among the British people, which may yet, despite the politicians, pull us through!

Today, however, the Press is not the only (scarcely even the main) medium of mass communication. It is therefore not surprising that the reviving interest in limericks has been evident also on television and radio. In January, 1971, the B.B.C.'s television programme 'Nationwide' put on a 'last line' competition and attracted rather more than five thousand entries. In April, its 'Look East' followed suit, and I like the play on 'Hosanna' in this verse:

> There once was a lady called Anna,
> In the choir she sang the soprana:

    The choirmaster said
    As she stood on her head,
"Hosanna, you show your hose Anna."[28]

In September, that immensely popular children's television programme, 'Blue Peter', announced its own competition, and within a
couple of weeks had received 8,229 entries for the judges to wade
through. Most, no doubt, were pretty mediocre, but a fair number
shewed real talent. One of them, forecasting the eventual massive
scale of the entry, also introduced the names of the programme's
three main presenters:

    There once was a programme – 'Blue Peter' –
    Asked for limericks with plenty of metre;
        They arrived host by host,
        Inundating the post,
    And buried poor John, Val and Peter.[29]

Others, like these three, had an admirably zany humour:

    There was a young lad called Davy,
    Who hated the food in the Navy;
        He couldn't have beef,
        In case his false teeth
    Would drop out and fall in the gravy.[30]

    There is a young boxer named Walter,
    Who comes from the island of Malta.
        One day in the ring,
        He stepped on a spring,
    And bounced all the way to Gibraltar.[31]

    There was a young cannibal, Ned,
    Who used to eat onions in bed.
        His mother said, "Sonny,
        It's not very funny,
    Why don't you eat people instead?"[32]

    Not long after this children's competition, I heard on an adult
entertainment programme a limerick about that light-hearted and
slight-breasted Liverpool singer, Cilla Black. As nearly as my
memory served me when I had quickly grabbed pen and paper, it
went like this:

    There was a young lady named Cilla,
    Who thought that nothing would fill 'er;

> To make herself plumper,
> She stuffed up her jumper
> Two melons wrapped up in a pillow.[33]

In the December of 1973 there were more limericks on 'Nation-wide', and by March, 1974, B.B.C's Radio Humberside had taken up the game. Some of those submitted by local residents for reading 'on the air' were quite the equal of many which have been produced by well-known authors. Here are two, from Hull and Flamborough respectively, in each case completing a verse whose first two lines had been set by the radio station:

> There was an old lady from Wawne,
> Who let out a terrible yawn;
> > Her dentures fell out
> > And she gave out a shout –
> She was about to take them to pawn.[34]

> A left-handed chef from Japan
> Sold hot dogs which he made in a van;
> > He found he was stranded
> > When he tried it right-handed,
> 'Cos he caught his bread rolls in the fan.[35]

But perhaps one of the most striking – even though it eventually turned out disappointing – indications of the degree to which limericks have begun once again to become fashionable, came a little later in 1974. The B.B.C. made Thackeray's six 'political' novels into a magnificently produced television series, 'The Pallisers'. On 11th May, one of the characters quoted a limerick and – naturally thinking that my ignorance of the verse must have been due to my far from perfect knowledge of that writer's works – I was quick off the mark to track it down. Back came the B.B.C's reply: the limerick was a complete invention by the dramatist who had adapted the novels for television!

To what extent, though, are present day 'show-biz personalities' in general interested in limericks, and how capable are they of producing good ones? Jean Harrowven recently set out to find the answer to this question. Deryck Guyler offered her a non-rhyming (in my view, also non-amusing) four-liner. Brian Rix provided merely a variant of the much-misused 'young lady from Leeds, who swallowed a packet of seeds'. Those sent by Spike Milligan and Roy Castle were not up to much. Benny Hill, Max Bygraves and Charlie Chester did rather better, and one by Eric Sykes was also rather good. But, by and large, the evident interest of present-day enter-

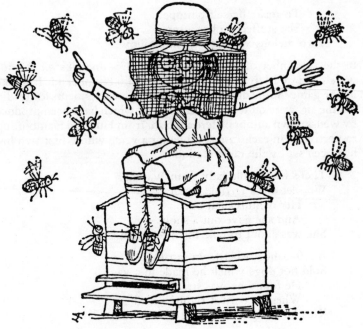

There was a young lady from Blythe,
Who foolishly sat on a hive,
As the bees buzzed around,
With a terrible sound,
She said, 'Oh why don't you bee-hive?'

**Gillian Hunt
Age: 9**

TWO LIMERICKS BY YOUNG CHILDREN

This and facing page – from B. Baxter & R. Gill, 1972, *The Blue Peter Book of Limericks*
(illustrated by Peter Firmin), London, Piccolo/B.B.C., Pan Books.

There was a young butcher from York,
Whose face was as round as a cork,
The reason he said,
Was the air in his head,
Which he'd swallowed while taking a walk.

Julia Wright
Age: 9

These two verses were among the many thousands submitted for the competition conducted by the B.B.C. children's programme, 'Blue Peter'.
N.B. The 'bee-hive'/'behave' punning rhyme had earlier appeared in 'There was a young apiarist, CLIVE' in Langford Reed's 1937 *My Limerick Book*.

tainers in limericks was not matched by anything approaching equal quality of invention. Bob Monkhouse, however, introduced his own name in a clever manner:

> "In a monast'ry," cried Friar Tuck,
> "Lewd brothers are pushing their luck;
>> So are lecherous abbots
>> With unwholesome habits –
> There's a Monkhouse for that sort of muck!"[36]

Richard Murdoch, radio veteran of 'Much-Binding-in-the-Marsh', appropriately provided a verse upon a Norfolk place-name:

> There was an old lady of Weasenham,
> Whose bed clothes had too many fleas in 'em.
>> So she covered her sheeting
>> With masses of Keating
> Which made all the fleas in 'em sneeze in 'em.[37]

The best of the lot came from two other radio veterans, Ted Ray and Arthur Askey. The former (who, sadly, died within a few weeks of writing to me with amended wording) wrote:

> A comedy fiddler named Ray
> In an orchestra started to play,
>> But a rival, 'tis said,
>> Struck poor Ted on the head,
> And he swore in a 'VIOLINT' way.[38]

and the latter, who was still evergreen in his television appearances at the age of seventyseven, produced this:

> A lively young lady named Kate
> Said, "The leak in the bath, it can't wait."
>> Came the plumber next minute
>> While she was still in it;
> Now she's a cute plumber's mate.[39]

Can it be mere coincidence that they both hail from the city of perpetual punning and quick-fire wit, Ted Ray having gone as a boy to the Liverpool Collegiate School and Arthur Askey to the Liverpool Institute?

The academic world, in earlier periods the special home of the sophisticated limerick (although the more obvious and slightly vulgar variety was quite popular with music hall audiences), has also begun once more to favour this form of verse. Visiting St. Andrews University in the summer of 1971, and browsing at a notice-board in the marine research laboratory, I came across a protest against what had evidently been some recent act of arboricide. A limerick (in the original, quite unpunctuated) ran thus:

A marine Professor was he
Who sanctioned the death of a tree.
When asked, "Why this mess?"
Said he could not care less,
Since it had nothing to do with the sea.[40]

Then followed, in a variety of hands, a series of verses on the same topic. Most of them were of less than mediocre quality – which applies even to one writer who at least had recognised that fact:

The death of a tree is a sad thing – I know it,
For it's taken a long time to grow it,
But there is a lesson to learn,
Though inner fires may burn,
Zoologists should not try to be poets.[41]

Naturally, as a biologist, I was reluctant to accept the wide generalisation of the final line. Thus it happened that, having met in the laboratory a young woman research worker who was studying marine slugs, I presented her with this effort:

There was a young woman called Ross,
Whose husband became very cross
When she filled all their jugs
With sassenach slugs
Preserved in his whisky *écosse*.

By 1973, specialised mathematical limericks were beginning to reappear. Six by W.A. Dodd were printed in the British journal, *Mathematics in Schools*. Two of them illustrated neatly the current movements towards metrication and towards 'modern' mathematics:

A modern young lady called Rita
Buys ribbon and cloth by the metre.
She gets bacon and ham
Weighed out by the gram
And orders her milk by the litre.

There was a young lady called Kate,
Whose maths was right up-to-date.
She said "It is fun
When three threes are one-one,
Which they are with modulo 8!"[42]

It was in the same year that the *American Mathematical Monthly* published Leo Moser's verses, the best of which the reader has already seen. Also in 1973, Lancaster University's Professor of Religious Studies, Ninian Smart, wrote a light-hearted but basically serious article entitled 'Coarse [spelling *sic*] Work Assessment', which included this comment upon tutor-student relationships in academe today:

> Though our students are quite pulchritudinous,
> There's a thing that is always eludin' us:
>   Though we pinch and we leer
>   And seduce them with beer,
> Our conduct is unturpitudinous. [43]

By the summer of 1975, Britain's still fairly young Open University was conducting a limerick competition in its newspaper, *Open House*. The trouble was, most of the entries were not limericks. Someone in the Social Science department, for example, produced this awful effort:

> From Harold Wilson came the cry:
> 'Let's educate the masses
> But as we can't afford the bricks
> We'll do away with classes'. [44]

Moreover, "Virtually, all those entries which were more or less in limerick form were lacking in either rhythm, rhyme, wit or good taste consonant with even the permissive standards of today"[45]. The verse adjudged best of the bunch won the prize with this pretty poor specimen:

> A hairy young Scotsman called Porteous
> Was always so meek and so courteous
>   Till pay negotiations
>   Exhausted his patience –
> Now listen and hear just how frAUT he is. [46]

Obviously, the less said about the rest of those submitted, the better. It really would be lamentable if, among the university's staff, there were no one capable of producing something better than this competition evoked.

Fortunately, there are still some writers among us who have valuably contributed to the recent limerick revival and who are capable of producing verses of the very highest quality. One of these is Paul Jennings, a regular contributor to *Punch* and *The Spectator*, and author of *Oddly Enough* (1951), *Even Oddlier* (1952) and *Next to*

Oddliness (1955). In 1974, he presented in a Sunday magazine the following splendid comments upon the contemporary scene:

> An L.S.E. graduate said,
> "As a student, of course, I was red;
>> But now I'm with Shell
>> Let the proles go to hell,
> My pension is safe till I'm dead."
>
> The statesman's great art, that of fixn,
> Would have been more effective in Nixn
>> If he'd understood
>> That the bad and the good
> Are for keeping apart, not for mixn.
>
> All newspaper boardroom agenda
> Since Murdoch, have had some addenda;
>> Must *everyone* plan
>> For the dirty old man
> Who only wants female pudenda?
>
> The comics who go on TV,
> From pressing anxiety free,
>> Don't need to hear laughter –
>> It's all dubbed in after;
> *They* laugh as they pocket their fee.
>
> A unisex man who got wed
> To a unisex woman, soon said
>> "We have come to the end
>> Of this curious trend
> And find duosex better in bed."[47]

Even the Mother of Parliaments in session has now started giving birth to limericks. Early in March 1972, a Committee of the House of Commons was considering the Housing Financing Bill, and Mr. Arthur Latham (Labour, Paddington North) had this to say of Mrs. Sally Oppenheim (Conservative, Gloucester):

> The Honourable Lady for Gloucester,
> Friendships with tenants did foster;
>> When they realised the fact
>> They were caught in the Act;
> At the next election they lost her.[48]

Much more interesting, by reason of the identity of the perpetrator, was a somewhat later occasion in the House of Lords. The debate was during the Committee stage of the Consumer Credit Bill, and the particular point was the precise definition of a 'relative'. Lord Aberdare, presumably impatient of much of the quibbling which had been going on, moved an amendment that the definition should include 'Uncle Tom Cobleigh and All'. Whereupon the Opposition spokesman on trade and consumer affairs drily declaimed:

> The clause is in principle clear;
> No reference to Uncle or Peer;
>   But the clause is so wide
>   That, all joking aside,
> We think he should think again here.[49]

"I hope you will not judge my poetic qualities too harshly . . .", the author of this limerick wrote to me. "The verse . . . was concocted in 90 seconds in response to the allegation from the other side of the House that I represented a 'metrical frivolity' "[50]. And the name of the Noble Lord? He was, of all people, the Earl of Limerick!

XVI

An Unholy Hierarchy

Repeatedly one remarks upon the contributions which have been made by men of the cloth to the limerick art, and especially at its higher levels. For some strange reason, this seems to apply especially to those who would claim to be priests in the apostolic succession rather than to those who perhaps see themselves as being more in the line of the prophets. Possibly the former have that greater degree of theological assurance which permits them to treat even their own church and its doctrines with occasional levity, or perhaps there is something about nonconformism in religious belief which goes with solemnity in literary expression. One is uncertain whether to predicate an excess of frivolity among the orthodox or a surfeit of sobriety among the dissenters. More probably, it is none of these things, but simply that until fairly recent times the former category of cleric had more often been educated in the Oxbridge tradition.

Since Mother Church has contributed so generously to our common heritage of limericks, it would seem ungrateful if an agnostic were not to return the compliment – and how better than by a batch of uniformly religious relevance? However, since it is limericks that we are concerned with, there will (I hope) be no reactions of resentment among the religious if my verses deal rather with the delinquencies than with the devotions of their subjects.

In this oecumenical era, it might appear almost improper to shew preference for any one religion over another; and yet, since the anglosaxon culture within which limericks have flourished has its roots set firmly in the soil of christendom, it is only equitable to concentrate on this one among the world's great religions. Thus, the moral obliquities of bonzes, brahmins, cantors, fakirs, lamas, levites, muftis, mullahs, pharisees, rabbis *et hoc genus omne* have been left to the perhaps tenderer mercies of later pens.

Yet, even after the exercise of this self-denying ordinance, one is left with the problem of sheer scale, and I have sought some reduction by total exclusion of the distaff side. Nuns, sisters, mothers superior, abbesses, prioresses and sundry other *religieuses* were all

223

tempting targets, but at them I have aimed not a single shaft. Whether, in these days of women's liberation, this act of charity will be properly appreciated, or whether it will be characterised as yet another manifestation of male pig chauvinism, only the future will unfold.

But even this act of positive sex discrimination leaves too many possible targets. Therefore, the thinning-out process has been pursued a stage further by deciding not to deal with archimandrites, capitulars, cenobites, metropolitans or missionaries – inviting as they all were. I also considered omitting all men not in full holy orders, but that might have been taken to imply (most unjustly) that the entire laity was laudable and only the priesthood peccant. So, while excluding from stricture such lesser ranks as acolytes, almoners, beadles, sacristans, sidesmen and thurifers, I have made at least token inclusion of a chorister, a lay preacher, a sexton and a verger.

Within these self-imposed restrictions, without which my verses might have become unconscionably many, I present, in approximate rank-order, and all (with the deliberate exception of the last one) starting with the classic phrase 'There was', my uncomplimentary catalogue of twenty priestly and ancillary imperfections, 'An Unholy Hierarchy':

> There was a priapic old Pope,
> Laid hands on each novice with hope;
> > He said, "Peter's dome
> > Provides a good home –
> Provided you offer me scope".

> There was a promiscuous Primate,
> Who said that, at this day and time, it
> > Is right to embrace
> > One of each faith and race
> In our oecumenical climate.

> There was a proud pompous old Prelate,
> Who said, on arriving in hell, "It
> > Is quite a disgrace
> > That *I* have to face
> The final tribunal-appellate".

> There was an adulterous Abbot,
> As randy as any old rabbit;
> > He'd even been known
> > (Indeed, he was prone)
> With neighbouring nuns to cohabit.

There was an appalling old Prior,
Who was quite an unprincipled liar;
    He'd swear black was white,
    That daytime was night,
Or heaven as hot as hell-fire.

There was a permissive young Bishop,
Who said to 'square' vicars, "Oh pish! Op-
    inions *do* vary –
    Pray don't be contrary!
What's wrong with a porn-cannabis shop?"

There was an abhorrent Archdeacon,
Who loved to find failings to sneak on;
    His joy was profound
    Whenever he found
A deacon his rancour to wreak on.

There was a disgusting old Dean
Who explored every crude magazine
    From cover to cover –
    Agog to discover
The mean or unclean or obscene.

There was a vainglorious Canon,
Disdained a mere eucharist fanon;
    As mystical host
    He used buttered toast
And flaunted a gaudy gonfanon.

There was a chrysophilist Rector,
To sin was a sincere objector;
    But he never had qualms
    About stealing alms –
He claimed, as a coinage collector.

There was a vinicolous Vicar,
Unduly addicted to liquor;
    He said, "There's no sin
    In whiskey or gin –
The spirit thus enters much quicker".

There was a Perpetual Curate,
Whose language was hypersulphurate –
    While, as for his thinking,
    It was not merely stinking,
But perfectly foul and suppurate.

There was a most maudlin old Monk,
Who was almost incessantly drunk;
    Each day he would hide a
    Full flagon of cider
Or firkin of flip in his bunk.

There was a fat fraudulent Friar,
Begged alms to rebuild a church spire;
    But they found he had fled,
    Having sold all the lead
To a shady itinerant buyer.

There was a most cupid Confessor,
Who counselled each contrite transgressor,
    "If you'll put an amount
    To my private account,
Your penance will be so much lesser".

There was a licentious Lay Preacher
Who, meeting a maid, would beseech her
    To let no false pride
    Interfere if he tried,
While laying on hands, to unbreech her.

There was a necrophilous Sexton,
Who had all the parish perplexed. On
    The north of the nave
    He dug up a grave –
At noon, when there should have been sext on.

There was a vile molochite Verger,
Who, paid as baptismal submerger,
    Could see nothing wrong
    In submerging too long –
To earn a fresh fee as a dirger.

There was a concupiscent Chorister,
Who one day deflowered a young florist. Ere
    Away he could walk,
    She snipped off his stalk –
And thenceforth he came to abhor Istar.

The sins of the Church Universal,
So varied and quite quaquaversal,
    Need patience supernal
    And time sempiternal
For fully effective rehearsal.

Dare one still hope, after the above excess of execration of ecclesiastics, for at any rate a minor benediction from any among them who happen also to be limerick-lovers?

XVII

An Amorous Alphabet

Much as I dislike mere dirt and reluct at coproglossia, I must confess to a curious captivation by erotically allusive verse. But only under certain conditions. It must be genuinely tender, or really witty, or outrageously funny. Or, in other cases, it may be marked by verbal felicity or clever construction or some enticing epigrammatic quality. And I prefer it to be free from mere crudity of language and nastiness of thought.

Perhaps such selectivity may seem somewhat puritan. After all, some people say, does not every normally hormonised human being have powerful sexual urges, and what is wrong with giving them free rein? There may be a great deal wrong. It is the very fact that we have urges of such great power which necessitates self-discipline, for no society worthy of the name can long survive in the absence of some generally accepted degree of libido-regulation. And, since literature so powerfully inter-acts with life, it is well to guard even against excessive literary excitation. Still, the enjoyment of lively limericks seems a harmless enough way of occasionally indulging in sensual fantasy.

Being blessed with a wife who shares my amorist inclinations, and who fortunately enjoys hearing my metrical inventions almost as much as I enjoy composing them, I not infrequently emit light-hearted amatory verses. They are rarely put to paper, but in the spring of 1972 a dozen were written down and thus preserved from oblivion. We were lazing in Djerba, that desert island of the lotos-eaters whose delights were so long ago found so alluring by Ulysses and his men. My wife, usually less torpid than me at high temperatures, periodically wandered along the littoral in search of previously unseen sea-shells, leaving me lying semi-comatose. And, while she was away, the candent sun combining with the cooling breeze to generate in me a languorous concupiscence, fascinating Tunisian place-names sometimes lazily formed themselves semi-consciously into limericks. Here are those which I found energy enough to record:

228

As they lay in the sun at Chenini,
He said, "Surely a garment so teeny
    And foreign to Venus
    Should not come between us?
So why not remove your bikini?"

In the heat of the midday at Douz,
We go to our room for a snooze;
    But somehow, it seems,
    We never have dreams –
For a snooze is not quite what we choose.

A couple lay down by the Tanit,
And it was the wife who began it.
    She said, "Come and nestle
    Your mast by my vessel,
And, when you are ready, please man it."

A sailor, at Sidi ben Saïd,
Said, "Now I shall sleep, for I'm tired" –
    That's not what he said
    When he saw on his bed
A nubile and naked young naiad.

A Khalif who came from Kabili
Complained that his hareem was chilly;
    So all his wives said,
    "Then let's go to bed
And let us not dally or dilly."

One day by a tree at Tabarka,
Her husband was heard to remark, "A
    Fine head of hair! –
    But I much prefer
The curls that are denser and darker."

How happy that man at Houmt-Souk,
Who went with his wife to a nook;
    They first played with Fanny,
    But soon found a cranny:
Of all that she gave, he partook.

A dusky young damsel of Djerba,
So torrid that nothing could curb her,
    Lay down on the beach
    And said, "I beseech
The service of Arab or Berber".

The troglodyte maids of Matmata,
Outdoors, only giggle and chatter;
    But deep in their cave
    They must misbehave –
Else how should they grow so much fatter?

A man and his wife at Mellita
Were sparking inside their bed-sitter;
    There was no suspicion
    Of faulty ignition,
For he was a competent fitter.

A couple, sight-seeing Ksar,
Were reckoned a trifle bizarre
    When they gave way to passion
    In far-reaching fashion
Not far from the busy bazaar.

At dusk, in the dunes of Tozeur,
They said, "Do you think that we dare?"
    As the sun sank right down,
    They returned to the town –
And shook out the sand from their hair.

Occasional casual compositions such as these may be amusing enough, and that is their sufficient justification. But there is a good deal of truth in a remark once made by Denis Norden – that limerick-making is a talent like wiggling your ears: you've either got it or you haven't. And, if you've got it in any appreciable degree, the pleasure of easy wiggling may eventually pall. Sometimes, therefore, one welcomes a severe technical challenge, for the sheer intellectual pleasure of overcoming it. In the composition of limericks, there are several possible ways of setting oneself a long hard run with high hurdles instead of a short smooth canter over soft turf.

One of these ways is to accept the discipline of never using any but genuine geographical locations; for faking place-names (as it is evident that many limerick-makers do), and thereby evading the problem of finding three rather than two line-ending rhymes, is rather like pinching pennies from a blind man's plate: it could seem rewarding only to a rascal devoid of both sensitive conscience and professional pride. Then, to provide the mentally muscular pleasure of sustained struggle, one can go for a substantial series of verses posing some common problems. It occurred to me that an amorous alphabet might be worth attempting, the whole collection to satisfy several self-imposed criteria. All twentysix verses, I decided, were to begin with an indefinite article; each first-line-ending 'key-word' (with the exception of 'X' which was to be utilised in its special sense of signifying indeterminacy) was to be a genuine British location; each person specified was to be pursuing some occupation connected or at least not inconsonant with the place; and each verse, although erotically allusive, was preferably to be tangentially rather than blatantly so. Here, then, is my amorous alphabet (and I assure my readers that, not far from Down St. Mary in Devon, there really is a little hamlet called 'Zeal Monachorum'):

An angler who lived in Argyll,
Tore his kilt as he clambered a stile:
    You might think he'd choose
    At least to wear trews –
But his wife wears a satisfied smile.

A prudish young preacher in Bude,
Who everything lewd had eschewed,
    Would gladly lie down
    With his wife in a gown,
But he thought it was rude in the nude.

A railwayman, running from Crewe,
Said, "How I regret that so few
    Lady passengers dream
    That I'm still full of steam,
Or else they'd be forming a queue".

An electrical dealer from Distance
Said, "Ma'am, can I be of assistance?";
    But he got quite a shock
    When she took off her frock
And said, "Will you test my resistance?"

A linen-maid working at Eton
Said, "Hubby, I hope you've your heat on?
    Forgive the inquiry,
    But I feel quite fiery,
And that's why the floor's got a sheet on."

A musical maiden from Frome
Allowed her friend's fingers to roam;
    He taught her the score –
    Then gave an *encore*
On her other erogenous dome.

A landlady living in Gower
Had passions of primitive power –
    No masculine lodger
    Could possibly dodge her
Demands to embed in her bower.

A happy young housewife in Hale
Believed in hot peppers and quail;
    She said such a supper
    Would make her man tup her
With fervour and quite without fail.

The bride of a banker in Iver
Took on a small bet for a fiver;
    Straight after the marriage
    She stripped in the carriage
And drove from the church like Godiva.

A jolly young joiner from Jarrow
Found a fissure excessively narrow;
    When the query came, "Why
    Not at least have a try?"
He replied, "I'm a *beau*, not an arrow".

A curate, who cured in Kilcane,
Said, "Bishop, why do you complain?
    If a deaconess begs
    With wide open legs,
How can a kind curate refrain?"

A marriage adviser in Leeds
Said, "What your wife patently needs
    Is husbandly passion
    In every known fashion,
With nice variation of speeds".

A maid on a farm outside Mold
Once said to a shepherd, "I'm told
    That you have a fine ram.
    Now, I'd make a good dam,
So why not come into my fold?"

A newspaper novice in Norton
Said, "Here's some good news to report on:
    I've found since I wed
    That a lithograph bed
Is not the best bed to disport on."

An ostler who lived outside Otley
Had a wife, who welcomed him hotly;
    They both liked a ride,
    With him first astride
And then in positions all motley.

A presbyter, preaching in Perth,
Said, "Sinners abound on this earth";
    So, straight after dinner,
    He sought out a sinner –
And wantoned for all he was worth.

A fervent fox-hunter at Quorn
Felt he ought to make use of his horn;
    So, crying out, "Zounds!
    I'll not follow hounds",
He lay with his lass on the lawn.

A rural dean, riding by Rake,
Met a maid by the side of the lake;
    He said, "Let us praise
    The Lord and his ways –
And then of our pleasure partake".

A milliner maiden in Sankey
Said, "Let us have no hanky-panky!"
    But after a while
    She said, with a smile,
"For what you have given, I thank 'ee".

A museum assistant at Tring
Gave each bird an identity ring:
    One bird could not fly,
    But she knew how to lie –
And how to play yang to his ying.

A lock-keeper's lass in Upavon
Had locks that were black as a raven;
    On her head they were straight,
    But they curled near the gate
Which led to the innermost haven.

A bride, who lived just outside Valley,
Said, "So far we've only been pally;
    But, now that we're wed,
    Just take me to bed –
And see that you don't dilly-dally".

A mason, who married in Warwick,
Had a column decidedly doric;
    For the rest of her life
    His gratified wife
Was happy, and even euphoric.

A prominent person in X
Was of quite indeterminate sex
    And had great renown
    As quean of that town:
But was it *regina* or *rex*?

A young engineer at York
Said, "When you arrive at the fork,
    Don't veer right or left:
    Go straight up the cleft,
With a touch of rotational torque."

A zealot from Zeal Monachorum
Was sadly devoid of decorum:
    He had a proclivity
    For amorous activity
In public, in front of the forum.

And now, taking pre-emptive action against any who might feel inclined to criticise these twentysix stanzas on grounds either ethical or literary, let me humbly admit:

My verses above, alphabetical,
Could scarcely be reckoned ascetical;
    And, what's even worse is,
    My amorous verses
Are not even very poetical.

Nevertheless, *amorem amo*.

XVIII

A Collegiate Collation

Since so many limericks have been produced by academics, it is surprising that so comparatively few are based upon the names of universities and colleges. In the whole of Lear there is not a single one, and in Reed's *Complete Limerick Book* there are but five (although, admittedly, some of the best produced since then have made clever play upon collegiate nomenclature). Nor do very many limericks puncture the pedantic pretensions of the professorial. The culpabilities of clergymen, the lapses of lawyers, the failings of physicians, the scrupulosity of schoolmasters – all these targets have frequently been found too tempting for limerick-makers to resist. But academics *quâ* academics have in the main been left unmolested. This cannot have come from any general generosity of spirit towards fellow-scholars, for in few places is the air so thick with caustic conversational arrows as in the groves of academe. Perhaps there is sufficient catharsis in the post-prandial conversation of combination rooms, and hence no need to compose verses vilipending tutorial colleagues. And yet that can be only a small part of the explanation, for many more limericks are lightheartedly laughable than are wantonly wounding.

Another minor mystery is why – although there are brilliant exceptions which severely prove this rule – the limerick has tended to flourish better on the banks of Cam than by those of Isis. And this tendency goes back a long way – indeed, one of the earliest traced usages of the word was in an 1898 issue of *Cantab*. Could this preferential development be connected with the fact that for centuries the Cantabrigian has characteristically been less establishment-orientated than the Oxonian? Not only is it true that, while the limerick must have rhyme and rhythm, it need not have reason; it is also true that it is generally better without too much reverence. Oxford sided with King Charles, Cambridge with Cromwell; and it was in the latter place that, while King James I was riding through the streets, piss-pots were emptied out of upper windows. Throughout the present century, the Cabinets of British

235

governments (Conservative, Labour and Liberal alike) have been crowded with those who have succeeded in the Schools rather than with those who have triumphed in the Triposes. And it seems still to be quite commonly the case that, whereas the Oxford man walks down the street as if he owns it, the Cambridge man walks down the street as if he doesn't care a damn who owns it.

At any rate, it occurred to me to compose a collection of libellous limericks upon the names of Cambridge colleges. Very soon I began to suspect a much more cogent reason than any of those already adumbrated for such compositions being relatively rare: many of the colleges have names for which the finding of two rhymes, together with the required stressing, is far from easy. Possibly, as even some of my closest friends have on occasion indelicately hinted, there is just a slight streak of stubbornness in my nature: at any rate, this discovery of difficulty determined me to do the job properly and cover the colleges completely. Moreover, not one of the verses was to use the traditional opening, 'There was a . . .', and every one was in some way, either openly or hemicryptically, to refer to some special feature of the particular college.

In my undergraduate days there were twenty full colleges at Cambridge. Since then, two new undergraduate colleges have been founded, three approved societies or approved foundations have become full colleges or virtually so, and there have been four new foundations to cater especially for graduates. However, although this raised the number of possible targets to twentynine (it may by now have gone even higher), I finally decided to stop at the twenty-seventh in order of date of foundation – thereby terminating with the one whose name could do double service, both for itself and for the university as a whole. Here, then, as an act of impious *pietas* towards my first *alma mater*, and with each verse preceded by a 'potted' characterisation of the college, is my collection, 'A Collegiate Collation':

Peterhouse was founded in 1284 by Hugo de Balsham, Bishop of Ely. It is the only Cambridge College with a deer park:

> A ferocious young Fellow of Peterhouse
> Said, "This has become too effete a House;
>   Our deer are too tame" –
>   Things have not been the same
> Since he set free the beasts from a cheetah house.

Clare College was founded in 1326 (as 'University Hall') by Richard de Badew and was refounded about 1339 (as 'Clare House';

later, 'Clare Hall') by Lady Elizabeth de Clare, grand-daughter of
Edward I:

> A corpulent classic at Clare
> Said, "Calories I must forswear";
>   So strong was his will,
>   He fasted until
> He'd slimmed into clar(e)ified air.

Pembroke College was founded in 1347 (as 'The Hall of Valence
Mary') by Mary, widow of Aymer de Valence, Earl of Pembroke,
and was later liberally endowed and given its present name by Henry
VI. The poet Thomas Gray found that "The Spirit of Lazyness (the
Spirit of the Place) begins to possess even me", and some say that the
place still has rather more than its share of rowing and riding men. It
is commonly referred to as 'Pemmer':

> An amateur jockey at Pemmer
> Was 'gated' to seven pip-emma.
>   He was seen at Newmarket
>   In a pub after dark: it
> Presented an awkward dilemma.

Gonville and Caius College was founded in 1348 (as 'Gonville Hall')
by Edward Gonville, Vicar-general of Ely, and was refounded in
1558 by Dr. John Caius, physician to Edward VI and Queen Mary. It
is especially known for medical studies:

> A porter at Gonville and Caius
> Said, "No lady visitors, please!
>   For I fear you would hear
>   What's not fit for your ear –
> These medics swear worse than bargees."

Trinity Hall was founded in 1350 (as 'The College of the Scholars
of the Holy Trinity of Norwich') by William Bateman, Bishop of
Norwich. It is especially known for legal studies:

> A lawyer at Trinity Hall
> Said, "At the Old Bailey, recall,
>   The Code Napoleonic
>   Is thought quite moronic;
> And yet it's respected in Gaul."

Corpus Christi College was founded in 1352 by the Cambridge
Gilds of Corpus Christi and of the Blessed Virgin Mary, but was
commonly called 'Benet [St. Benedict] College' right up to the early

nineteenth century. Its library contains the manuscript of St.
Jerome's Latin version of the Gospels:

> A latinist, gild Corpus Christi,
> Of post-roman manners naught wist he –
>   For symposial sport
>   He swigged down the port,
> And in the decanter then pissed he.

King's College was founded in 1441 by King Henry VI as a higher-
level sister-foundation to his Eton College. Its chapel and choir are of
world renown:

> A young choral scholar at King's
> Looked just like a cherub, *sans* wings;
>   But he had a proclivity
>   For amorous activity
> And other un-angelic things.

Queens' College was founded in 1448 (as 'The Queens' College of
St. Margaret and St. Bernard') by Margaret of Anjou, consort of
Henry VI (hence its rather bawdy undergraduate song, 'The Jolly
Old Monks of St. Bernard') and was refounded in 1465 by Elizabeth
Widville, consort of Edward IV (hence the plural form, Queens',
with apostrophe after the 's'). Its most famous member was Eras-
mus, who complained about the quality of its food and beer. It is
especially distinguished in oriental studies:

> A sinologue student at Queens'
> Complained of a slug in his greens –
>   And yet dishes Chinese
>   Contain oodles of these,
> Especially in chicken *chow miens*.

St. Catharine's College was founded in 1473, to the honour of 'saint
Katerine the virgin', by Robert Wodelarke, Chancellor of the University and Provost of King's. It is commonly referred to as 'Cat's':

> A young *coquette*, courting in Cat's,
> Proceeding beyond friendly pats,
>   Said, "You'll find that my breasts
>   Are beneath tatted vests –
> Pray take out my tits from my tat(t)s."

Jesus College was founded in 1497, on the site of the rather scandalous Benedictine nunnery of St. Radegund, by John Alcock, Bishop
of Ely (hence its punning badge of a cock). Its most famous member

was Thomas Cranmer. Its boat club has very frequently been head of the river:

> A cox(cks) to his tutor at Jesus
> Said, "Sir, from all reading release us;
>   If to books I keep going,
>   I lose time from rowing,
> And that, Sir, would greatly displease us."

Christ's College was founded in 1505, on the basis of an earlier foundation of 'God's House for poure scolers', by Lady Margaret Beaufort, Countess of Richmond and Derby, the mother of Henry VII. Its most famous members were John Milton and Charles Darwin. Some say that its mulberry tree garden is haunted:

> A sorcerer's room-set at Christ's
> Was plagued by perverse *poltergeists*;
>   When he found them too frisky,
>   He sought solace in whisky
> And swallowed it neat and un-iced.

St. John's College was founded in 1511, on the site of an earlier Augustinian 'Hospital of the Brethren of St. John the Evangelist', by the same Lady Margaret (acting posthumously through her executors). The close-traceried windows of its 'Bridge of Sighs' across the Cam were so designed to ensure effective nocturnal enclosure of its undergraduates:

> A sizeable sizar of John's,
> When caught climbing in by the dons,
>   Explained with deep sighs,
>   "I'm of too great a size
> And so I got stuck in the *pons*."

Magdalene College was founded in 1542, on the basis of an earlier Benedictine 'Monks College of Buckingham', by Thomas, Baron Audley of Walden, Lord Chancellor of England. Its most famous member was Samuel Pepys, of whom it was noted, "Peapys . . . solemnly admonished for having been scandalously over-served with drink":

> A masterful Master of Magdalene
> Sent down a promiscuous lordling.
>   He said, "Lord Lewdd keeps
>   In the same set as Pepys –
> That's no place for keeping a bordel in".

Trinity College was founded in 1546, on the combined sites of the earlier foundations of 'Michaelhouse', 'King's Hall' and 'Physwick's Hostel', by Henry VIII. It is much the largest college of the University. Its most famous members were Francis Bacon and Isaac Newton, and it is especially known for scientific and mathematical studies:

> A philosopher Fellow of Trinity
> Said, "Geometry shows this affinity:
>   Concavo-convex is
>   Symbolic of sexes,
> While arrows denote masculinity."

Emmanuel College was founded in 1584, on the site of a suppressed Dominican community, by Sir Walter Mildmay, Chancellor of the Exchequer under Elizabeth I. It was a Puritan foundation, whose Fellows were strictly enjoined to ensure that the behaviour and conversation of its scholars were at all times seemly. Its most famous member was John Harvard, who emigrated to Massachusetts and there founded Harvard College in the Cambridge of that State:

> An eavesdropping don at Emmanuel
> Was told, "If you're wise, dear man, you'll
>   Abandon that habit –
>   Or you'll grow like a rabbit,
> Or end up with ears like a spaniel."

Sidney Sussex College was founded in 1596, on the site of an earlier Franciscan foundation, by the anti-papist Lady Frances Sidney, Countess Dowager of Sussex (acting posthumously through her executors). Its most famous member was Oliver Cromwell, of whom it was noted that he was "more famous for his exercises in the fields than in the Schools". Nevertheless, the College tends to be placed well in Tripos lists. It is commonly referred to as 'Sidney':

> An over-sexed Scholar of Sidney
> Subsisted on sweetbreads and kidney;
>   He gained first position
>   In Carnal Coition –
> He had the right diet, though, did'n' 'e?

Downing College was founded in 1800 by Sir George Downing (acting posthumously through his executors) and was to have had a 'Great Court' even larger than Trinity's. Unfortunately, protracted litigation with members of the family, who wanted the inheritance for themselves, cost so much in lawyers' fees that not enough remained to complete the grand design:

> An architect, planning at Downing,
> Said to the surveyor, "The crowning
>> Conceit of my brain
>> Has gone down the drain –
> And all but the lawyers are frowning."

Girton College was founded in 1869 (originally at Hitchin) by Emily Davies and other pioneer feminists, as a university college for women. In 1873 it moved to Girton, just on the outskirts of Cambridge. Its members took the same studies and degree examinations as the men – although, strangely, it did not legally become a 'College of the University' until 1948:

> A giddy young girl up at Girton,
> When found with a man, had no skirt on.
>> She explained to her tutor,
>> "He thought I looked cuter –
> The subject is one he's expert on."

Newnham College was founded in 1871 by Anne Jemima Clough and others, as the second Cambridge college for women. It also became a full 'College of the University' in 1948:

> A modern young maiden at Newnham
> Wore trousers – but how did she woo in 'em?
>> For friendly caresses
>> I much prefer dresses:
> There's very much more you can do in 'em.

Selwyn College was founded in 1882 (as a 'Public Hostel' conducted on the principles of the Church of England) and was named in memory of George Selwyn, Bishop of New Zealand and later of Lichfield. It became an 'Approved Foundation' in 1926 and a full 'College of the University' in 1958:

> A potulent Preacher at Selwyn
> Said, "Don't let the forces of hell win;
>> If communion wine
>> With whisky combine,
> Men's love for pure spirit might well win."

Hughes Hall was founded in 1885 (as the 'Cambridge Training College for Women') and was later named after Elizabeth Phillips Hughes. It became a 'Recognised Institution' in 1949 and an 'Approved Society' in 1968:

> A tired trainee at Hughes Hall
> One day on her blackboard did scrawl,

"I've quite had my fill –
Do just as you will;
You're driving me right up the wall!"

Fitzwilliam College was founded in 1887 (as 'Fitzwilliam Hall';
from 1924, 'Fitzwilliam House') to provide a centre of corporate life
for non-collegiate (and especially for mature) students. It became a
full 'College of the University' in 1966. It is commonly referred to as
'Fitzbilly':

A forty-year-old at Fitzbilly
Had a passion for strong piccalilli;
    But, just for a change,
    He would widen his range
With a mixture of chutney and chilli.

St. Edmund's House was founded in 1896 (for the fostering of
studies in the spirit of a Roman Catholic community) by Henry
Fitzalan Howard, fifteenth Duke of Norfolk. It became an
'Approved Society' in 1965 and an 'Approved Foundation' in 1974:

A man of St. Edmund's House
Was sadly deficient in *nous*;
    When received by the Pope,
    He expressed the warm hope
That all was quite well with his spouse.

New Hall was founded in 1954 (as a 'Recognised Institution') by an
Association formed to promote a third Cambridge foundation for
women. It became a full 'College of the University' in 1972:

A modest young maid of New Hall
Met a man at a fancy dress ball;
    He said; "Isn't it rude
    To be totally nude?" –
She replied, "I am Eve ere the Fall."

Churchill College was founded in 1960 as a national tribute to
Winston Churchill. It is especially committed to scientific,
mathematical and technological studies:

An ultra-high-thermist at Churchill
Contracted one winter a rare chill;
    To his doctor he said,
    "I've a cold in my head,
And low temperature suits my research ill."

Darwin College was founded in 1964 (and named in tribute to Charles Darwin) by Gonville and Caius, St. John's and Trinity. It specially provides for research students:

> A doctorate-hunter at Darwin
> Wrote a thesis: 'Did Persia's Great Shah win
>> The fight at Ras Khaim,
>> Or, as some scholars claim,
> Did the Sultan of Old Zanzibar win?'

And finally, to conclude this collegiate collation:

University College was founded in 1965 by the University. It also specially provides for research students:

> The members of our great University
> Display the most striking diversity:
>> Some wise and some foolish,
>> Some saintly, some ghoulish,
> And some of the utmost perversity.

Floreat semper Cantabrigia!

XIX

A Tribute of 'Learics'

The latter-day revival of limericks has been conspicuously lacking in one thing. Nobody seems even to have tried to recapture that unique combination of whimsey, neologising, crypto-nostalgia, sublimated sadism and sheer concentrated absurdity which was so characteristic of Edward Lear.

So, if imitation be the sincerest form of flattery, I round off this volume by presenting my personal tribute of twenty 'learics', set down in the three-line format which he sometimes favoured, to the immortal memory of the first great master of the limerick art:

There was an Old Man of Dundee, set out for a swim in the sea,
But the lobsters and crabs took turns to make grabs
At the toes of that Man of Dundee.

There was an Old Woman of Beverley, outwitted the verger most cleverly,
To the tower she did climb, and pealed a full chime;
That bell-ringing woman of Beverley.

A funny old Frenchman in Nantes, he roars and he raves and he rants.
The reason: a dog and a bristly hog
Have torn two big holes in his pants.

There was a Young Maiden of Chard, who knitted lambs' wool by the yard.
When she kept 'dropping' stitches, she said, "*Baa!* these breeches
Will have gaps in unless I try hard."

There once was a Couple from Hull, were feeding some crumbs to a gull;
When the gull got too greedy, they said, "We won't feed 'ee!"
That crumbious Couple from Hull.

There was a Young Man of St. Bees, who had the most knobbly knees;
So, just for a 'lark', he stood still in the park,
Where they looked like the trunks of old trees.

There was an Old Man of Montrose, who had most peculiar toes.
They grew with such strength, and became such a length,
That he tied them in 'butterfly' bows.

There was an Old Man of Blantyre, who played all day long on a lyre;
All the dogs and the cats and the mice and the rats
Sat round and sang songs as a choir.

There was a Nizam of Mysore, who had a protuberant jaw;
When he opened it wide, or turned to one side,
His head would get stuck in the door.

There was an Old Lady of Rise, who always hoped for a surprise;
At the Great Exhibition, she fulfilled her ambition,
When they gave her poke-bonnet a prize.

There was a Princess of Perugia, whose eye-balls got huger and huger,
Till they got so tremendous that they looked quite horrendous,
That Ugly Princess of Perugia.

A musical Mermaid of Stockholm each day combed her hair with a rock comb;
To keep clean her tail, she stood in a pail,
As she sang to the sailors of Stockholm.

There was a Mad Dervish from Dab'a, did nothing but jibber and jabber,
Till he went to Maldive and there learned to dive,
And now he's a champion crabber.

A pukka Mem-sahib of Delhi delighted in wibwobble jelly;
She stewed annelids with squoogious squids,
And made herself sick with that jelly.

There was an Old Man of Cawnpore, who laid himself down on the floor.
He explained, "On these mats I can play with the cats,
And that's why I lie on the floor."

There was a Proud Lady of Pett, who affected a gold-rimmed lorgnette;
She froze with one look all ranks below Duke;
That far too proud Lady of Pett.

A Savant, who lived on Vesuvius, said it stood on a plum-pudding pluvious.
When they asked him to prove it, he replied, "I can't move it,
And so it is impossiproovious".

A Widow, who lived by the Humber, kept kittens too many to number;
She fed, I surmise, on tabby-cat pies,
That *mews*-ical Widow of Humber.

There was an Old Manxman of Peel, who ate five roast pigs at a meal.
He was such a great glutton, he burst every button;
That pork-I-pine Manxman of Peel.

One day, as Folk stood on the pier, they said, "That Old Man looks most queer!
From the shape of his nose, and his twiddly toes,
We think it must be Mr. Lear."

O magister! te saluto.

REFERENCES

To be read in conjunction with the Bibliography

Chapter I

LIMERICKS IN GENERAL

[1] A., *Times Lt. Supp.*, 6 February 1969

[2] A., qu. Reed, L., 1924, 103

[3] Knox, R., oral circ., Cambridge, 1930s

[4] A., *loc. cit.*

[5] Wells, C., 1902, xxi

[6] De Quincey, T., qu. *op. cit.*, xx

[7] Wyndham Lewis, D.B., 1936, xx

[8] A., qu. Wells, C., 1925, 63

[9] A., qu. Reed, L., 1924, 69

[10] A., qu. Baring-Gould, W.S., 1968, 153

[11] Lear, E., qu. Jackson, H., 1947, 172

[12] A., *Punch*, 1863, qu. Reed, L., 1934, 107

[13] Lear, E., 1846, qu. Jackson, H., 1947, 25

[14] Prowse, W.J., qu. *Camb. Hist. Engl. Lit.*, XIII, 162

[15] Inge, C., qu. Reed, L., 1924, 40

[16] A., qu. MacCord, D., 1945, 216

[17] A., qu. Untermeyer, L., 1963, 89

[18] 'Twain, M.', qu. Cerf, B., 1960, 28

[19] 'Carroll, L.', qu. Wells, C., 1920, 839

[20] Holmes, O.W., qu. Untermeyer, L., 1963, 24

[21] A., qu. *op. cit.*, 70

[22] A., oral circ., New York, 1950s

[23] Shaw, A., qu. Cerf, B., 1960, 124

[24] A., qu. Wells, C., 1920, 951

[25] Bergson, H., qu. Roberts, M., 'Wit and Humour', *Camb. Encycl.*

[26] Hazlitt, W.C., qu. Rhys, E., 1928, viii

[27] Butler, S., 1901, 152

[28] A., qu. Reed, L., 1924, 137, 106

[29] A., oral circ., Liverpool, 1920s

[30] A., qu. Untermeyer, L., 1963, 62

[31] A., qu. *op. cit.*, 117

[32] Legman, G., 1964, 439

[33] Ditto, *loc. cit.*

[34] Boccaccio, G. (C 14), tr. Rhys, E., 1928, 171

[35] Wright, F.A., 1925, xii

[36] Aristophanes (C 5-4 B.C.), tr. *op. cit.*, xiii

[37] Ditto, tr. Rogers, B.B., 1915, 223

[38] Baring-Gould, W.S., 1968, 17

[39] A., *Times Lit. Supp.*, 6 February 1969

[40] Amis, K., *Observer Mag.*, 30 September 1973

[41] Herbert, A.P., 'Foreword', Reed, L., 1934, vii

[42] MacCord, D., qu. Brock, H.I., 1947, 14

Chapter II

HOW PLEASANT TO KNOW MR. LEAR!

[1] 'M.H.', *Notes and Queries*, 9 November 1898, 408

[2] Reed, L., 1924, 37

[3] Roberts, M., *Chambers's Encyc.* (1967 edn.), XIV, 600

[4] Lear, E., 1872, introd.

[5] Sharpe, R.S.(?), 1822

[6] Lear, E., qu. Jackson, H., 1947, xiv

[7] Ditto, qu. *op. cit.*, xv

[8] Ditto, 1846 (1864 edn.), prelims.

[9] Ditto, qu. Jackson, H., 1947, xxiii

[10] Ditto, qu. *op. cit.*, vii

[11]Jackson, H., 1947, x
[12]Brock, H.I., 1947, 5
[13]Lear, E. (? 1846), Liverpool Picton Library (cat. P821.8)
[14]Ditto, *op, cit.*, plates 1, 2, 3
[15]Ditto, *op. cit.*, plates 28, 86
[16]Ditto, 1846 (1864 edn.)

[17]Ditto, 1846, qu. Jackson, H., 1947, 30
[18]Untermeyer, L., 1963, 15
[19]Lear, E., 1846, qu. Jackson, H., 1947, 33
[20]Ditto, 1846, qu. *op. cit.*, 31
[21]Ditto, 1846, qu. *op. cit.*, 53, 51, 17
[22]Reed, L., 1924, 21

Chapter III

WHY 'LIMERICK'?

[1]*Oxf. Engl. Dict.* (1933 edn.), VI, 298
[2]*Webster's 3rd New Internat. Dict.* (1961 edn.), II, 1312
[3]*Americ. Heritage Dict. Engl. Lang.* (1969 edn.), 758
[4]*Funk & Wagnall's New Standard Dict.* (1949 edn.), I, 1436
[5]*Univ. Dict. Engl. Lang.*, 1932, 675
[6]*Encycl. Dict.*, 1909, suppl. vol., 331
[7]*Everyman's Encyc.* (1967 edn.), VII, 587
[8]*Encyc. Brit.* (1970 edn.), XIV, 37
[9]Legman, G., 1974, ix
[10]Murray, J.M., *Notes and Queries*, 10 December 1898, 479
[11]Reed, L., 1924, vii
[12]Ditto, *op. cit.*, 18
[13]Ditto, 1937, x
[14]A., French tradnl. children's verse.
[15]A., qu. Boswell, J., 1791 (1906 'Everyman' edn.), II, 243, f.n.
[16]*Children's Encyc.* (1960 edn.), VI, 235
[17]*Reader's Guide to Literary Terms* (1961 edn.)
[18]*Encyc. Americ.* (1968 edn.), 521
[19]*Brewer's Dict. Phrase & Fable* (1970 'Century' edn.)
[20]Cohen, J.M., private communication to C.B., 7 April 1974
[21]Brock, H.I., 1947, 4

[22]Boas, G., *English*, Spring 1965, 15
[23]Wells, C., 1925, iii
[24]Reed, L., 1924, viii
[25]Opie, I. & P., 1951, 38
[26]Thackeray, W.H., 1843, *Irish Sketch Book* (1903 'Caxton' edn.), 219
[27]Ditto, 1855, *Lyra Hibernica* (1899 'Pocket Book' edn.)
[28]O'Toumy (Tuomy) (1706-1775), qu. Harrowven, J., 1976, 18
[29]Ditto, tr. Mangan, J.C., qu. Hoagland, K., 1947, 186
[30]Macgrath, A., (1723-179?), tr. Mangan, J.C., qu. *op. cit.*, 187
[31]Legman, G., 1974, 1xii
[32]*Cantab.*, 6 October 1898
[33]Kipling, R., 1899 (1908 edn.), 201
[34]M.H., *Notes and Queries*, 19 November 1898, 408
[35]Murray, J.H., *Notes and Queries*, 10 December 1898, 470
[36]Russell, M., *Irish Monthly*, February 1898, qu. Partridge, E., 1949, 252
[37]Weekley, E., 1952, 237
[38]*Engl. Dialect. Dict.*, 1898, III, 609
[39]Scott, W., 1814, *Waverley*, qu. *Oxf. Engl. Dict.* (1961 edn.), VI, 301
[40]Borrow, G., 1851, *Lavengro*, qu. *Oxf. Engl. Dict.* (1961 edn.), *loc. cit.*

Chapter IV

PIONEERS AND PRECURSORS

[1]Legman, G., 1964, 430
[2]A., 1820-21, qu. *Oxf. Dict. Nurs. Rh.*, 267
[3]Ditto, qu. *op. cit.*, 329
[4]Ditto, qu. Opie, I. & P., 1973, 152

[5]Ditto, qu. De Vries, L., 1965, 117
[6]Ditto, qu. *loc. cit.*
[7]Sharpe, R.S.(?), 1822, qu. *Oxf. Dict. Nurs. Rh.*, 241
[8]Ditto, qu. *op. cit.*, 91

9 Ditto, qu. *op. cit.*, 359
10 Ditto, qu. Harrowven, J., 1976, 32
11 'A Lady', 1823, qu. De Vries, L., 1965, 36
12 *Punch*, 13 December 1845
13 A., (tradnl.), qu. *Oxf. Dict. Nurs. Rh.*, 206
14 Ditto, qu. *op. cit.*, 147
15 A., oral circ., qu. Opie, I. & P., 1959, 100
16 Ditto, qu. *op. cit.*, 103
17 Ditto, qu. *loc. cit.*
18 Ditto, qu. *op. cit.*, 111
19 A., oral circ., Hertfordshire, 1940s
20 A., qu. Opie, I. & P., 1959, 95
21 Ditto, qu. *op. cit.*, 6
22 Ditto, qu. *op. cit.*, 112
23 A., oral circ., Merseyside, 1930s
24 A. (tradnl.), qu. *Oxf. Dict. Nurs. Rh.*, 114
25 Ditto, qu. *op. cit.*, 113
26 Piccini (?), c.1780, qu. *op. cit.*, 60
27 Southey, R.(?), c.1820, qu. *op. cit.*, 100
28 Legman, G., 1964, 434
29 Dobson, H.A. (1840-1925), qu. *Oxf. Bk. Engl. Verse* (1939 edn., 1006)
30 Hunt, L. (1784-1859), qu. Emerson, R.W., 1875
31 Moore, T. (1779-1852), *Poetical Works* (1881 edn., 232)
32 Ditto, *op. cit.*, 233
33 Ditto, *op. cit.*, 250
34 Peacock, T.L. c.1811, qu. Brett-Smith, H.F.B. & Jones, C.E., 1931, VII, 400
35 Wilberforce, W., 1821, qu. *op. cit.*, 452
36 Peacock, T.L., 1821, qu. *op. cit.*, 147
37 O'Flaherty, C. (1794-1824), qu. Hoagland, K., 1947, 390
38 Bishop, M., qu. Baring-Gould, W.S., 1968, 38
39 Ramsay, A., 1724 (1871 edn., I, 63)
40 Ditto, *loc. cit.*, II, 116
41 A., c.1640, qu. Legman, G., 1964, 434
42 A. (C 17), 'Roxburgh Ballads', qu. Pinto, V. de S. & Rodway, A.E., 1957, 136
43 Dunbar, W. (b. 1460), qu. Kinley, J., 1958, 21
44 Ditto, qu. *op. cit.*, 44
45 A., c.1226, qu. *Oxf. Bk. Engl. Verse*, 1
46 A. (C 14), Harleian MS. 7322, qu. Swann, R. & Sidgwick, F., 1934, 102
47 Elizabeth I (?), qu. Baring-Gould, W.S. 1968, 25
48 Wisdome, R. (d.1568), qu. Legman, G., 1953, xvii
49 A., c.1606, qu. *op. cit.*, xviii
50 Shakespeare, W., *King Lear*, Act III, Sc.4 (1960 edn., 67)
51 A. (? C 16), qu. D'Israeli, I., 1839, 286
52 Shakespeare, W., *Hamlet*, Act IV, Sc.5 (1936 edn., 104)
53 Ditto, *Othello*, Act II, Sc. 3 (1957 edn., 40)
54 Ditto, *The Tempest*, Act II, Sc. 2 (1921 edn., 39)
55 Jonson, B., 1621, qu. Morley, M., 1890, 260
56 Herrick, R., 1648, qu. Emerson, R.W., 1875
57 Ditto, qu. Pinto, V. de S. & Rodway, A.E., 1957, 269
58 Gay, J., 1728, *The Beggar's Opera* (1972 edn., 39)

Chapter V

WHAT PRECISELY IS A LIMERICK?

1 Moore, T. (1779-1852), qu. *Oxf. Bk. Engl. Verse*, V, 694
2 Brontë, P., 1811, qu. Brontës (1905 'Haworth' edn.), IV, 525
3 Darton, W., 1797, *A Present for Little Girls*, London, Darton & Harvey, qu. De Vries, L., 1965, 59
4 A., oral circ., tradnl.
5 A., qu. *Oxf. Dict. Nurs. Rh.*, 435
6 Hopkins, J.H. (1820-1891), qu. Routley, E., 1961, 138
7 Sidney, P. (1554-1586), qu. Swann, R. & Sidgwick, F., 1934, xiii

[8]Gilbert, W.S., 1877, *The Sorcerer*, qu. Swinton, M., n.d., 23

[9]Ditto, 1881, *Patience*, qu. *Selected Operas (First Series)*, 1949, 67

[10]Ditto, 1888, *Yeoman of the Guard*, qu. *op. cit.*, 76

[11]Ditto, qu. Fenn, G.M., 1871 (1887 edn.), 145

[12]Untermeyer, L., 1963, 10

[13]A., qu. Letts, J., 1973, 44

[14]A., qu. *op. cit.*, 75

[15]A., qu. Wells, C., 1920 (1941 edn.), 950

[16]A., qu. Roberts, M., 1942, 295

[17]A., qu. Untermeyer, L., 1963, 107

[18]Chesterton, G.K., 1933, 155

[19]Douglas, N., qu. Baring-Gould, W.S., 1968, 26

[20]Gilbert, W.S.(?), qu. Roberts, M., 1942, 295

[21]Lear, E., 1846, qu. Jackson, H., 1947, 7

[22]A., *Punch*, 1920, qu. Reed, L., 1934, 131

[23]Beckson, K. &'Ganz, A., 1961, 117

[24]Ridout, R. & Witting, C., 1964, 176

[25]*Webster's New Colleg. Dict.*

[26]Cohen, J.M., *Encyc Brit.* (1970 edn.), XIV, 38

[27]*Encyc. Americ.* (1959 edn.)

[28]Baring-Gould, W.S., 1968, 24

[29]Knox, E.V., *Encyc. Brit.* (1951 edn.), XIV, 130

[30]Omond, T.S., 1903, 139

[31]Campion, T. (c. 1575-1620), qu. *op. cit.*, iii

[32]Swinburne, A.C., qu. *loc. cit.*

[33]Bysshe, E., 1702, qu. Saintsbury, G., 1910, 16

[34]Coleridge, S.T., 1816, qu. Coleridge, E.H., 1912, I, 213

[35]Ditto, qu. *op. cit.*, 215

[36]Omond, T.S., 1903, 6

[37]Hopkins, G.M., qu. McChesney, D., 1968, 16

[38]Ditto, c.1883, 'Author's Preface' (*MS*), qu. Gardner, W.H., 1953, 9

[39]Ditto, 'Pied Beauty', qu. *op. cit.*, 30

[40]Gilbert, W.S., 1869, *Bab Ballads*, qu. Wyndham Lewis, D.B., 1936, 244

[41]A., *Times Lit. Supp.*, qu. Baring-Gould, W.S., 1968, 24

[42]Fadiman, C., 1957, 270

[43]Jennings, P., 'There was an old rhyme', *D. Telegraph Mag.*, 22 November 1974

[44]Bishop, M., 'On the Limerick', *N.Y. Times Bk. Rev.*, 3 January 1965

[45]A., qu. Baring-Gould, W.S., 1968, 30

Chapter VI

POPULARITY POST-LEAR

[1]A., 1864, qu. Wells, C., 1925, 16

[2]Ditto, qu. *op. cit.*, 5

[3]Ditto, qu. *op. cit.*, 9

[4]Ditto, qu. *op. cit.*, 17

[5]Ditto, qu. *op. cit.*, 7

[6]A., *Punch*, 1863, qu. Reed, L., 1934, 108, 110, 111

[7]Kernahan, C., qu. Reed, L., 1924, 14

[8]Rossetti, D.G., qu. Rossetti, W.M., 1911, 275

[9]Ditto, qu. *op. cit.*, 274

[10]Ditto, qu. *op. cit.*,275

[11]Ditto, qu. *op. cit.*, 274

[12]'Carroll, L.', qu. Ireson, B., 1965, 223

[13]'Carroll, L.(?)', newspaper cutting (*Whitby Gazette*?), n.d., pasted into C.B.'s copy of Reed, L., 1924

[14]Galsworthy, J., qu. Reed, L., 1924, 140

[15]Bennett, A., qu. *op. cit.*, 54

[16]Kipling, R., qu. Wells, C., 1902, xxxii

[17]Stevenson, R.L.(?), qu. Reed, L., 1924, 37

[18]Russell, B., qu. Wells, C., 1920, 39

[19]Hicks, S., qu. Reed, L., 1924, 57

[20]Coburn, C., qu. *op. cit.*, 133

[21]Wells, C., 1902, xxxii

[22]Euwer, A., qu. Untermeyer, L., 1963, 52

[23]Dulac, E., 1908

[24]A., *London Opinion*, 1907, qu. Reed, L., 1924, 24

[25]Rhodes, R., 1907, qu. *op. cit.*, 28

[26]Reed, L., 1924, 25

[27]*op. cit.*, 23
[28]*Punch,* 8 January 1908, qu. Reed, 1934, xv
[29]A., *Punch*, 2 March 1904, qu. *op. cit.*, xiv
[30]A., *Punch*, 1892, qu. *op. cit.*, 15
[31]A., *Punch*, 1892, qu. *op. cit.*, 9
[32]A., *Punch*, 1902, qu. *op. cit.*, 8
[33]A., *Punch*, 1904, qu. *op. cit.*, 10
[34]A., *Punch*, 1904, qu. *op. cit.*, 81
[35]A., *Punch*, 1904, qu. *op. cit.*, 18
[36]A., *Wipers Times*, 31 July 1916 (1973 repr.), 122, 119, 116
[37]A., *Punch*, 1918, qu. Reed, L., 1934, 36
[38]A., *Punch*, 1918, qu. *op. cit.*, 35
[39]A., *Punch,* 1918, qu. *op. cit.*, 32
[40]A., *Punch*, 1918, qu. *op. cit.*, 34
[41]A., *Punch,* 1919, qu. *op. cit.*, 37
[42]Holt, E.C., *Punch*, 21 July 1920, qu. *op. cit.*, 77-79
[43]A., *Punch*, 1924, qu. *op. cit.*, 130

[44]A., *Punch*, 1919, qu. *op. cit.*, 58
[45]A., *Punch,* 1925, qu. *op. cit.*, 134
[46]A., *Punch*, 1918, qu. *op. cit.*, 19
[47]A., *Punch*, 1924, qu. *op. cit.*, 27
[48]Braley, B., 1925, qu. Baring-Gould, W.S., 1968, 68
[49]Wells, C., 1925, iii
[50]Bellamy, W., qu. Wells, C., 1925, 21
[51]Christgau, F.G., qu. *op. cit.*, 26
[52]Burgess, C.B., qu. *op. cit.*, 23
[53]Robinson, E.M., qu. *op. cit.*, 25
[54]Reed, L., 1924, xi
[55]Inge, C., qu. Reed, L., 1924, 41
[56]A., qu. *op. cit.*, 47
[57]Knox, R., qu. *op. cit.*, 44
[58]A., qu. *op. cit.*, 49, 50
[59]Reed, L., *op. cit.*, 59, 58
[60]A., qu. *op. cit.*, 70, 60
[61]'Beaumains', qu. *op. cit.*, 89
[62]Kennington, A., qu. *op. cit.*, 85
[63]A., qu. *op. cit.*, 96

Chapter VII

THE LIMERICK'S RANGE

[1]Opie, I. & P., 1951, 2
[2]Untermeyer, L., 1963, 10
[3]Brock, H.I., 1947, 13
[4]A., *Punch*, 13 December 1845
[5]Kennedy, J., qu. Reed, L., 1924, 85
[6]A., qu. *op. cit.*, 125
[7]A., qu. Brock, H.I., 1947, 30
[8]'Pete', *Sunday Post*, 3 February 1974
[9]Hendrie, R., *Sunday Post*, 10 February 1974
[10]Pearson, Mrs. M., *loc. cit.*
[11]Nash, O., 1954, 66
[12]A., qu. Untermeyer, L., 1963, 34
[13]Aiken, C., 1963, 5
[14]A., qu. Reed, L., 1924, 134
[15]A., qu. *op. cit.*, 71, 62, 120
[16]A., qu. Baring-Gould, W.S., 1968, 176, 112
[17]Warren, Mrs., qu. Reed, L., 1924, 133
[18]O'Brien, Sister D., *Teachers' World*, 1 February 1974
[19]Children (ages 10 & 12), qu. Rowe, A.M., 1967, I, 16

[20]A., qu. *Daily Telegraph*, 25 March 1974
[21]Reed, L., 1928, 55
[22]A., *Punch*, 1921, qu. Reed, L., 1934, 20
[23]A., *Punch*. 1918, qu. *op. cit.*, 17
[24]A., *Times Lit. Supp.*, 16 February 1969
[25]Joyce, J., qu. Gogarty, St. J., 1937, 297
[26]A., qu. Letts, J., 1973, 49
[27]A., qu. Wells, C., 1920, 835
[28]Dodd, W.A., *Mathem. in Schools*, II (3), 16 May 1973
[29]Hilton, A.C. ('Edward Leary'), 1872, qu. MacCord, D., 1945, 218
[30]A., qu. Reed, L., 1924, 107
[31]Moser, Leo, *Americ. Mathem. Monthly*, 80(8), 902, October 1973
[32]Ditto, *loc. cit.*
[33]Carter, H.L., qu. Baring-Gould, W.S., 1968, 18
[34]Dodd, W.A., *Mathem. In Schools,* II (3), 16 May 1973

[35]Strachey, J.St.L., qu. Reed, L., 1924, 55

[36]Buller, A.H.R., *Punch*, 19 December 1923

[37]Ditto, qu. Baring-Gould, W.S., 1968, 18

[38]A., qu. Untermeyer, L., 1963, 110

[39]A., qu. Letts, J., 1973, 47

[40]Brookes, P., *Radio Times*, 20 December 1975

[41]A., qu. Letts, J., 1973, 33, 30

[42]A., qu. *op. cit.*, 33, 35

[43]A., qu. Untermeyer, L., 1963, 84

[44]A., qu. Reed, L., 1924, 126

[45]A., oral circ., Cambridge, 1930s

[46]A., oral circ., ditto

[47]Ashley-Montagu, R.F., qu. Meynell, F. & V., 1924 (1938 edn.), I, 253

[48]Joad, C.E.M., qu. *loc. cit.*

[49]A., qu. Letts, J., 1973, 49

[50]A., qu. Reed, L., 1924, 87

[51]A., qu. Cerf, B., 1960, 20

[52]A., qu. Baring-Gould, W.S., 1968, 96

[53]A., qu. Wells, C., 1925, 39

[54]A., *Punch*, 1925, qu. Reed, L., 1934, 44

[55]A., qu. Letts, J., 1973, 52

[56]A., *Punch*, 1926, qu. Reed, L., 1934, 44

[57]Reed, L., 1924, 48

[58]A., qu. Wells, C., 1925, 51

[59]Inge, C., qu. Reed, L., 1924, 51

[60]A., qu. Reed, L., 1937, xi

[61]A., qu. Untermeyer, L., 1963, 67

[62]A., qu. Letts, J., 1973, 48

[63]A., qu. Untermeyer, L., 1963, 154

[64]Crowley, A., qu. Legman, G., 1964, 447

[65]Holt, E.C., *Punch*, 1920, qu. Reed, L., 1924, 91

[66]A., qu. *op. cit.*, 93

[67]A., qu. *op. cit.*, 92

[68]A., newspaper cutting pasted into C.B.'s copy of Reed, 1934

[69]Belloc, H., 1940 (1950 edn.), 172

[70]A., qu. Untermeyer, L., 1963, 46

[71]Rank, M.O., qu. Cerf, B., 1960, 46

[72]Osborne, F.J., 1920s, letter dated 21 September 1973 to C.B.

[73]A., qu. Untermeyer, L., 1963, 144

[74]Reed, L., 1928, 105

[75]Marquis, D., qu. Baring-Gould, W.S., 1968, 67

[76]A., 1914

[77]Adam Smith, J., 1953, Preface

Chapter VIII

SOME MASTERS OF THE ART

[1]Legman, G., 1974, xiii

[2]Lear, E., 1846, qu. Jackson, H., 1947, 38

[3]Ditto, qu. *op. cit.*, 16

[4]Legman, G., 1974, vii

[5] *loc. cit.*

[6]Ditto, *loc. cit.*

[7]Untermeyer, L., 1963, 15

[8]Thorneley, T., 1936, 61

[9]Ditto, *loc. cit.*

[10]Ditto, *op. cit.*, 53

[11]Ditto, *op. cit.*, 55

[12]Ditto, *op. cit.*, 57

[13]Ditto, *op. cit.*, 54

[14]Ditto, *op. cit.*, 56, 53

[15]Ditto, *op. cit.*, 53

[16]Ditto, *op. cit.*, 55

[17]Ditto, *op. cit.*, 57

[18]Ditto, *op. cit.*, 53

[19]Ditto, *loc. cit.*

[20]Ditto, *op. cit.*, 59

[21]Ditto, *loc. cit.*

[22]Ditto, *op. cit.*, 56, 62

[23]Ditto, *op. cit.*, 60

[24]A., qu. Douglas, N., 1928 (1969 edn.), 18

[25]? P. Heseltine, qu. *op. cit.*, 80

[26]A., qu. *op. cit.*, 77

[27]A., qu. *op. cit.*, 42

[28]Douglas, N., *op. cit.*, 11

[29]A., 1864, qu. Wells, C., 1925, 11

[30]Euwer, A., 1917, qu. *op. cit.*, 24

[31]A., qu. *op. cit.*, 48

[32]A., qu. *op. cit.*, 55, 85

[33]Wells, C.(?), *op. cit.*, 86, 87, 90

[34]Ditto, 1906, 207; 2nd *v*., qu. Baring-Gould, W.S., 1968, 66
[35]Cohen, J.M., *Encyc. Brit.* (1970 edn.), XIV, 37
[36]Reed, L., 1924, 37
[37]A., qu. Reed, L., 1924, 50
[38]A., qu. *op. cit.*, 67, 61
[39]Halliday, A.E., qu. *op. cit.*, 85
[40]Taylor, H., qu. *op. cit.*, 96
[41]A., *Tit-Bits*, c.1922, qu. *op. cit.*, 84
[42]Reed, L., 1928, 15
[43]Ditto, *op. cit.*, prelim. note
[44]Ditto, *op. cit.*, 47, 63

[45]Ditto, *op. cit.*, 13, 109
[46]Ditto, *op. cit.*, 56, 48
[47]Ditto, *op. cit.*, 52, 54, 82
[48]Ditto, 1934, 1
[49]Ditto, 1937, 13
[50]Ditto, *op. cit.*, 15, 25
[51]Ditto, *op. cit.*, 31
[52]Ditto, *op. cit.*, 36
[53]Ditto, *op. cit.*, 42
[54]Ditto, *op. cit.*, 51
[55]Ditto, *op. cit.*, 64
[56]Ditto, *op. cit.*, 105
[57]Ditto, *op. cit.*, 115

Chapter IX

THE RISQUE, THE RIBALD AND THE RANCID

[1]Bennett, A., qu. Reed, L., 1924, 15
[2]Shaw, G.B., qu. *op. cit.*, 13
[3]Herbert, A.P., 1934, vii
[4]A., *Sporting Life,* qu. Baring-Gould, W.S., 1968, 1
[5]Legman, G., 1964, 427
[6]Boston, R., *Guardian*, 16 October 1976
[7]Cohen, J.M., *Encyc. Brit.* (1970 edn.), XIV, 37
[8]A., qu. Holland, V., 1967, prelim.
[9]Bishop, M., qu. *op. cit.*, 1
[10]Swinburne, A.C., qu. Baring-Gould, W.S., 1968, 74
[11]'Carroll, L.', qu. Woollcott, A., 1939, 792
[12]A., qu. Reed, L., 1924, 50
[13]Untermeyer, L., 1963, 135
[14]A., qu. *op. cit.*, 142, 143, 135
[15]A., oral circ., Hull, 1960s
[16]A., qu. Untermeyer, L., 1963, 85
[17]A., qu. Baring-Gould, W.S., 1968, 107
[18]A., qu. Letts, J., 1973, 93, 61
[19]A., oral circ., Chelsea, 1950s; varied by C.B.
[20]A., oral circ., London, 1940s; varied by C.B.

[21]A., qu. Holland, V., 1967, 58
[22]A., oral circ., Cambridge, 1930s
[23]A., qu. Holland, V., 1967, 10
[24]A., qu. Baring-Gould, W.S., 1968, 82
[25]A., qu. *op. cit.*, 95
[26]A., qu. Letts, J., 1973, 55
[27]A., qu. Baring-Gould, W.S., 1968, 106
[28]A., oral circ., Cambridge, 1930s
[29]Herford, O., qu. Baring-Gould, W.S., 1968, 64
[30]A., qu. Jennings, P., *D. Telegr. Mag.*, 22 November 1974
[31]Aiken, C., 1963, 31
[32]A., qu. Harris, F., 1922-27 (1948 edn.), II, 260
[33]A., qu. Baring-Gould, W.S., 1968, 185
[34]A. qu. Legman, G., 1964, 396
[35]A., oral circ., London, 1950s
[36]A., qu. Baring-Gould, W.S., 1968, 16
[37]Fadiman, C., 1957, 274
[38]Marquis, D., qu. Baring-Gould, W.S., 1968, 21
[39]Quiller-Couch, A., 1939, xiii
[40]Auden, W.H., qu. *N.Y. Rev. of Books*, 12 May 1966

Chapter X

VARIANTS

[1]Opie, I. & P., 1951, vi
[2]A., qu. Reed, L., 1934, xii
[3]Dickens, C., 1865 ('Centennial' edn.), 14
[4]A., *Punch*, 1926, qu. Reed, L., 1934, 114
[5]A., *Punch*, 1932, qu. *op. cit.*, 136
[6]Reed, L., 1924, 77
[7]Ditto, 1928, 106
[8]Lear, E., 1846, qu. Jackson, H., 1947, 37
[9]A., qu. Reed, L., 1924, 96
[10]Nash, O., 1961, 53
[11]A., qu. Wells, C., 1925, 81
[12]A., qu. Baring-Gould, W.S., 1968, 110
[13]A., qu. Reed, L., 1924, 92
[14]Lear, E., 1846, qu. Jackson, H., 1947, 12
[15]A., qu. Reed, L., 1924, 102
[16]A., qu. Baring-Gould, W.S., 1968, 148
[17]A., *Times Lit. Supp.*, 16 February 1969

[18]Lear, E., 1846, qu. Jackson, H., 1947, 3
[19]Ditto, 1872, qu. *op. cit.*, 190
[20]A., qu. Reed, L., 1924, 92
[21]'R.D.', 1927, pl. XI
[22]A., qu. Baring-Gould, W.S., 1968, 47
[23]A., qu. *loc. cit.*
[24]A., qu. *op. cit.*, 113
[25]A., qu. *loc. cit.*
[26]Lear, E., 1846 & 1872, qu. Jackson, H., 1947, 177, 28, 42
[27]A., oral circ., London, 1950s
[28]A., qu. Reed, L., 1924, 49
[29]A., qu. Baring-Gould, W.S., 1968, 124
[30]A., oral circ., Cambridge, 1930s
[31]A., qu. Reed, L., 1924, 130
[32]A., (Monkhouse, C.), qu. *op. cit.*, 95
[33]Reed, L., 1937, 115
[34]A., qu. Baring-Gould, W.S., 1968, 115
[35]A., *Punch*, 1863, qu. Reed, L., 1934, 108
[36]A., qu. Untermeyer, L., 1963, 133

Chapter XI

SEQUENCES

[1]A., *The Pearl*, February 1880, qu. Legman, G., 1974, 76; possibly from a Robert Burns original
[2]A., *Princeton Tiger, N.Y. Press, Chicago Tribune*, qu. Baring-Gould, W.S., 1968, 28
[3]Reed, L., 1924, 75
[4]Kernahan, M., qu., Reed, 1924, 72
[5]Wells, C., 1925, 91
[6]A., *Punch*, 1926, qu. Reed, L., 1934, 97-103
[7]Euwer, A., 1927, qu. Baring-Gould, W.S., 1968, 73
[8]Reed, 1937, 54, 138

[9]Ditto, 1937a, 9, 11, 10, 23, 31, 49, 24, 73
[10]A., c.1938, 'Lapses in Limerick', qu. Legman, G., 1974, 172
[11]Belloc, H., 1940(1950 edn.), 173, 174, 178
[12]Crisp, Q., 1943, 7, 8, 11, 19, 28
[13]A., 1943, 'Socially Conscious Pornography', *Unexpurgated*, qu. Legman, G., 1974, 196, 198, 199
[14]Bulley, S., *Daily Mail*, 7 August 1971
[15]Tattersall, A., *Univ. Lond. Bulletin*, January 1973

Chapter XII

LINES IN LESSER TONGUES

[1]Untermeyer, L., 1963, 12

[2]Douglas, N., 1928 (1969 edn.), 16, 19

[3]Spencer, T.J., qu. Baring-Gould, W.S., 1968, 27

[4]A., qu. Wells, C., 1902 (1958 edn.), 267

[5]A., qu. *loc. cit.*

[6]Boccaccio, G., 1384 (1966 Mursia edn.), 381

[7]Brown, P.M., personal communication to C.B., 12 February 1974

[8]Aquinas, St. Thomas (1225-1274), 'Oratio', in Roman Catholic Church, (1955 edn.), 35

[9]Norman, A.F., personal communication to C.B., 5 January 1974

[10]A., *Punch*, 1918, qu. Reed, L., 1934, 36

[11]Reed, L., 1937, 22

[12]A., qu. Reed, L., 1924, 121

[13]A., qu. *loc. cit.*

[14]A., qu. Wells, C., 1925, 37

[15]A., *Punch*, 1925

[16]du Maurier, George, qu. Reed, L., 1924, 53

[17]Ditto, qu. Wells, C., 1937 (1950 edn.), 263

[18]A., qu. Untermeyer, L., 1963, 141

[19]Wallace, J.E., unidentified newspaper cutting, n.d., pasted in C.B.'s copy of Reed, L., 1924

[20]A., qu. Reed, L., 1924, 122

[21]Joyce, J., qu. Baring-Gould, W.S., 1968, 67

[22]A., qu. *op. cit.*, 100

[23]A., qu. Reed, L., 1924, 118

[24]A., *Granta*, ?1924, qu. Elvin, L., private communication to C.B., 22 January 1978.

[25]A., qu. *op. cit.*, 103

[26]Knox, R., qu. *op. cit.*, 82

[27]Lancaster, Sir Osbert (?), qu. Boston, R., *Guardian*, 16 October 1976.

Chapter XIII

INGENIOUS TYPOGRAPHICS

[1]A., *Punch*, 1896, qu. Reed, L., 1934, 91

[2]Phillips, C.K., *Punch*, 1904, qu. *op. cit.*, 94

[3]Webb, W.S., qu. Reed, L., 1924, 65

[4]A., *Punch,* 1928, qu. Reed, L., 1934, 92

[5]Mannock, P.L., qu. Reed, L., 1924, 61

[6]A., qu. *op. cit.*, 60

[7]A., qu. Holland, V., 1967, 66; orthography coordinated by C.B.

[8]A., qu. Reed, L., 1924, 61

[9]Bloomfield (Bishop), qu. *op. cit.*, 42

[10]Knox, E.V., *Punch*, 1928, qu. Reed, L., 1934, 66

[11]A., qu. Reed, L., 1924, 61, 63, 60

[12]A., marginal *MS* in Kingston upon Hull Public Library copy of Reed, 1928; orthography coordinated by C.B.

[13]Knox, E.V., *Punch*, 1928, qu. Reed, L., 1934, 65

[14]A., qu. Baring-Gould, W.S., 1968, 173

[15]A., probably *Punch*, pasted in C.B.'s copy of Reed, L., 1934

[16]A., qu. Wells, C., 1906, 203, 207

[17]A., qu. *op. cit.*, 203

[18]Nash, O., 1954, 64

[19]A., qu. Wells, C., 1925, 79

[20]A., qu. Cerf, B., 1960, 111, 101, 114, 112

[21]A., qu. Reed, L., 1924, 62

[22]Mannock, P.L., qu. *loc. cit.*

[23]A., qu. Baring-Gould, W.S., 1968, 165

[24]A., qu. Untermeyer, L., 1963, 107

[25]A., qu. Letts, J., 1973, 17

Chapter XIV

THE 'PROSE' LIMERICK

[1]Knox, R., *Times* (?), qu. Holland, V., 1967, 96

[2]A., *Punch* (?), cutting pasted into C.B.'s copy of Reed, L., 1934
[3]Bibby, C., *The Teacher*, 27 June 1969

Chapter XV

THE LATTER-DAY REVIVAL

[1]Burgess, W.S., qu. Baring-Gould, W.S., 1968, 59

[2]Ross, A.I., qu. *op. cit.*, 63

[3]A., 1969, comic postcard seen by C.B. in Thirsk

[4]Bulley, S.C. (Bishop), *Daily Mail*, 7 August 1971

[5]Wauchope, M.O.C., *Sunday Times*, 31 October 1971

[6]Rushton, S. (age 12), *The Teacher*, 10 December 1971

[7]Collins, S. (age 13), *loc. cit.*

[8]Askew, G., *Yorkshire Post*, 13 December 1972

[9]Young, K., *op. cit.*, 14 December 1972

[10]*Sunday Mirror*, 27 May 1973

[11]*op. cit.*, 3 June 1973

[12]Hughes, D.C., *op. cit.*, 10 June 1973

[13]Walsh, R., *loc. cit.*

[14]O'Halloran, L., *op. cit.*, 3 June 1973

[15]Saxby, R., *loc. cit.*

[16]Marlow, S., *Daily Mirror*, 8 September 1973

[17]Cox, A.P., *Daily Mail*, 8 September 1973

[18]Chandler, M., *loc. cit.*

[19]Macdonald, R., *loc. cit.*

[20]Duncan, W., *Sunday Post*, 10 February 1974

[21]Buchan, W.J., *loc. cit.*

[22]Laird, J.D., *op. cit.*, 17 February 1974

[23]Ogilvy, R.F., *op. cit.*, 17 February 1974

[24]A., *op. cit.*, 31 August 1975

[25]Burns, E., *op. cit.*, 7 September 1975

[26]Faulds, J., *op. cit.*, 14 September 1975

[27]Author wishes not to be named, *loc. cit.*

[28]Williams, L., qu. Harrowven, J., 1976, 96

[29]Jones, A. (age 9), qu. Baxter, B. & Gill, R., 42

[30]Coleman, R. (age 10), qu. *op. cit.*, 74

[31]McDermott, D. (age 13), qu. *op. cit.*, 38

[32]Nash, G. (age 11), qu. *op. cit.*, 69

[33]A., 'Cilla' programme, B.B.C. T.V., 6 November 1971

[34]Clarke, Mrs., B.B.C. Radio Humberside, 4 March 1974

[35]Ingle, Mr., B.B.C. Radio Humberside, 25 February 1974

[36]Monkhouse, Bob, qu. Harrowven, J., 1976, 120

[37]Murdoch, R., qu. *op. cit.*, 119

[38]Ray, T., qu. *op. cit.*, 115 (amended for C.B. by Ted Ray)

[39]Askey, A., qu. *loc. cit.*

[40]A., 1971, notice-board in St. Andrews University marine research laboratory

[41]A., 1971, *loc. cit.*

[42]Dodd, W.A., *Mathem. in Sch.*, May 1973, II, 3, 16

[43]Smart, N., *Times Higher Educ. Supp.*, 11 May 1973

[44]A., *Open House* (Open University), 2 July 1975

[45]'Junius', *loc. cit.*

[46]'Artifax', *loc. cit.*

[47]Jennings, P., *Sunday Telegraph Mag.*, 22 November 1974

[48]Lathan, A., qu. *Yorkshire Post*, 7 March 1972

[49]Limerick, Earl of., qu. *Guardian*, 7 May 1974

[50]Ditto, personal letter to C.B., 13 May 1974

Bibliography

Where a work was published anonymously or the name of an author has not been traced, the symbol 'A' is used.

Where there is some uncertainty about author's name, date of publication, place of publication or name of publisher, the symbol '?' is used.

Pseudonyms etc. are given, within single quotes, with cross-references to real names where known.

Dates of birth and/or death are sometimes given, within parentheses, where date of writing and/or first publication is unknown.

Since in this field the border-lines between author, anthologiser, editor etc. are sometimes very blurred, no such distinctions are indicated.

Some titles of publications which have not been seen by C.B. are included, as at least providing a lead for future scholars.

A., 1820/21, *The History of Sixteen Wonderful Old Women, illustrated by as many engravings; exhibiting their Principal Eccentricities and Amusements.* London, Harris and Son, Corner of St. Paul's Church-yard. (Date on title-page is 1821, but first page of text gives 1 May 1820.)

A. (Sharpe, R.S.?), 1822, *Anecdotes and Adventures of Fifteen Gentlemen.* London, John Marshall.

A., 1864, *The New Book of Nonsense: a Contribution to the Great Central Fair, Philadelphia, in aid of the Sanitary Commission.* Philadelphia, Ashmead & Evans.

A., 1864a, *Ye Book of Bubbles. In aid of the Sanitary Commission, Philadelphia.* New York, Endicott.

A., 1864b, *Inklings for Thinklings.* Philadelphia, Sanitary Commission.

A., 1868, *A New Book of Nonsense.* ?, ?.

A., 1870, *Cythera's Hymnal, or Flakes from the Foreskin: a Collection of Songs, Poems, Nursery Rhymes, Quiddities etc.* 'Oxford: Printed at the University Press, for the Society for Promoting Useful Knowledge' (actual publisher unknown).

A., c.1913, *Geography without Groans: a Few Words on the Use of Limericks in County Council Schools* (pamphlet). London, ?.

A., 1914, *The Book of William [Kaiser Wilhelm]: with Apologies to Edward Lear.* London & New York, Warne.

A., 1916–18, *Wipers Times* etc. (facsimile reprint, ed. Beaver, P., 1973. London, Peter Davies).

A., 1923, *Cleopatra's Scrapbook.* 'Blue Grass, Kentucky', ?.

A., 1933, *Heated Limericks.* 'Paris' (actually, probably Havana), privately printed for Erotica Biblion Society.

A., 1935–38, *Lapses in Limerick* (MS.). Ann Arbor, Michigan.

A., 1940s, *The Bagman's Book of Limericks*. Paris, Excel Books.

A., 1941–47, *Index Limericus* (card index). Berkeley, California.

A., 1943, *Unexpurgated*. Los Angeles, 'Bidet Press'.

A., 1945, *From Bed to Verse: An Unabashed Anthology*. Wiesbaden, illicit printing by members of U.S. Army of Occupation.

'A Lady', 1823, *Little Rhymes for Little Folks: or, a Present for Fanny's Library*. London, John Harris.

Adam Smith, Janet, 1953, *The Faber Book of Children's Verse*. London, Faber.

Aiken, Conrad, 1963, *A Seizure of Limericks*. London, W.H.Allen.

Aquinas, St. Thomas (1225–1274), 'Oratio S. Thomae Aquinatis'. *vide* Roman Catholic Church, *Vade Mecum Sacerdotis* . . .

Aristophanes, 422 B.C., *The Wasps*. *vide* Rogers, B.B. and Wright, F.A.

Armitage, John, 1960, *Children's Britannica*. Chicago & London, Encyc. Brit. Co.

Baring-Gould, W.S., 1968, *The Lure of the Limerick: an uninhibited history*. London, Hart-Davies (also 1970, 'Panther' edn.).

Barrère, A. & Leyland, C.E., 1897, *A Dictionary of Slang, Jargon and Cant*. London, Bell.

Baxter, Biddy & Gill, Rosemary, 1972, *The Blue Peter Book of Limericks*. London & Sydney, B.B.C. with Pan Books.

Beaver, P., *vide* A., 1916–18.

Beckson, Karl & Ganz, Arthur, *A Reader's Guide to Literary Terms*. London, Thames & Hudson.

Beilenson, Peter, 1940, *Peter Pauper's Limerick Book*. New York, 'Peter Pauper Press'.

Bell, T., 1821, *Kalogynomia, or the Laws of Female Beauty: being the elementary principles of that science* (1899 edn.). London, Walpole.

Belloc, Hilaire, 1940, *Selected Cautionary Verses* (1950 edn., Harmondsworth, Penguin).

Bishop, Morris, 1942, *Spilt Milk*. New York, Putnam.

Boccaccio, Giovanni, 1348, *The Decameron* (1966 Milan 'Mursia' edn.).

Borrow, George Henry, 1851, *Lavengro: the Scholar, the Gypsy, the Priest*. London, Murray.

Boswell, James, 1791, *The Life of Samuel Johnson, LL.D.* (1906 'Everyman' edn., London, Dent).

Brett-Smith, H.F.B. & Jones, C.E., 1931, *The Works of Thomas Love Peacock* (VII, *Poems and Plays*). London, Constable; New York, Gabriel Wells.

Brewer, Ebenezer Cobham, 1870, *Dictionary of Phrase and Fable, giving the Derivation, Source, or Origin of Common Phrases, Allusions, and Words that have a Tale to Tell*. London, Cassell (also 1970 'Centenary' edn., ed. I.H. Evans).

Brock, H.I., 1947, *The Little Book of Limericks*. New York, Duell etc. (also 1969 reprint, Freeport, N.Y.).

Brontë, Patrick, *vide* Turner, J.H. and Ward, Mrs. H.

Butler, Samuel, 1901, *Erewhon Revisited* (1927 edn., London, Cape).

Butler, Tony, 1970, *The Best Irish Limericks*. London, Wolfe Publ. Co.

Bysshe, Edward, 1702, *The Art of English Poetry*. London, ?.

'Carroll, Lewis' (C.L. Dodgson) (1832-2898), *vide* Woollcott, A.

Cerf, Bennett, 1960, *Out on a Limerick: a Collection of over 300 of the World's Best Printable Limericks: Assembled, Revised, Dry-cleaned and Annotated by Mister Cerf*. New York, Harper; 1961, London, Cassell.

Chesterton, Gilbert Keith, 1933, *All I Survey: a Book of Essays*. London, Methuen.

Close, K.R., 1930, *How to Write a Prize-Winning Limerick*. Florida, U. of Miami.

Cohen, J.M., 1952, *Comic and Curious Verse*. Harmondsworth, Penguin.

———, 1970, 'Limerick', *Encyclopaedia Britannica*. Chicago & London, Encyc. Brit. Corpn.

Coleridge, Ernest Hartley, 1912, *The Complete Poetical Works of Samuel Taylor Coleridge* . . . . Oxford, Clarendon Press.

Coleridge, Samuel Taylor (1772-1834), *vide* Coleridge, E.H.

Cornish, G.A., 1968, *The Encyclopedia Americana* ('International' edn.). New York, Americana Corpn.

Cornish, Kenneth, 1948, *Nonsense Verse*. Durban, Knox Publ. Co.

Crisp, Quentin, 1943, *All This and Bevin Too*. London, Nicholson & Watson.

Darton, F.J. Harvey, 1932, *Children's Books in England: Five Centuries of Social Life* (1958 edn.). Cambridge, C.U.P.

Darton, William, 1797, *A Present for a Little Girl*. London, Darton & Harvey.

Davidson, Angus, 1938, *Edward Lear: Landscape Painter and Nonsense Poet* (also 1950 edn., Harmondsworth, Penguin).

Davidson, Angus & Hofer, Philip, 1953, *Teapots and Quails, and Other New Nonsense*, London, Murray.

Davidson, Thomas, 1898, *Chambers's English Dictionary: Pronouncing, Explanatory, Etymological* (1929 reprint). Edinburgh & London, Chambers.

Davies, Randall, *vide* 'R.D.'

Dawson, Lawrence, *J. Walker's Rhyming Dictionary of the English Language* (1924 edn.). London, Routledge; New York, Dutton.

De Vries, Leonard, 1965, *Flowers of Delight* (selections from Osborne Collection of Early Children's Books). London, Dobson.

Dermody, Thomas, 1807, *The Harp of Erin*. London, Richard Phillips.

'Derry Down Derry', *vide* Lear, Edward.

Dickens, Charles, 1865, *Our Mutual Friend*. ('Centennial' edn., London, Heron).

D'Israeli, Isaac, 1791-1834, *Curiosities of Literature* (1854 edn.). London, Edward Moxon, (orig. publ. anonymously).

Dodgson, Charles Lutwidge (1832-1898), *vide* 'Carroll, Lewis'.

Douglas, [George] Norman, 1928, *Some Limericks: Collected for the use of Students, & Ensplendour'd with Introduction, Geographical Index, and with Notes Explanatory and Critical*. Florence, Orioli (privately printed) (And many other *sub rosa* edns.; openly printed as *The Norman Douglas Limerick Book*, New York, Grove Press, 1967 and London, Anthony Blond, 1969).

Drake, ?. 1949, *A Book of Anglo-Saxon Verse* . . . . Oakland, California, 'Concavo-Convex Press'.

Dulac, Edmund, 1908, *Lyrics, Pathetic and Humorous, from A to Z*. London & New York, Warne.

Dunbar, William (b. ? 1460), *vide* Kinley, J., 1958.

'E.R.' *vide* Rhys, Ernest.

Emerson, Ralph Waldo, 1875, *Parnassus*. Boston, James Osgood (1969 edn., New York, Garrett Press).

Euwer, Anthony, 1917, *The Limeratomy: a Compendium of Universal Knowledge for the More Perfect Understanding of the Human Machine, Done in the Limerick Tongue* . . . . New York, James Pons.

Fadiman, Clifton, 1957, *Any Number Can Play*. Cleveland & New York, World Publ. Co; Canada, Nelson, Foster & Scott.

Fenn, George Manville, 1871, *The World of Wit and Humour* (1887 reprint). London, Paris & New York, Cassell.

Fitzgerald, Penelope, 1977, *The Knox Brothers*. London, Macmillan.

Funk, C.F., *Funk & Wagnall's New Standard Dictionary of the English Language* (1949 edn.). New York & London, Funk & Wagnall.

Gardner, W.H., 1953, *Poems and Prose of Gerard Manley Hopkins* (1963 edn., Harmondsworth, Penguin).

Gay, John, 1728, *The Beggar's Opera* (1972 edn., London, Davis-Poynter).

Gilbert, William Schwenk (1836-1911), *Selected Operas* (First series, 1949 edn.). London, Macmillan.

———, *vide* also Fenn, G.M., 1871 and Swinton, M., n.d.

Gogarty, Oliver St. John, 1937, *As I was going down Sackville Street* (1954 edn., Harmondsworth, Penguin).

Gorey, Edward (? pseud.), 1954, *The Listing Attic*. New York, Duell, Sloan & Pearce; Boston, Little, Brown.

Graham, Harry J.C. ('Col. D. Streamer'), 1899, *Ruthless Rhymes for Heartless Homes*. London, E. Arnold.

Grose, Francis, 1785, *A Classical Dictionary of the Vulgar Tongue*. London, S. Hooper.

———, 1811, *Lexicon Balatronicum: a Dictionary of Buckish Slang, University Wit, and Pick-pocket Eloquence* . . . *by a Member of the Whig Club*. London, no publ. named.

Hale, Susan, 1919, *Nonsense Book: a Collection of Limericks*. Boston, Marshall Jones.

Halliwell, James Orchard, 1842, *The Nursery Rhymes of England, Collected Principally from Oral Tradition*. London, Percy Society.

'Harde, Dick', n.d., *Lusty Limericks & Bawdy Ballads* (mimeograph). U.S.A.

Harris, Frank, 1922-27, *My Life and Loves* (1948 edn., Paris, Obelisk Press).

Harrowven, Jean, 1976, *The Limerick Makers*. London, Research Publ. Co.

Harvey, Paul, 1946, *The Oxford Companion to English Literature*. Oxford, Clarendon Press.

Herrick, Robert, 1648, in Emerson, R.W., 1875.

Hoagland, Kathleen, 1947, *1000 Years of Irish Poetry: the Gaelic and Anglo-Irish Poets from Pagan Times to the Present*. New York, Devin Adair; London, Falcon Press.

Holland, Vyvyan, 1967, *An Explosion of Limericks*. London, Cassell.

Hopkins, J.H. (1820–1891), *We Three Kings . . .*, in Routley, E., 1961.

Hopkins, Gerard Manley, c.1883, *Author's Preface* (MS.), in Gardner, W.H., 1953.

Hunt, Leigh (1784–1859). *Song to Ceres*, in Emerson, R.W., 1875.

Iveson, Barbara, 1962, *Verse that is Fun*. London, Faber.

——, 1965, *The Faber Book of Nursery Verse*. London, Faber.

Jackson, Holbrook, 1947, *The Complete Nonsense of Edward Lear*. London, Faber.

Jonson, Ben, 1621, *vide* Morley, H., 1890.

Kinley, James, 1958, *William Dunbar: Poems*. Oxford, Clarendon Press.

Kipling, R., 1899, *Stalky and Co*. London, Macmillan.

——, 1926, *Debits and Credits* (1949 edn.). London, Macmillan.

Lear, Edward, 1846 (?). *A Book of Nonsense (by Derry Down Derry)*. Probably privately printed Presentation issue. Liverpool Picton Library, P.821.8, (possibly 1854).

——, 1846, *A Book of Nonsense* (various edns., London, Routledge *et al.*).

——, 1872, *More Nonsense Pictures, Rhymes, Botany &c.* (various edns., London, Routledge *et. al.*).

——, *vide* also various collections, especially Davidson A. & Hofer P., 1953; Jackson, H., 1947; Liebert, H.W., 1975; and Rhys, E., 1927.

Legman, Gershon [George Alexander], 1964. *The Horn Book: Studies in Erotic Folklore and Bibliography*. New York, University Press Inc.

——, 1974, *The Limerick: 1700 Examples, with Notes, Variants and Index*. London, Jupiter Books (orig. publ. 1953, Paris, Hautes Etudes).

Lehmann, John, 1977, *Edward Lear and his World*. London, Thames & Hudson.

Leland, Charles Godfrey (L.L.D.?), 1863, *Ye Book of Copperheads*. Philadelphia, Leypoldt.

Letts, John, 1973, *A Little Treasury of Limericks Fair and Foul*. London, Pan Books.

Liebert, Herman W., 1975, *Lear in the Original: Drawings and Limericks*. New York, Kraus; London, O.U.P.

'Liza Jane', *vide* Thurtle, Ida.

'L.L.D.', *vide* Leland, Charles Godfrey.

Logue, Christopher, *vide* 'Vicarion'.

McChesney, Donald, 1968, *A Hopkins Commentary*. London, U.L.P.

MacCord, David, 1945, *What Cheer!: an Anthology of American and British Humorous Verse; Gathered, Sifted, and Sorted . . . .* New York, Coward-McCann; Toronto, Longmans.

Meynell, Francis & Vera, 1924, *The Weekend Book*. London, Nonesuch Press (also 1938 edn., Harmondsworth, Penguin).

Milligan, Spike, 1968, *Silly Verse for Kids,* Harmondsworth, Penguin.

Morley, Henry, 1890, *Masques and Entertainments by Ben Jonson.* London, Routledge.
Nash, Ogden, 1954, *Many Long Years Ago.* London, Dent.
——, 1961, *Good Intentions.* New York, Grosset & Dunlop.
'Negri' (? pseudon.), 1945, *King Henry had Six Wives: Limericks of History.* Lower Chelston (?).
Noakes, Vivien, 1968, *The Life of a Wanderer,* London.
Omond, T.S., 1903, *A Study of Metre* (1920 reprint). London, De La More Press.
Opie, Iona & Peter, 1951, *The Oxford Dictionary of Nursery Rhymes.* Oxford, Clarendon Press.
——, 1959, *The Lore and Language of Schoolchildren.* Oxford, Clarendon Press.
——, 1973, *The Oxford Book of Children's Verse.* Oxford, Clarendon Press.
Peacock, Thomas Love, *vide* Brett-Smith, H.F.B. & Jones, C.E., 1931.
Pinto, Vivian de Sola & Rodway, Allen Edwin, 1957, *The Common Muse: an Anthology of Popular British Ballad Poetry, XVth – XXth Century.* London, Chatto.
Quiller-Couch, Arthur, *The Oxford Book of English Verse, 1250-1918* (1939 edn.). Oxford, Clarendon Press.
'R.D.' [Randall Davies], 1912, *A Lyttel Book of Nonsense.* London, Macmillan (1925 2nd., Kensington, Cayme Press).
——, 1923, *A Little More Nonsense.* Kensington, Cayme Press.
——, 1927, *Less Eminent Victorians.* London, Peter Davies.
Ramsay, Allan, 1724, *A Tea-Table Miscellany: A Collection of Choice Songs, Scots & English* (1871 edn., Glasgow, John Crum).
Reed, [Herbert] Langford, 1924, *The Complete Limerick Book: the Origin, History and Achievements of the Limerick, with about 350 Selected Examples.* London, Jarrolds.
——, 1928, *The Indiscreet Limerick Book: 200 New Examples.* London, Jarrolds.
——, 1934, *Mr. Punch's Limerick Book.* London, Cobden-Sanderson.
——, 1937, *My Limerick Book.* London & Edinburgh, Nelson.
——, 1937a, *The New Limerick Book.* London, Herbert Jenkins.
Rhys, Ernest ('E.R.'), 1927, *A Book of Nonsense by Edward Lear with Struwwelpeter and Other Absurdities by Various Authors* ('Everyman's Library'). London, Dent; New York, Dutton.
Ridout, R. & Witting, C., 1969, *The Facts of English.* London, Ginn.
Roberts, 'Michael' [William Edward], 1942, *The Faber Book of Comic Verse.* London, Faber.
Rogers, B.B., 1915, tr. Aristophanes, *The Wasps.* London, Bell.
Roget, Peter Mark, 1852, *Thesaurus of English Words and Phrases, Classified and Arranged so as to Facilitate the Expression of Ideas and to Assist in Literary Composition* (also several later edns.). London, Longman, Brown, Green & Longman.

Roman Catholic Church, (1955 edn.), *Vade Mecum Sacerdotis* . . . . Ratisbonae, Puslet.

Rossetti, Dante Gabriel, *vide* Rossetti, William M.

Rossetti, William M., 1911, *The Works of Dante Gabriel Rossetti* (rev. & enl. edn.). London, Ellis.

Routley, Erick, 1961, *University Carol Book*. Brighton, Freeman.

Rowe, A.W., 1967 et seq., *Active Anthologies*. London, Blond Educational.

Saintsbury, George, 1910, *Historical Manual of English Prosody*. London, Macmillan.

Scott, Walter, 1814, *Waverley: or 'Tis Sixty Years Since* (1816 edn.). Edinburgh, Archibald Constable.

Shakespeare, William (1564-1616), *Hamlet* (1936 edn.), *King Henry V* (1947 edn.), *King Lear* (1960 edn.), *Othello* (1957 edn.), *The Tempest* (1921 edn.). Cambridge, C.U.P.

Sharpe, Richard Scrafton (?), 1822, *Adventures and Anecdotes of Fifteen Gentlemen*. London, John Marshall.

Skeat, Walter W., 1879-82, *An Etymological Dictionary of the English Language* (1924 impr.). Oxford, Clarendon Press.

'Streamer, Col. D.', *vide* Graham, Harry J.C., 1899.

Steinberg, S.H., 1953, *Cassell's Encyclopaedia of Literature*. London, Cassell.

Swann, Robert & Sidgwick, Fank, 1934, *The Making of Verse: a Guide to English Metre*. London, Sidgwick & Jackson.

Swinton, Marjory, n.d., *Lyrics from Gilbert & Sullivan Operas*. London & Glasgow, Collins.

Thackeray, William Makepeace, 1843, *Irish Sketchbook*. London, Chapman & Hall (1903 edn., in *Yellowplush Papers &c.*, London, Caxton Publ. Co.).

———, 1855, *Lyra Hybernica*. London, Bradbury & Evans (1903 edn. as above; also 1899 'Pocket Book' edn.).

Thorneley, Thomas, 1936, *Provocative Verse and Libellous Limericks*. Cambridge, Heffer.

Thurtle, Ida ('Liza Jane'), 1969, *Let's Laugh a Little*. Ilfracombe, Stockwell.

Turner, J. Horsfall, 1898, *Brontëana: the Rev. Patrick Brontë, A.B.: His Collected Works and Life*. Bingley, T. Harrison.

Untermeyer, Louis, 1963, *The Pan Book of Limericks*. London, Pan Books (orig. publ. 1962, London, W.H. Allen).

'Vicarion, Count Palmiro' [Logue, Christopher], 1955, *Book of Limericks*. Paris, Olympia Press.

Ward, A.W. & Waller, A.R., 1907-27, *The Cambridge History of English Literature*. Cambridge, C.U.P.

Ward, Mrs. Humphrey, *The Life and Works of Charlotte Brontë and her Sisters* . . . (1905 'Haworth' edn.). London, Smith, Elder.

Weekley, Ernest, 1952, *A Concise Etymological Dictionary of Modern English*. London, Secker & Warburg.

Wells, Carolyn, 1902, *A Nonsense Anthology*. New York, Scribner's (1958 edn., New York, Dover; London, Constable).

————, 1920, *The Book of Humorous Verse*. New York, Doran (1941 edn., New York, Halcyon House).

————, 1925, *Carolyn Wells's Book of American Limericks*. New York & London, Putnam (Knickerbocker Press).

————, 1937, *The Rest of My Life*. Philadelphia, Lippincott.

Woollcott, A., 1939, *The Collected Works of Lewis Carroll*. London, Nonesuch Press; New York, Random House.

Wright, F.A., 1925, *Greek Social Life*. London, Dent; New York, Dutton.

Wright, Joseph, 1878, *The English Dialect Dictionary: being the Complete Vocabulary of All Dialect Words still in use or known to have been in use during the last two hundred years*. London, Frowde; New York, Putnam.

Wyndham Lewis, D.B., 1936, *The Nonsensibus*. London, Methuen.

Index to Limericks

This index is based upon selected 'key-words'
(commonly, but not always, the last words of first lines)
which indicate persons or places or themes of verses.

General Index

Titles of books, newspapers and periodicals are not indexed comprehensively but only where they have especial relevance.